A LION IN COURT

A LION

VINCENT HALLINAN

IN COURT

G. P. Putnam's Sons, New York

Published simultaneously in the Dominion of Canada by Longmans Canada Limited, Toronto

Library of Congress Catalog Card Number: 62-18278

Second Impression

Manufactured in the United States of America

Van Rees Press • New York

This volume is respectfully dedicated to those other Hallinans—Vivian, Patrick, Terence, Michael, Matthew, Conn and Daniel—all of whom are brave soldiers in the war for human equality and emancipation.

Contents

Introduction

A FAIRLY recent development in psychology is called the "Looking-glass Image Theory." Its basic principle may be stated as: "We tend to become the kind of people which we believe others consider us to be."

The idea appears to be sound. Ordinary experiences give us examples to illustrate it. A skinflint is suddenly publicized in the newspapers for an act of seeming generosity. All at once he finds himself—and probably undeservedly—the recipient of his fellow citizens' respect. This gives him a new and pleasant sensation, a warm feeling. He tries to retain it and ends up a genuine philanthropist.

On the other hand, there's an old adage: "If you want to hang a man, start by getting him a bad name." A shrewder suggestion might be to get him the bad name and he will hang himself. Many girls and boys have been ruined by accepting the denunciation: "You're no good!" After this has been repeated often enough by parents, teachers, juvenile court judges and others whom they have been taught to respect, they conform to that judgment. Their downward careers are not in defiance of the condemnation but in acceptance of it. Prisons are full of people who in their adolescence surrendered to such destructive criticism.

9

Yet, whatever else may have shaped my own character and directed my course of conduct, I don't believe it can be blamed on the Looking-glass Image influence.

I have always refused to conform just for the sake of conformity. Also, I could never be sure what the Image looked like. I fear that I have ended up a study in paradox. It would be difficult to find out what my general reputation is, since people's opinions of me cover a wide spectrum. One would have to arrange a composite from the reflections of many mirrors, each distorted by its own biases and prejudices.

The chief reason for this diversity of views is that most of them have been arrived at by reading newspapers. These journals have a capacity for painting people in the most fantastic shapes and colors. Also, they agree with Emerson that a foolish consistency is the hobgoblin of little minds, and they change the picture from day to day. Once you have become "news," everything you do outside the house justifies another look.

For many years now I have been "news." My notices have varied. As a youth they were on the sports pages as a football star, and in scholastic circles as the pride of the Jesuits. Later I was under attack as a crusading young attorney who took on the entrenched powers of the San Francisco courts. In the forty years that followed I have been praised and vilified as a defense attorney in a variety of noted murder trials. I made national headlines when I took over the defense of the ILWU labor leader Harry Bridges. When I went to prison the headlines garnered me more fame. I was dubbed the emissary of the Reds when I ran for president on the ticket of the Independent Progressive Party.

Meanwhile, my opinions and views have stirred up fury and admiration. Those who shared my opinions on the particular issue involved sang my praises—but only when I personified their hopes and convictions. Those who recoil from the somewhat radical notions I sometimes advocate express their fear and hatred of them in personal hostility to me as an individual.

Still, there is one department in which opinion of me remains fairly consistent. That is the one which involves my ability as a lawyer. In my first year of practice I astounded my youthful compeers by earning a fee of $20,000, and from that time on I have never heard of anyone who believed I was less than highly competent at my trade.

Law is a rough, tough game. It is played by a lot of cool, cunning, calculating customers. It invites that kind of people. The great majority of them work hard. They keep abreast of the latest decisions. They figure out quirks and tricks to get around difficulties. They prepare their cases meticulously. They interview witnesses carefully, and get everything out of them which they can, including things which never happened. If they're in the district attorney's office, they have trained investigators and the state's authority to find all these things for them. A sincere but bumbling defense lawyer would get short shrift in a contest with such adversaries. Some such have found their way into the criminal courts. They usually end up selling Fuller brushes.

Neither is humility consistent with success as a trial lawyer. Humble people don't take on fate. A man who will take responsibility for the liberty and lives of others must have considerable self-confidence, or be entirely callous. Almost all the great trial lawyers I have known were as vain as peacocks, although most of them managed to conceal their vanity. Looking back on my own career, I cannot honestly pretend that I was distinguished by any considerable modesty. I just wasn't made that way. Almost all my disasters came from charging ahead with full knowledge of what might happen. It never occurred to me that I might lose. When I was a young fellow I'd take on anyone in a fist fight. I seriously believed that I could lick Jack Dempsey. Thirty years later, when I first landed in a prison, I felt much the same sensation, even though the outfit I had been fighting was a pretty formidable heavyweight itself—the United States Government.

So, as you can well see, the mirror gets very distorted when I look at myself. The adjectives come smashing home. When I was a moppet, running the streets of San Francisco, it was "little shanty Irish cat-licker." As a law student and semi-pro football player, such descriptions as "brilliant" and "hard-hitting" popped up. I was to become a "mad dog" when I defended Harry Bridges. In prison I was a "troublemaker" and a "nigger lover." When I state my political views, I am usually tabbed as a "radical," and by more free-swinging editors, even a "Communist."

All this confusion makes it difficult to know where to begin. But maybe as good a place as any is in San Francisco over fifty years ago.

Part I

My Early Years

CHAPTER 1

Hallinan vs. Heaven

WHEN I was about nine years old, my career in life was set. I was to become a lawyer. While this decision was my father's, he was impelled to it by a certain entity or personage whose very identity was then, and continues to be, an unfathomable mystery. The title of this *deus ex machina* was repeated a thousand times in our home; scarcely a visitor departed without having heard the significant part he had played in our family history. Yet he was but a disembodied spirit, a vibration in the ether, a name that was recited.

That name was Spivlo V. Mahoney.

But if only a name, it was indeed a name to be conjured with. And conjured with it was to a glorious purpose. In a critical moment it had been interposed between the Hallinans and injustice, and had turned its thrust aside.

This is the role it played in the small drama of our family troubles. We were poor. My parents were Irish immigrants. My father worked as a conductor on the California street cable cars in San Francisco twelve hours a day, and got one day a month off. His monthly salary was $70. On this he supported his family which then contained seven children.

He was singularly honest and honorable. His head was scarred from policemen's clubs wielded in bitter strikes to raise the wages and shorten the hours of the company's platform men, but he scorned to knock down a nickel of the fares he collected for it. If his principles amounted to bigotry and his loyalties to fanaticism, at least they were not for sale. He would burn at the stake before he would betray a cause or a friend.

When the great earthquake and fire of 1906 devastated San Francisco, we were living in a four-room cottage in its western addition. The rent was about $12 a month. The house had a basement which ran its full length and width. When the fire was over, this basement became desirable storage space for people who had managed to remove their furniture from their homes before the flames reached them. Our landlord proposed to capitalize on this windfall. As it was impossible that we could pay more than our present rent, he served us with a 30-day notice to vacate the premises. The eviction of our family, with its numerous small children, was catastrophic. There was no place to go.

In those days, before the automobile, streetcars were the general means of conveyance. Prominent persons were regular passengers on my father's car, and he was friendly with many of them. Among the more cordial was Charles Heggerty, attorney for the Southern Pacific Railroad Company. My father hastened to this giant of the bar with our sorry problem. The magnanimous Heggerty gave it his full attention. Having read the notice, he perused a section of the Code and said:

"I'm pretty sure this notice is legally defective. When the thirty days are up, they'll file an unlawful-detainer action. Try to avoid being served as long as possible. Meanwhile, I'll look up the authorities on this, and we'll see if we can't kick the case around for awhile."

As the ominous day approached, my father proceeded to follow the lawyer's instructions. He never answered the doorbell in person nor left the house without inspecting its environs from behind the curtains. The older children, as well as all the immediate neighbors, were alerted for anyone who looked like a process server. If a suspicious character was observed in the vicinity when my father was due home from work, one of us met him around the corner to warn him. He then detoured into the rear entrance of the house behind ours, climbed the back fence, and thus avoided the danger.

The cable company's platform men were enlisted in this campaign of evasion. If a stranger boarded a car, inquiring for Pat Hallinan, each played his part. The conductor—it might be my father himself—called out to the motorman, "What car is that fellow Hallinan on?"

The reply usually was: "That one that just passed us. Hop off and run after it. He'll stop at the next corner."

A wave to the conductor of the other car insured that it wouldn't stop. After a chase of two or three blocks the process server gave up. To prevent being brought within the jurisdiction of the court while turning in his car at night, my father had another stratagem. The conductor preceding him met him a block from the carbarn, took over his position, and turned in his vehicle also.

After some four months of this the plaintiff's lawyers enlisted the aid of the company officials. My father was called to the superintendent's office where a deputy sheriff was waiting to serve him.

Then Heggerty really began kicking the case around. The courts were in a chaotic condition, and it was not difficult to procure delays, even in an unlawful-detainer action which had precedence. A demurrer or two were sustained, and it was another three months before the plaintiff finally got his case to trial. It was then that our good genius emerged to confound him.

Spivlo V. Mahoney!

As my father told it a thousand times: "When they had finished their case, Charley Heggerty says: 'Your Honor, I move for a nonsuit.' 'On what grounds, Mr. Heggerty?' says Judge Van Nostrand. 'On the grounds,' says Charley Heggerty, 'that the notice to vacate is fatally defective.' 'Have you any authority for that?' says Judge Van Nostrand. 'I have, Your Honor,' says Charley Heggerty, 'it's Spivlo v. Mahoney.' "

"And," my father would continue in his most impressive tones, "do you know that Judge Van Nostrand *had never heard* of Spivlo v. Mahoney?"

Over the many years that I heard this saga repeated I never lost my wonder and concern at the monumental ignorance of Judge Van Nostrand in never having heard of Spivlo v. Mahoney. It wasn't until I was a lawyer myself and saw the thousands of books and recognized that there were numberless decisions in them that I realized the wonder would have been if Judge Van Nostrand *had* heard of Spivlo v. Mahoney.

At any rate, it must have been of convincing authority, for the nonsuit was granted and the plaintiff had to start all over again. Altogether it took him eighteen months to get us out of that cottage. Even then, with his back to the wall, Heggerty was able to bluff a settlement under which we agreed to move out and the landlord waived all the back rent. This, then, was the incident which determined my career.

It was not possible to find a home in the burned-out city, and we moved to Petaluma, a town about thirty miles north of San Francisco. We chose that location because some family friends lived there. My father continued to live and work in San Francisco, and his meager pay had to be stretched still further.

We rented another four-room cottage for $6 a month. It was a poor little house, misplaced in the poshest part of Petaluma—such as that was. We had neither gas nor electricity, and did our cooking on a wood stove. We had no carpets on the floor. There was a bathtub, but the water pipes were not connected to it, and we used it to store potatoes.

The place had a sizable backyard where we raised chickens and planted vegetables. We were poor all right, but never hungry. The Hallinan kids were active, noisy and quarrelsome. We dismayed our snooty neighbors, but we were proud little barbarians and cared not a hoot for their ill opinion.

The years of our growing up were not happy ones. We were the "bridge" generation. Our parents were Irish and our children would be Americans, but we were neither. Imposed upon us were the traditions, the bigotries and the superstitions of our ancestry, but there were none of our own age with whom to share them. We were aliens in the land of our birth.

Any opportunity to enlarge our horizons was restricted by another factor: my mother and father were fanatical Roman Catholics. Whatever intellectual stirrings might have once moved them had been long surrendered to the dictates of the Church. So far as they were concerned there was no redemption outside of the Church, and nobody but a Catholic was worthy of their friendship.

We children were trapped in the web of these concepts. That is not to say we mistrusted or sought to evade this situation. That would have saved us. Instead, we accepted it wholeheartedly. We willingly sacrificed the happiness of childhood to a dark superstition.

Of course, despite our poverty, we had to go to St. Vincent's Academy, the parish school maintained by the Sisters of Charity of the Blessed Virgin Mary. It was about a mile and a half from our home, and there was a five-dollar-a-month tuition for the five of us; in addition we had to buy our own books. The public school was only half as far away and books and tuition were free, but to go there would have been unthinkable.

When I think of our family, it is Annie who dominates the picture. Cast in better circumstances she might have amounted to something. She was honorable to a fault and of unflinching courage. Her mind was clear and discerning within the narrow bounds in which it was permitted to move. All her high qualities were withered in the arid soil of a prudish morality and bigoted religiosity.

She was about twelve years old when we moved to Petaluma; our sister Mary was a year younger, and I two years younger than Annie. Then there were twin girls about six, a brother Jerry who was four, and Emily about two.

Annie rode herd on this outfit. When we started off for school in the mornings, the twins walked first, Mary and I followed, and Annie—a foot taller than either of us—brought up the rear. We were punctual attendants at every school session, and our appearance at any given point was as regular as the clock. To add to the attraction, the twins were pronouncedly cross-eyed.

The interest in our entourage was doubled and redoubled on Saint Patrick's Day. That was our real national holiday, far more important than the Fourth of July, and we sallied forth wearing rosettes of broad green and orange ribbons, the streamers reaching to our knees. They were a permanent décor, carefully stored away for the next year, much like our Christmas-tree ornaments.

At first our daily passage past the public school was a recurring nightmare. We walked past with eyes fixed ahead, ignoring the jibes of the juvenile Protestants. Finally a few of them made the error of extending their annoyance beyond jeers and insults. They crossed to the opposite sidewalk, barred our path, and proceeded to push us around.

Annie was a handsome child with delicate features and a sensitive face. Under all her feminine appearance, however, was the courage of a lion and the fury of a tornado. Now she hurled herself upon our tormentors like the Charge of the Irish Brigade at Fontenoy. Right and left flew her little fists, and in seconds the whole contingent of assailants were in full retreat, bloodied and dismayed. They fled behind the safety of their school fence whence they regarded our small Amazon with awe. From then on, so long as Annie was with us, we were free from molestation.

Circumstances soon took me from under her wing. My classes ended an hour or so earlier than hers, and I had to walk home alone. On my first such trip I was waylaid by two urchins about my own age who proceeded, in the fashion of small boys, to bully me to the last extreme. I cannot remember now what indignities they imposed upon me. Time charitably erases such bitter memories, but I will never forget the misery of those homeward walks. I found roundabout ways of avoiding the malignant pair, but they discovered them and again confronted me, releasing me only after reducing me to tears and humiliation.

There was a pretty little girl in my class whom I greatly fancied. One afternoon she visited a relative who lived near my home, and we walked together. Chatting with my small inamorata, I failed to notice that we were on the street where my two tormentors lived until I was horrified to observe them moving toward us.

Their smirking countenances were upon us before I could plan strategy or retreat. One of them seized my jacket. Pride rose above fear to save the day. It was one thing to endure degradation when no one was watching; it was another to suffer it in the presence of a lady love. Abruptly I swarmed upon my assailant with both fists flying. I caught him a wondrous blow in the belly. To my astonishment he fell to the ground, gasping and bawling. I turned on his companion, pounding him about the face and head. He ran.

Never will I forget the elation which possessed me as we continued our walk. More than the admiration of my small friend was the enormous satisfaction of having found and proven myself. Never again would I passively accept indignity or injustice; never again would I show the white feather or shrink from a fight.

Soon this noble sentiment turned into a less commendable one. I had uncovered a dangerous talent. I could fight; battle was exhilarating. There was nothing to fear. Willie Slocum was the biggest boy in our class. He was a head taller than I and was active and robust. He too had bullied me, and I could scarcely wait for the next day to take that up with him. He accepted the challenge with some surprise.

The rumor of an impending battle spread quickly. After school the entire male student body assembled to watch it. The odds were against me, but my victory of the preceding day furnished an invincible inspiration. I sailed in with abandon. In a short while Willie quit. In the excitement I did not notice when I was struck myself, and it was not until some minutes after the fight that I discovered I had a black eye.

Far from being discomfited by this, I was immensely proud of it. I headed for home, purposely taking the street where my enemies of yesterday lived. I hung around for some time, waiting for them to appear. I would have unhesitantly attacked both of them, but they failed to show up.

When I got home the black eye was a different matter. My mother was outraged. She had seen my erstwhile opponent, knew

how much bigger than I he was, and did not believe my story
of victory. Then Annie came home and agreed with her. It was
quite impossible that I should have beaten Willie Slocum. Tomorrow she would fix him. I argued and implored, but to no avail.
Next morning Annie waylaid Willie Slocum in the school yard
and beat the hell out of him.

We were drowned in religion. Everything in our lives was
regulated by the tenets of the Church. We lay helpless in its
embrace, like embryos in the amniotic fluid. My mother accepted
reverses with a philosophical observation: "We must not repine
at our lot, though low it be cast, for we know not what God may
have in store for us."

Not that she was a devotee. She rarely went to church herself,
although she never permitted us to miss Mass except for the
most important reasons. She was short and fat and enjoyed eat-
ing. She always kept a case of bottled beer in the house. In her
youth she had been pretty, and her face was still handsome, but
her figure had disappeared in an excess of flesh. She could swear
like a trooper.

We raised chickens, hatching them under setting hens. Before
placing one of these on a clutch of eggs, they were sprinkled with
holy water and we all said a short prayer. If the hen showed an
inclination to wander from the nest, a candle was lighted to the
Blessed Virgin.

No sharp distinctions were made in the family between religion and other forms of superstition. Annie went the whole route.
She would no more open an umbrella in the house than she
would eat meat on Friday. If she forgot her purse or gloves, she
would not dare return for them, believing that disappointment
would attend her errand. She would stand across the street, yelling
for someone to bring the misplaced article to her.

At least half our school day was spent in religious exercises or
instruction. We were drilled in a catechism which answered the
profoundest problems of the universe with glib assurance. The
mystery of man's fate was solved in two replies:

Q. Who made you?

A. God made me.

Q. Why did God make you?

A. God made me to know Him and love Him, to serve Him in this world and to be happy with Him forever in the next.

Samuel Johnson once said that those in the lower walks of life are rather driven by the force of fear than attracted by the prospect of good. So it was with our observance of the rules by which we should serve Him in this world. The promised reward fell short of satisfaction, but the alternative was terrible. Heaven, with its eternity of playing harps and singing hosannas, was not particularly attractive, but Hell would make the hardiest tremble. Indeed, Paradise was delineated quite sketchily, but Hell was described with such minuteness of detail that one would suppose that the nuns who instructed us concerning it had just completed a Cook's tour of the region.

The suffering in Hell is worse than anything that can be imagined. The souls of the damned burn with the most excruciating pain. There is never a moment's respite from their agony, and they never get used to the torments they endure. The fires of Hell are real, yet they give no light, and one suffers in absolute darkness. The groans and screams of the lost souls add constantly to the terrors of the region. Even worse than these or than the flames is the awful remorse and grief that one feels for having offended God and brought himself to this terrible fate.

All this goes on for Eternity. It is almost impossible to conceive what Eternity means, but if the world were a solid steel ball, and every hundred years a little bird flew by and just brushed it with his wing, by the time he had worn it completely away Eternity would be just beginning.

One of the greatest pains in Hell is the bitter envy of seeing the happy souls in Paradise. On the other hand, those blessed souls in Heaven have no sorrow or sympathy for the damned. They know that these are being justly punished for their sins. Indeed, the sight of God's justice being vindicated against the wicked in Hell adds to the pleasures of those who are saved. If you were

in Heaven and should see your own mother or your brother or
sister burning in Hell, you would not feel the least bit sorry for
them, because you would know that they had merited their punishment by offending against the goodness of God.

During Lent and retreats these lectures were supplemented by
visiting priests. The nuns' accounts were but pale ghosts of the
robust descriptions with which we were then regaled. As a matter
of fact, the visitor's merit was measured by the degree to which
he could exceed his confreres in creating and maintaining an
atmosphere of terror.

Our every thought and action was governed by precise rules.
Deviation from these were recited and corrected in Confession.
Our black-robed mentors were the repositories for God's penal
code. In this ambient, curiosity was stifled. There were subjects
which it was sinful to think of, let alone discuss. I do not know
how we got to learn that sex was one of these, since nobody dared
mention it. Anything which touched it even collaterally was
taboo.

An example of this occurred in history class, when we discussed the family of George Washington. The Sister asked, "Who
was Martha Washington?"

When there was no answer, she questioned each pupil in turn.
Some guessed that she was George Washington's mother, others
his sister. Most of the class said simply that they did not know.

When all had been asked, the Sister said, "Why, she was his
wife."

We glanced at each other in some consternation. At least half
the class had known all along that Martha Washington was
George Washington's wife, but they wouldn't dare say so. We
were astonished that the nun had used the term.

Over all was the aura of death. Its insignia of the gibbet and
skull were everywhere. In each room hung a crucified Christ. Our
daily diet was of murder and torture. We memorized the san-
guinary passages from the Right Reverend Richard Gilmour's
Bible History and recited in class the fate of the Christian martyrs:
"Many were exposed to wild beasts; others thrown into the Tiber.
Some were beheaded; some were crucified; others rolled up in

pitch and at night burned to light up the public gardens . . . They scourged Peter and John; stoned St. Stephen; cast St. James head-long from the roof of the Temple and beat out his brains with a fuller's mallet . . . On the 29th of June in the year 67, St. Paul was beheaded on the Ostian Way, just outside the walls of Rome; while St. Peter was crucified on Mount Janiculum within the walls."

These were the glories of our faith. We should not lament the fate of these heroes, but rather rejoice in it. Life is not important, it is only a vale of tears, a place of sorrow and misery, whose goal is death. Its temptations must be resisted and its pleasures renounced. Suffering and sacrifice are the way to Heaven.

Thus was the happiness of childhood smothered in the ashes of death. Thus was the promise of our youth strangled in a circlet of thorns. After eight years of this regimen the children, particularly the girls, emerged with senses of sin and shame which remained with them for life. Their capacities for pleasure had been warped and shrunken. Forever after there would be something dirty in anything connected with sex and even with love.

Inculcated with all the morbid renunciation of life and pre-occupation with death, was one active sentiment. We learned anti-Semitism at its origin. All the crimes which men had com-mitted were overshadowed by one enormous transgression—the murder of the Son of God Himself, the Crucifixion of Christ.

It was the Jews who had perpetrated this monstrous deed. If the Romans had been the immediate executioners, the Jews had driven them to it. They had cried out to Pilate: "Crucify Him! Crucify Him!" And when the Roman washed his hands of the Saviour's blood they had accepted its guilt. "His blood be upon us and upon our children!"

Our *Bible History* recited the sanction of that defiance in ring-ing terms: "For eighteen hundred years has the Blood of Christ been upon the Jews. Driven from Judea—without country, with-out home—strangers amongst strangers—hated, yet feared—have they wandered from nation to nation, bearing with them the visible sign of God's curse. Like Cain, marked with a mysterious sign, shall they continue to wander until the end of the World."

We learned with satisfaction the fate of the more immediate transgressors "In the year 69 the Jews revolted against Rome, when Titus, the Roman general, collected an army and besieged Jerusalem, surrounding the city with vast fortifications. Soon famine, then pestilence, set in. The city was torn by factions from within, while the Romans battered down the walls from without. Neither young nor old were spared. Jerusalem was doomed. The prophecy of Christ was about to be fulfilled. Forewarned, the Christians had fled. Within one year, more than one million Jews died from pestilence or were killed by the Romans. The city was taken, the Temple burned, the people sold into slavery and thus dispersed over the world as we now find them without country or king. Truly the Blood of Christ is upon them."

Let it not be assumed that I was a reluctant conscript in this strange company. I embraced its tenets with surprise but without doubt, and accepted its disciplines with eager innocence. In a short time I was an altar boy. It was very thrilling to serve at Mass, moving about on the altar, ringing the bell before the Host was uncovered, pouring water and wine over the priest's fingers, and rattling back Latin answers to his mysterious pronouncements.

It was even more exciting to march out with a lighted taper to ignite the candles just before the ceremony commenced. Then I was the central figure on the stage. In full view of the assembled worshippers, I would move solemnly about my duties, genuflecting before the altar on each passage, all resplendent in red cassock and white surplice.

To be sure, it was painful to get up at five when I had to serve six-o'clock Mass, or to give up my evening when it was my turn to officiate at Vespers, but these annoyances had their compensations. The warmth and lights of the church, the crowded pews, the music of the choir and the fumes of incense, suffused one with a sense of power and mystery.

Indeed, on one occasion during Vespers I underwent an astonishing experience. I was standing at the foot of the altar, swinging the censer, exhilarated by the emotions which the circumstances aroused, when suddenly there were no walls nor candles, no church nor priest nor worshippers. I was alone in a mighty void, possessed of an immense exaltation. I felt that I was one with Infinity and that I wanted to cry out: "I know! I understand!" Far out on the margins of the vision lights flashed out and disappeared. For a moment I experienced supreme happiness.

Abruptly the transport ceased and I was back in the little church, swinging the censer. I looked around in surprise. Apparently nothing had happened to arouse anyone's notice. I wondered if I should call out and tell of my experience. Then reality took over, and I said nothing about it.

Years later, reading William James' *The Varieties of Religious Experience,* I found my own analyzed. What had happened to me was a form of hypnosis induced by the lights, the music and the other circumstances of the ceremony acting upon a mind disposed to religious ecstasy. You get the same reaction with hashish.

Indeed, I finally discovered that this experience has been shared by the most irreligious. I was narrating the event to a number of friends, and before I could finish, Bill Herron, an attorney with whom I was associated, interrupted with startled eagerness. "By God, Vin," he cried, "that's exactly the way I feel when I'm drunk!"

In 1912 I was fifteen, and we moved back to San Francisco. Long before, the Sister Superior at St. Vincent's had advised my parents to send me to St. Ignatius College. I was considered a brain storm and worthy of nothing less than the Jesuit Fathers, the master teachers of the world.

Accordingly I enrolled first in the high school and later the college conducted by these paragons of education. The division of studies under them was about the same as at the Petaluma convent—that is to say, at least half of our time was assigned to learning the principles, history and defense of the Roman Catholic Church.

The Jesuits have conducted this ·school in San Francisco for many years. When their buildings were destroyed in the earth-quake and fire of 1906, they moved to a two-story wooden build-ing at Hayes and Schrader streets, and it was there I received what passed for an education. I put in the three years of high school, and four more getting an A.B. degree, in their "univer-sity." There were six in our graduating class. About half of the preceding four years had been used up in Christian Apologetics and Ethics. The first was a series of arguments sustaining the divinity of the Roman Catholic Church, the infallibility of the Pope, the villany of Protestantism, and other items of similar importance. Ethics was a distillation of morals fashionable dur-ing the Middle Ages.

In addition, we studied Greek and Latin, both as tedious pieces of drudgery. Neither the teachers nor the pupils considered them languages, and we learned the conjugations of verbs without understanding their significance. We also studied geometry and plane and spherical trigonometry, without having the faintest idea of what they were all about. The teachers shared in this confusion. Examinations were passed by writing out the problems in small lettering on cards which were handed back and forth during the tests. There was also a course in chemistry, conducted by a clownish old priest who barely knew the difference between a Bunsen burner and a thermometer. A primitive sort of Physics course was most rewarding, since, among other things, we killed several rats trapped on the premises by placing them in bell jars and pumping out the oxygen.

Voltaire said that he spent fourteen years with the Jesuits and learned nothing but Latin and nonsense. Butler, in his history of civilization in Europe, stated that, in reward for completing a course at a Spanish university, you would come out knowing less than when you went in. My own conclusion is that if you spend eight years on a Jesuit education, you must use approxi-mately half of the remainder of your life unlearning what they have taught you. A few years ago, when I was suspended from the bar, I wished to enroll at the University of California to study Russian. I had another secret purpose: I had watched four of my sons win, in succession, the middleweight intramural boxing championship at that school. I was about sixty years old, but was certain I could duplicate their feats. A transcript of my credits at Saint Ignatius High School and College were duly transmitted to the Berkeley campus. Altogether, including an A.B. and an LL.B. degree, they were insufficient to procure enrollment at the University of California as a freshman.

The law school was held at night from 7:30 to 9:30. It was permissible to attend it during the last two years of the day course. I kept quite busy those two years. Each morning at seven o'clock I opened Tim McCarthy's corner grocery store, some two blocks from my home. I worked there until eight, went home for breakfast, and then walked a mile and a half to school. At four o'clock I was back at the grocery store and worked until six. I went home to dinner, hiked out to law school, and hiked back again when classes were over. On Saturdays and holidays I worked in the grocery store all day. Meanwhile, I had a few other activities. I was captain of the college football team and editor of the school magazine.

To tell the truth, our studies involved little time or energy. None of us paid the slightest attention to the courses, except in devising ways to cheat our way through examinations. So long as we were well saturated in theology, the Jesuits did not give a whoop about our proficiency in science or mathematics. We knew as much about them as the teachers did, which was precious little.

When we entered law school it was different. This was something extremely practical. I think it was the first time in my life I ever studied anything. I had the highest marks of the thirty students in the freshman class. All but five or six pupils worked during the day, and were grimly serious about their law courses.

Somewhere along the line I got a job in Daniel A. Ryan's law office. It was an ideal setup. Ryan was brilliant and experienced, but lazy. I started in serving papers and doing similar chores, but in a very short while he had me looking up law and writing briefs on appeal. More important, he had me sit at the counsel table with him on every case he tried. I caught on fast. At that time it was not necessary to be admitted to the bar to practice in the justice's court, and very shortly Ryan turned over to me

all those small pieces of litigation which were tried in that jurisdiction. This was a wonderful opportunity and I did not neglect
it. Never were cases better prepared than those which I handled
in the San Francisco Justice's Court. The opposing counsel were
usually a great deal older and busier and could not take that
much time and effort. I would go from house to house, ringing
doorbells to find witnesses for a traffic accident involving a $50
repair bill, and I would bemuse the court with decisions from
distant jurisdictions. I had an unbroken string of victories. I was
a hungry fighter.

One day I got a phone call from a firm which I had twice
bested in the justice's court. They wanted to have a talk with
me. They offered me $300 a month to come into their office and
handle their justice court cases. It was a terrible temptation;
Ryan was paying me $40 a month, and a salary of $300 exceeded
my fondest hopes. Nevertheless, I turned it down. I was looking
at the long haul. There was much I had yet to learn from Ryan,
and I had not been hard put to defeat these gentlemen.

Presently I was faced with a new development. New legislation
had been enacted to govern admissions to the bar. Up to this
time, the examinations had been conducted by the justices of
the District Court of Appeals, and it was felt that they were not
sufficiently exacting in their requirements. A board of bar
examiners was created to perform the task. There was much
discussion and concern among the candidates for the first examination to be conducted by the new board. It was supposed that
its examination would be much harder than those of former years.
I heard that many who contemplated taking it intended to defer
their application to the next examination, and meanwhile to hit
the books harder than they had been doing.

I made what turned out to be a shrewd guess. I figured that
in their first venture the bar examiners would actually be more
conscientious *and* lenient than they would be at any subsequent
time. I also guessed, from the number who were dropping out,
that the applicants would be relatively few in number, and
that a larger proportion could be safely passed without intruding
too much upon the monopoly enjoyed by those already admitted.

I put in my application. I had a hard time combining schoolwork, employment by Ryan and private reading, to make up the minimum period of study required for eligibility.

My bet paid off. The new board, in its first examination, passed a higher percentage of candidates than was ever admitted before or since, and lo! there among the fortunate names was mine! I was twenty-two years old, and already a golden path had opened at my feet. My chief recollection is that I was still walking on air when I boarded a streetcar, and that I wanted to tell somebody else about it. I turned to a passenger standing near me and blurted out, "I just passed the bar examination!" Then I noticed his seedy clothing, his face already old, the lines of care and labor etched upon it. He looked at me dully for a moment, as though he recalled the examinations he had not passed, the paths that had never opened. I had an instant of confused embarrassment; then his face softened, and a slow smile spread across his features. He put out his hand. "Good Boy," he said. "Congratulations." I had told nobody of my intention to take the examination, and everyone was astonished at my success. All except Ryan. "I'd have been surprised if you hadn't passed it," he exclaimed. "I'll bet you know a damn sight more law than any of the bar examiners!"

A few days after I was admitted I had my first venture in the Superior Court. Ryan represented a man named Martin Raglan, who kept a saloon on the corner of Powell and Eddy streets. When his lease expired, he found that the premises had been rented to other tenants at a higher rental. Meanwhile, he had installed a mahogony and plate-glass partition which—under all the authorities which I was able to find—constituted a part of the real property. Raglan determined that he would not have the advantage of this installation. He returned to the saloon with an ax and demolished the partition. However, he had overlooked the fact that he had deposited $500 with the landlord as security for the observance of the lease, which, among other things, required him to leave the premises in good condition upon its termination.

The landlord now contended that the partition had become

part of the real property, that Raglan had violated the lease by destroying it, and that he was not entitled to the refund of the $500 deposit. Raglan employed Ryan to collect the money for him, and a suit was filed. Ryan had me research the law on the subject, and I was forced to inform him that his case appeared pretty hopeless.

Shortly after nine o'clock on the morning of the trial Ryan phoned me at the office. "The Raglan case is on for trial this morning," he said. "Go on out there and try it!"

"Mister Ryan," I protested, "I can't win that case!"

"You damn well can!" he roared. "Get out there and win it!"

I hurried out to court. I was certain of a defeat, but did the best I could. The landlord was represented by Charles Christin, an able and experienced practitioner. We were both dumbfounded when, at the conclusion of the testimony and without waiting for argument, the trial judge announced: "Judgment for the plaintiff for five hundred dollars."

"Why, Your Honor," protested Christin, "I can't understand that decision."

"It was the plaintiff's property," the Judge replied doggedly. "He had a right to do what he wanted to with it."

When I returned to the office Ryan accosted me fiercely. "Well," he demanded. "What happened?"

"We won," I informed him, somewhat confusedly.

He lay back in his chair and roared with laughter. "The only reason I sent you out to try it," he explained, "was that I thought it couldn't be won and I didn't want to give Charlie Christin the satisfaction of licking me."

My religious convictions persisted into my young manhood. I enlisted in an officers' training camp of the U. S. Navy during World War I, and I frequently served Mass. When I was admitted to the bar I was still keeping the Sacraments.

Then, out of the blue, it happened. One night I waited on a street corner to transfer to a trolley car. Nearby was a bookstore, and a rack of secondhand volumes stood outside its window. I killed time by glancing through them. My eye caught a title.

It was a collection of essays by Thomas Paine. I picked it up gingerly and thumbed through it, mildly curious to see what the Dirty Little Atheist had to say. I stopped at a sentence. It said: "Of all the arguments for the Divinity of Christ, that based on his miracles is the most obvious—as though Almighty God would go around like a showman, doing tricks to prove he was telling the truth."

The logic of the statement hit me like a thunderbolt. My eyes and mouth popped open. I bought the book and started reading it. When the car came along, I could scarcely take my eyes off the text to board it and pay my fare. The trip home took twenty or twenty-five minutes, and by the time it ended I was a complete atheist.

It is improbable that my faith has actually been destroyed by that one volume. More likely the termites of doubt had been gnawing away the foundations of its curious structure without my noticing them. Subconsciously I was ready for a slight push to demolish it.

Thinking back, I recalled an incident during my last year at St. Ignatius College which supports this conclusion. A retreat was in progress and was being observed with the customary solemnity. We were required, during recess, to abstract ourselves from every wordly thought and to confine ourselves to religious contemplation. Play, amusement and even conversation were forbidden. The boys moved about the schoolyard, regarding its surface with thoughtful miens, or sat reading religious tracts— all under the scrutiny of black-robed ecclesiastics.

Our senior class members, contemptuous of these disciplines, gathered surreptitiously in one of the upper rooms, where we discussed sports and other such topics. From this we were led to harass our more devout fellows in the yard below by throwing chalk and other objects at them.

Immediately after the noon recess Father Nicholas Bell, the prefect of discipline, came to our room. He was a big man, imposing in black soutane and biretta, with a long rosary suspended from his belt. He had the face of a classic fanatic, with glistening eyes, bushy brows, aquiline nose and heavy jaw.

Without preliminaries, he began in reasonable enough tones: "During the noon recess, while the other pupils were observing their devotions, a number of boys in this room were throwing chalk at them. I want everyone who was in this room at noontime to stand up."

None did.

Bell drew himself to his full height. "I'm going back to my office," he said, "and I want every boy who was in this room at noontime to be there within five minutes. If any one of them isn't there within that time . . ." He raised his right hand above his head, his fist clinched. His frame shook with passion, and his voice rose to a thunderous pitch, *"May the curse of the Living God fall upon him!"*

He wheeled and strode from the room.

I glanced at my fellow culprits, mildly amused at this extravagance. To my astonishment, I beheld them tumbling from their desks and hastening on the heels of the grim old disciplinarian. I kept my seat, calmly confident that the Living God would not bother to respect an invocation based on such trifling grounds. The other wretches were suspended and required to bring their parents for a briefing on their misconduct.

Nothing happened to me.

CHAPTER 2

My Legal Debut

WHEN I first entered the legal field in San Francisco, it contained some of the ablest jury-trial lawyers in the country. Nathan Coombs Coghlan, Edwin V. McKenzie, John Taafe and Frank Murphy were its outstanding criminal defense advocates.

Of these, I consider McKenzie to have been foremost. He had none of the flashiness which sometimes illuminates a trial performer. He was of medium height, stockily built, with an inclination to overweight, and prematurely bald. In the courtroom he was easy, confident and vigorous. His mind was alert, discerning and ingenious, and he had a capacity for hard work which was little short of genius.

His mother had died when he was four years old. Some nine years later his father had remarried. Ed could not endure the new household, and at thirteen, took off into the wide world strictly on his own. He first worked his way to England to see the coronation of Edward VII, and then over the continents, finally settling in Mexico, where, at the age of nineteen, he set himself up in business as an electrician. How he acquired this trade the Lord only knows. At any rate, he was sufficiently proficient two years later to procure a job in San Francisco's electrical department, and was soon promoted to inspector.

Meanwhile, his brother Harry, two years older than he, had

stayed close to the paternal hearth and had graduated from Santa Clara College. Pending his bar examinations, he had procured a clerical appointment in the district attorney's office.

Ed became interested in his brother's lawbooks. He began reading them with avidity and pored over them night and day. The bar examinations were four months away when he started. Both brothers took it. Harry, with a college degree, flunked; Ed, with a grammar-school education, passed.

With the help of his brother's coaching, Harry made it on the next attempt. He remained in the district attorney's office for a few years, while Ed entered the services of Nate Coghlan, then the outstanding criminal lawyer in the state.

Eventually the McKenzies formed their own partnership, and the pattern of their previous relationship persisted. Harry was never more than a run-of-the-mill advocate; Ed leaped quickly to recognition as one of the ablest in the community.

The curious contradictions in the McKenzie brothers and their fates persisted to the end. Harry was a great athlete; he was of powerful build, almost as broad as he was tall. He had been a football star in college and later on the Olympic Club squad, and was an excellent boxer. He was once attacked in the courtroom by Deputy District Attorney Jim Brennan, himself a formidable figure. He was twice McKenzie's size and had been the pride of Stanford University's athletic teams. Harry knocked him out with a single punch.

When he was fifty-two years old, Harry McKenzie dropped dead. Ed's health had been uncertain for years. Shortly after his brother's death he sustained a severe heart attack. It was then discovered that he was suffering from chronic diabetes. Degenerative processes continued until he was operated on for cancer. a colostomy was necessary, and for the last eleven years of his life his bowels emptied through an orifice in his abdomen. During all that time recurring cardiac crises obliged him to keep close to an oxygen tent, and he was continually in and out of the hospital. He died at seventy-two.

Up to the end he maintained an office in his home, where he was in constant consultation with other lawyers, weighing their evidence and planning their stratagems. Edwin McKenzie was a complete lawyer. He was a profound student of substantive and procedural law, and he knew all its quirks, but his forte was the analyses and presentation of facts. He had a strong scientific bent and had acquired a considerable education in physics and chemistry. He could seize upon a detail which escaped the average eye and turn it into a decisive factor.

He once represented a man named Hickman, who was accused of the strangulation murder of a young woman. There was strong circumstantial evidence of the defendant's guilt, but McKenzie detected a flaw in it which he used with persuasive force. The defendant was a veteran ship's officer. The scarf with which the victim had been killed had been tied with a "granny" knot. This is a faulty way of tying a square knot, and no expert seaman would make such a fastening. This single factor weighed the scales for an acquittal in a case which otherwise leaned toward a conviction.

Often a significant fact will be noted by counsel, but will not be sufficiently exploited. The lawyer may recognize its value, but fail to develop it so as to convince a jury. Such an instance occurred in one of McKenzie's most celebrated cases. During a "Preparedness Day" parade in San Francisco in 1916, a bomb was exploded, killing several spectators.

Five persons were indicted for their murder. They were Tom Mooney, his wife Rena, and three associates—Billings, Weinberg and Nolan. The Mooneys were free-lance labor organizers with anarchistic bents. They had staged an abortive streetcar strike in San Francisco and had been suspected of a conspiracy to dynamite utility installations in its vicinity.

They were convicted in the press before their trials started. The district attorney's office dished out suspicions, innuendoes and conclusions which were distributed as facts. Later it was demonstrated that the entire case was a flagrant frame-up.

At that time the state laws required separate trials for each of the accused. Billings was tried first, and was convicted on the weirdest kind of testimony, including that of a woman who claimed to have seen him at the scene of the explosion through her "astral" body, though her physical entity was a couple of blocks away.

Tom Mooney was next brought to trial. He was defended by Burke Cochrane of New York. Cochrane was a Tammany Hall politician and renowned as an orator. His stature as a criminal lawyer would have to depend on something better than his conduct of the Mooney defense.

In the defendant's chambers the police had found a scrapbook containing numerous printed articles, most of them clipped from radical publications. Some of them advocated the overthrow of the existing social and political system by violent revolution. The district attorney attempted to bolster his case by questioning the defendant about these excerpts. Cochrane, without having examined the book and with the utmost folly, himself suggested putting the scrapbook in evidence.

The prosecutor seized the opportunity. On argument, he read the more inflammatory portions, with disastrous results to the defendant. Mooney was convicted and sentenced to hang.

The remaining defendants now procured McKenzie to defend them. He was reasonably sure that the indictments and convictions had been procured by fraud, and set out to verify his suspicions. His experience as an electrical inspector for the city enabled him to identify the telephone wires leading to the district attorney's office, and to trace them—by means of the colors on their insulation—into a complex located in the Monadnock Building on Market Street. He rented an office at that location, found the proper wire in the basement, and led a tap from it into his own suite. Listening in on the conversations which went on over it, he confirmed his suspicions and discovered means of exposing the prosecution's dishonesty.

Discussing this part of the case, he once confided to me, "Of course I knew that the Mooney case was a frame-up before I had heard a single word of the evidence."

This was a puzzling statement. "How did you know that?" I asked.

He smiled. "I can convince you *in one sentence* that the Mooneys are innocent," he said.

This was something still more challenging. There had been two convictions. Most people considered the defendants guilty. What opinions I had of the case were pretty much in the same direction. What was the single magic sentence which would undo all such beliefs?

Somewhat incredulously, I enquired: "What's the sentence?"

His eyes narrowed, and emphasizing each word, he replied: *"There never was a conspiracy of five people that one of them didn't turn state's evidence."* I brought my hand down on my thigh in a resounding acceptance of the argument. Take it from one instructed by long experience, it is conclusive.

To return to the item of evidence which had been ineffectual until McKenzie turned his peculiar talents upon it. A photo had been taken, from the roof of the Eilers Building, about a mile and a half from the scene of the explosion. It showed Tom and Rena Mooney near the parapet, and—what was of the greatest importance—it included a large clock in front of a jeweler's store on the opposite side of the street, with its hands only a minute or so from the time the bomb went off. If the timepiece was correct, it was demonstrably impossible for the Mooneys to have been at the scene of the outrage.

The prosecution attacked this exhibit with vigor. It introduced proof of the timepiece's customary inaccuracy, and also raised a strong implication that the picture had been taken long before the parade day, for the purpose of establishing an alibi. Sufficient doubt was cast upon the validity of the exhibit to destroy its efficacy.

In McKenzie's hands it was another story. The photo became conclusive proof of the defendants' innocence. More than a year elapsed before Rena Mooney was brought to trial. Meanwhile, the defense lawyer had numerous pictures taken from the same spot on the Eilers Building roof. He was then able to demonstrate that the shadows on the disputed photograph occurred only on the precise anniversary of the Preparedness Day parade and at almost the minute shown by the clock in the picture.

After many hours of deliberation the jury acquitted Rena Mooney. Weinberg was then brought to trial. It took a jury only ten minutes to return a verdict of Not Guilty. The indictment against Nolan was then dismissed.

The acquittal of his alleged accomplices, and an investigation by the United States Senate of the means used to convict him, dissipated any belief in the guilt of Tom Mooney. The state's attorney general stipulated that his conviction might be reversed, but the Supreme Court refused to accept this stipulation and affirmed the sentence. The governor then commuted it to life imprisonment. Mooney was offered a parole from prison, but refused to accept it, demanding a pardon. He spent twenty years in San Quentin before this was forthcoming, and died shortly after his release.

Edward A. Cunha was the assistant district attorney in charge of the Mooney case prosecutions. Years later he grudgingly conceded that Mooney probably had nothing to do with the bomb itself, but held obstinately to the contention that there had been no miscarriage of justice.

Cunha was a big, handsome man, and had a habit of reassuring himself by vigorous and emphatic assertion. Discussing the Mooney case, he said to me, "All right! The son of a bitch probably had nothing to do with making or setting the bomb—but it was his agitating that stirred up the fellow who did it, and under the rule of the Haymarket cases, that made him just as guilty as the one who actually did it."

I asked him: "What evidence is there that the person who set off the bomb had ever even heard of Mooney, let alone been influenced by him? Also, everybody knew that the Preparedness Day whoop-up was a preliminary to taking the United States into the war on the side of the Allies. Isn't it more likely that some German agent or pro-German fanatic did it?"

Ed shook his head. "You'll never convince me that Mooney didn't have it coming to him," he said obstinately.

So I didn't try.

Another of the great characters of the time at the San Francisco bar was an old-timer who was nursing the last flames of a once brilliant career. He was the flamboyant William F. Herron. Bill was brilliant, resourceful, generally broke and frequently drunk. From the time he was kicked out of Stanford University for printing an indecent poem in the student magazine he had run an erratic course. He was a bit over six feet tall, lean, and had white hair which he plastered back against his skull. He was one of those men one meets with occasionally, who—somewhere along the course of life—stops and says, "I like it here," and refuses to grow older. When he was in his deep fifties he continued to refer to himself as a "young lawyer."

He was almost lacking in a sense of humor, and what vestige he had never reached his own eccentricities. His ordinary expression was a saturnine scowl which never entirely disappeared. He would listen to an amusing story with an accommodating smile on his lips and his brows contracted in a puzzled frown.

Life to Bill was one long stage appearance. He never quit acting. He walked with a purposeful stride, as though he were really going somewhere. He never talked, he only declaimed. He discussed the most commonplace subjects in strident tones and dressed them up in classical allusions. He would stride dramatically into my office, stand on one leg, and rub his hands together. "I took a dip in the ocean this morning, Vin," he would enunciate fiercely, "and it was so goddamned cold that when I got out I stood shivering and shaking like King Henry the Fourth outside the palace of Pope Hildebrand. I don't mean Henry of Navarre you understand, but that Lancastrian one . . ."

Again, when an upcoming trial aroused his enthusiasm, he would confide in his own version of sotto voce, his hand cupped beside his mouth, and a "whisper" that could be heard on the next block: "We're going to win this one—and we're going to be so goddamned rich that we will clank when we walk like Jugurtha in his chains of gold, as is described by Crispus Sallust."

This "whisper" once brought him as close to embarrassment as it was possible for Bill to get. One of the Superior Court judges, Sylvain Lazarus, was quite deaf and required a hearing aid. He kept the battery portion on the desk in front of him and would manipulate it so as to adjust it to the tone of the person addressing him.

However, he also had the habit of turning the device off completely when he believed that the argument in progress was adding nothing to his understanding of the case. The lawyers would continue thundering while Lazarus insulated himself behind a curtain of silence. The judge's practice in this regard was known to Bill, as well as to many other lawyers.

Herron was debating a motion with another lawyer in Lazarus' court. His opponent was arguing vigorously, when Bill observed on the judge's face that look of calm contentment which had come to be recognized as accompanying his isolation from the world of noise.

Bill cupped his hand beside his mouth and "whispered" in stentorian accents to the other advocate, "You might as well shut up; he's got his hearing aid turned off and he isn't hearing a goddamned thing you're saying."

"Not this time, Mr. Herron," interjected the judge smilingly, "I'm not missing a word."

Bill's favorite expletive was "For Christ's sake," and he is the only person I have ever heard pronounce the "t" in that phrase distinctly. He always managed four syllables to it.

His boozing had ruined an otherwise promising career. He had been kicked out of several law firms for derelictions due to alcohol. He had once been employed by two leading lawyers, and for purposes of convenience in collecting it, they had assigned him a claim for $10,000. Following a trial, they recovered a judgment and the defendants appealed. They also knew Bill's weakness. While the appeal was pending they got him drunk, gave him $2,500, had him sign that the judgment was satisfied, and dismissed the appeal. Bill had a fling with the money, and it was some months later before his associates knew what had happened. They hurried back to court and had Bill's caper set aside on the basis that the satisfaction of the judgment had been procured by fraud and undue influence. Later the defendants had to pay the full amount, as well as losing the $2,500 they'd given Bill. But he was out of a job.

Yet, other lawyers sometimes needed Herron's brilliant mind. A wild case broke when a police spy, posing as a homosexual, infiltered a group which had gathered in a private home. There was a theatrical raid, several affluent men were taken in the trap, and the newspapers—dubbing the house the "Baker Street Club" —were off on their own orgy of sensationmongering. McKenzie took the case.

At the height of the scandal the lean, purposeful Herron made his usual dramatic entrance into McKenzie's office, attired in a badly frayed tweed suit, with a lawbook under his arm. "If I show you how to get the Baker Street Club off without a trial, will you give me a job?" he asked.

McKenzie agreed. Bill opened the book. "All right! Look here!" With a ragged fingernail, he pointed to a section. "Look at this! The acts technically known as *fellatio* and *cunnilingus* are hereby declared to be felonies . . . and so on."

McKenzie shrugged. "Yes?"

Herron beamed. "Don't you see? The state constitution requires all acts and parts of acts to be in the English language! These words are pure Latin. You won't find them in any goddamned English dictionary in the world! Hell! I can show them to you in Petronius Arbiter and half-a-dozen other poets of Rome in its decadent period. But not in any dictionary . . ."

Herron's classical lore won out. The Supreme Court held the statute unconstitutional and dismissed the defendants. The triumphant, white-haired Herron moved his books of poetry and his bottles into McKenzie's office. But it didn't last long. McKenzie spent so much time fighting disbarment proceedings instituted against his erratic associate that he finally had to send Herron back to the street.

It was about then that this colorful legal freebooter arrived on my doorstep. The District Court of Appeals had reversed a verdict which I had gotten against the Market Street Railway, my prime foe for years. My client was a ten-year-old boy whose feet had been cut off by a cable car. The jury had awarded him $50,000. But it had been annulled for alleged error on two unimportant instructions. Such corruption in the courts was an accepted problem in dealing with the all-powerful transit firm. A day or so later I was standing at the window, puzzling what my next move should be, when Herron came striding triumphantly in, his lean face flushed with enthusiasm, and I suspected, bourbon.

"I've just read the decision," he announced grandly, taking a Hamlet stance. "It's a goddamned outrage!" He paused, shifting rapidly to a Shylock pose. "I took the liberty of checking the instructions they found bad. I can show you half-a-dozen cases where the same court held those identical instructions proper." He cleared his throat. "I have some free time just now," he announced softly. "Let me write the petition for a hearing in the Supreme Court. If I don't get it, I won't charge you a cent."

I knew Herron and was wary. "First show me the cases," I hedged. I'd been searching for two days and hadn't found a clue.

Herron jubilantly pulled a crumpled bit of paper from his coat pocket. "Here they are!" He stepped briskly to my bookshelves and started pulling out volumes. He opened one California report, pointing to a page. I read it, confused. It had nothing to do with the matter at hand.

"You must have the wrong case," I said. "There's nothing here even remotely connected."

He shook his head, obviously saddened that his profession had declined to a state where such nincompoops as Hallinan could pass the bar. "Read the last line," he ordered.

It stated: "We have carefully considered the remaining instructions and find no error in them."

Herron grinned fiercely. "How many times have you seen that exact language in a decision? And how many lawyers bother to go out to the Appellate Court and look through the record to see what those 'remaining instructions' are? Here is one of them from that case you've just read."

He handed me a typewritten slip. The language on it was almost identical with one of the instructions in my case which the District Court had declared to be erroneous.

"Now," he went on triumphantly, "under the rule of *stare decisis*, when you prepared your instructions in this case you were entitled to rely on the court's ruling in the decision you have before you."

"Mr. Herron," I said, "you have a contract."

He drew up his petition for a hearing by the Supreme Court. It was a brilliant legal document. But it was something more, it had in it a ring of passion; it was a poetic cry for justice. The Supreme Court granted the hearing and affirmed the judgment.

And so began a turbulent association. Herron's imagination and vast legal lore saved us again and again in cases which had already been lost or rejected by other lawyers. Posed with a crisis, he would pace angrily, his brow furrowed, gesturing and muttering. Then he would explode. "I've got it! I've got it!" he'd shout.

Our reputation for winning tough cases spread. Even enemies would send clients. One woman came to us with a complicated contract matter which had already involved two separate trials, both of which she'd lost, and the decisions had become final. Herron, after a day of pacing, found a legal gimmick which would get the case before a jury on a new approach. We set out on a meticulous investigation. Our client had been badly overreached in her original contract. But the law was dead against her. Yet we found several tiny violations on the other side. By stringing them together, we barely got past a nonsuit and into court.

By then I was addicted to poetry too. I thundered and shouted before the jury, calling to their minds Portia's argument in *The Merchant of Venice,* and charged that if the Shylock in our case had been entitled under the law to his pound of flesh, he had forfeited it by squeezing even a few extra drops of blood from the heart of his unfortunate victim. Bill sat beaming as I spilled out the poetic allusions. We won.

While I was busy with these cases in my early law years, I was also ardently pursuing an avocation, playing football. I loved the game and was to continue to play it until I was thirty-eight years old.

This was no sand-lot scrimmaging either. I was captain of the college American football team, and after graduation played with club teams. Sometimes these were pretty poor, and sometimes we were Pacific Coast champions and played to big crowds. I ended playing Rugby for the San Francisco Olympic Club. Even then we were state champions. Though football interfered considerably with my law practice, I would sooner have given up the latter than the former. Dan Ryan always regarded with disgust the black eyes which I often carried to the office on Monday mornings following rough games on Sundays.

"Pretty soon," he used to remark sourly, "the lawyers will be calling you a football player and the football players will be calling you a lawyer."

Shortly after I passed the bar examinations I threw up my job with Ryan, including the $40 a month which it paid, and launched out for myself. I was wonderfully poor. My family consisted of my father and mother, a younger brother and six sisters. We lived in a five-room flat in a run-down section of San Francisco. Age and labor-union activities had retired my father; my oldest sister was a stenographer; another was a milliner's apprentice. Between us we supported the family in humble style.

A former schoolmate of mine had formed a law partnership with another young man, and they had two rooms in one of the cheapest buildings in the city. I made a deal with them. For $20 a month I was to have a desk in their reception room, with the right to use the other room in the improbable event that I should have a client to interview. This arrangement lasted only a month. At the end of that time they went broke. One of them took a job with an insurance company, and I took over the "suite," permitting the surviving partner to use the reception-room desk for nothing.

I had had a fantastic piece of luck. I had a girl friend who worked for the telephone company as a switchboard operator and was my principal source of business. If she heard that one of her fellow employees was having trouble with her mate, she did her utmost to steer her into my office. I will never forget the first of these. She wanted an annulment because of her husband's sexual impotency. She was quite young and had brought her mother and aunt along to expound the story.

The mother said, "You know, Mr. Hallinan, it's very difficult to discuss these things with a strange young man."

"Don't be hesitant," I assured her, "we're used to hearing all sorts of things; just speak out freely."

Thereupon the three launched into a discussion such as had never assailed my innocent ears. I could feel a great blush spreading over my features, and my best efforts to appear sophisticated impressed no one. Long afterward they laughingly told me how they had sympathized with my obvious discomfort. However, I got the girl the annulment, and this led to the stroke of good luck I have mentioned.

The mother and aunt had been left some money in the will of a deceased sister, but the document had been found after her death in a clothes closet, with the signature and the portions containing the devises to them cut out. The dead woman had left an only son, who would inherit the entire estate if there were no will. The two women put the matter in the hands of one of the best law firms in town.

A few days before the time expired in which they could offer the document for probate, the head of this firm informed them that the mutilated will was, in his opinion, worthless and that his firm could not undertake to represent them in asserting any claim under it. The law on the subject seemed clear. When a mutilated will is found among the effects of a deceased, it is presumed that it was mutilated by the maker, with intent to revoke it. The sisters had little to rebut the presumption, and the attorneys they had consulted felt that it would be a waste of money and effort to attempt to probate the document.

The day before the time would expire in which they could file a petition they consulted me about it. They had nothing to lose by turning it over to even the most inexperienced of lawyers. I supposed that we might at least get a small settlement out of it, and filed a petition for the probate of the will. Then I got to work on the law.

I found it wasn't nearly as strongly against us as the big attorneys had advised. In the first place, while all courts sustained the presumption I have mentioned, it was subject to important qualifications. The document we were depending on had been found by the dead woman's son, in a clothes closet, several weeks after her death. The majority of cases held that—for the presumption of revocation to apply—the mutilated document must be found "immediately" after death, and that the lapse of several days destroyed the presumption. So did its discovery by someone with an interest in destroying it—such as the son.

I found one case in an eastern state which held that the word "effects" meant the personal papers of the deceased, and that finding it elsewhere prevented the invocation of the presumption. Accordingly, I marshaled all the facts and law I could muster, and—the son having refused to settle for a nickel—we went to trial before a jury.

I will never forget that trial. It lasted four days, and I still believe that I didn't sleep a single wink on any of the nights preceding them. My opponent was an able and experienced man and persuaded the judge that I was wrong on the law. The court instructed the jury that the will was presumed to have been mutilated by the testator with intent to revoke it, and that we were obliged to overcome that presumption by clear and convincing evidence. We didn't have this and lost the case. I took an appeal, and the Supreme Court reversed the judgment. It ruled that the circumstances under which the will had been found were such that the presumption of revocation did not apply, and that the burden of proving revocation rested upon the son.

We hadn't done too badly on the trial, the jury being out a long time. This, with their main weapon taken away from them by the decision on appeal, persuaded our opponents to settle. It was a grand settlement, but the most astonishing thing about it was my fee. I had been working before and after school and during vacations since I was nine years old. The highest wages I had ever earned were Dan Ryan's $40 a month. And now, in my first year at the bar, my fee from that one case was $20,000!

This was away back in 1922. Twenty thousand dollars was one hell of a lot of money then. I bought a home for the family. It had eight rooms and cost $6,500. I also bought some new furniture for it and a phonograph. We used to wander around the rooms, gazing at them almost in unbelief at the sudden transition to luxury. I also bought a secondhand Chevrolet coupe and a desk, three chairs and a rug for the office. I was now a man of property.

CHAPTER 3

I Spar with a Giant

THE San Francisco into which I was born was a rough, tough place. It competed with a number of others for the title "The Wickedest City in the World" and somewhat gloried in the distinction. Prostitution was its major industry. The district around Pacific Street and upper Grant Avenue was known far and wide as the Barbary Coast. All manner of brothels, cribs and parlorhouses flourished in its environs. Gambling establishments, saloons, opium dens and clip joints of various types crowded in among them.

This was no pleasant, if illegal, garden of vice, but a region of deadly peril—sordid, thieving, murderous. Hatchetmen of Chinese tongs anticipated the gangsters of the Prohibition Era and gunned each other down in the streets. The city morgue was full of John Does, robbed and murdered in the back rooms of dives and dragged into neighboring alleys to be found by patrolmen on their rounds. High-school boys contracted gonorrhea and syphilis in the embraces of its female denizens.

If this last item smacks of exaggeration, I remember hearing with awe my classmates at St. Ignatius High School reciting their adventures in this formidable domain, and one of them—the son

of a prominent politician—displaying the chancre he had gotten
from a whore. Years later he was committed to an asylum, a
hopeless paretic.

It should be unnecessary to explain that this demimonde of
crime and vice could not have existed without the corruption of
the city government and—indeed—of its populace generally.
Even today San Francisco is actually graft- and vice-ridden. Its
police force boasts that gangsters cannot get a foothold in San
Francisco. Good reason: the cops do their own "protecting" and
keep the pay-offs in the family.

Lincoln Steffens, in his *Autobiography,* describes his researches into similar conditions in other large American cities.
He was puzzled at the tolerance displayed toward them by the
most responsible members of their communities. Prominent
people, high in the financial and social brackets, were not concerned by the presence among them of organized vice, nor by
disclosures that it maintained itself by bribery of law-enforcement
agencies.

Steffens solved the riddle. The Upper Crust was in no position
to get lofty about such things; it was up to its own neck in
political corruption. To be sure, it wasn't playing this game at
the police-sergeant level, nor concerned with the take of a
bookie joint. Its racket was acquiring public-utility monopolies;
its pay-offs went directly to the city fathers. Part of this remuneration consisted in closing its eyes to the cruder means by which
the politicos and their agents maintained their standard of living.

So it was in San Francisco. Its proudest names were deep in
graft. Its greatest fortunes were based on franchises for supplying
water, gas, transportation and other utilities, to the public, all
procured by wholesale bribery of its supervisors and other
officials. However, the tolerant spirit of San Francisco's pioneer
tradition permitted a departure from a certain delicacy of conduct which Steffens had noted in more effete communities. There,
the pillars of society disdained to participate in vulgar vices; here,
they owned the whorehouses.

This tolerance was in the web and woof of the city's life; it was
shared by *hoi polloi,* and it was no empty word. Shortly after

the turn of the century, a wave of reform, engendered by the jeremiads of the muckrakers, swept across the nation. When it arrived at San Francisco its force was broken in the face of this indifference. Disclosure of corruption among its political and social elite served rather to amuse than to outrage them. This attitude was a consistent one: the heroes of California tradition are mainly bandits; the Vigilantes, its most formidable law-enforcement agency, was completely lawless.

It is not to be understood that this sentiment was unanimous. Many residents of the city took law and order seriously. These rallied behind a corps of plumed knights, and launched a vigorous crusade against the forces of evil. Their purpose was noble, but their tactics were directed by the same ancestral distaste for legal niceties.

As their quarry was determined to escape ruin by whatever means and especially favored the foul, it was Greek against Greek. The opposing forces put on a legal three-ring circus which performed for almost five years. In all, 117 indictments were returned against assorted defendants. These included the mayor, the entire board of supervisors, the principal officers of all the public-utility corporations, various political bosses, fixers and bagmen.

When the final curtain was rung down on the numerous trials, appeals, proceedings and hearings, only one man had been sent to prison. He held no public office, nor was he an officer of one of the boodling corporations. He was the fixer and go-between for the bribegivers and -takers. He was also a cinch to be the sacrificial goat in the strongly Irish-Catholic community. He was a Jew.

I knew nothing of all this. I was still attending St. Vincent's Grammar School in Petaluma and working as an errandboy in a grocery store. Nine or ten years elapsed between the dismissal of the last indictment in the San Francisco graft cases and my innocent intrusion onto the stage where the drama had been performed. The audience had gone home and to sleep, the orchestra had moved to other theatres, and the actors had withdrawn to the wings.

Nevertheless, the season was by no means closed, nor were the Thespians unemployed. The scenery was changed and there were new faces at the rehearsals, but the scripts were substantially the same. A few of the old stars survived to make their impress on the growing generation, and fundamentally the traditional spirit persisted. However, there had been some chastening. Everything was as crooked as before, but on a more subdued tempo. This was true nationally. The swashbuckling robber barons were gone, and their sons had concluded that the creed of the Public Be Damned didn't pay. Even the oil trusts had become philanthropic. On the metropolitan scale, both the city fathers and the utility corporations had recognized the necessity for some discretion. Ruthlessness had become dangerous. The law had to be circumvented by legal means.

Even a few desultory crusaders were still in the chorus. About the time I finished law school the San Francisco Bar Association launched recall proceedings against two police-court judges whose techniques of collection were somewhat too raw. The electorate booted the careless magistrates out of office.

Personally, I was quite wide-eyed and ingenuous to all this chicanery. I supposed that the two acquisitive judges were exceptions and that their expulsion proved the invincibility of virtue. Thus, when I myself donned the white panache and found my feet tangled in the filaments of that very intrigue which had once controlled the power of the city, I kicked through them with a scorn which would probably have been considerably chastened by a clearer understanding of the true situation.

Among the flamboyant of the graft-case defendants had been James Coffroth. He headed a group of prize-fight promoters which were deep in the general corruption; the ring then, as now, being controlled by the shadiest of characters. In addition, he was overlord of all the protected gambling houses in the city. He was always described in the papers as "The Gambling Commissioner," which title—together with another distinction—invested him in the popular mind with respectability and even with the supposition of legality. This other distinction was that the judges of the Superior Court had appointed him secretary and jury commissioner of that court.

Nothing illustrates better than this one circumstance the cynicism and lawlessness of official San Francisco in those days. The magistrates, who were supposed to represent the law and upon whose decisions justice itself depended, thought nothing of placing in charge of the very portals of its temple a man whom they all knew to be a briber and corrupter of public officials: a man who had been saved from conviction only by the most consummate legal trickery; who openly flaunted state gambling laws; and who was a known associate of the most vicious and dangerous criminals in the city.

Coffroth served for a number of years as secretary and jury commissioner of the Superior Court. During all that time he conducted his gambling establishment in the full light of day, and his odds on everything from horse races to presidential campaigns were daily recorded in the local press. The more routine aspects of his gambling activities were handled by his partner Thomas Mulvey.

Age finally required James Coffroth to retire from the duties of his public office. His faithful performance of its obligations did not go unrecognized. The Superior Court judges magnanimously permitted him to name his successor as their secretary and jury commissioner. He named Thomas Mulvey.

This man was the engineer in charge of the machinery of justice when I first ventured into the Superior Court. He had the heart of a racketeer, but the suavity of an ambassador. He was tall, of medium build, and had a ruddy complexion; his graying hair was closely plastered against his head. As a badge of office, he affected cutaway coats and striped trousers. There was always a white carnation on his lapel.

Mulvey was soft spoken, courteous and deferential. This followed from long association with the domineering Coffroth. No one could remain long under the latter's domination and retain any of the outward aspects of a vigorous personality. But Mulvey was enormously alert and suspicious. He remained close to his work, fearful of disclosure or betrayal.

He and I became the antagonists in a duel which lasted for several years. Each of us miscalculated the other. I was ignorant of his character, his precedents and his associations, and underestimated his capacity for mischief. In fact, I regarded him with contempt and could not understand why judges and lawyers were afraid of him. I laughed at more than one warning that he was quite capable of having me knocked off.

Mulvey, for his part, misinterpreted my brashness. With his overly suspicious nature, he feared me much more than was warranted. He always believed that I was only the front man for a combination of powerful forces which were out to get him, and that I was tempting him to some excess which could be used to ruin him.

Both errors served me. He planned and plotted to destroy me, but always by some legally justifiable means. I was concerned only in disclosing his dishonesty in the selection of jury lists and the other affairs of the Superior Court, and to procure safeguards against it. I was not the least concerned with his efforts at retaliation, and felt entirely competent to take care of myself. My bravado led to one of the liveliest clashes in my career at the bar.

During those first years of my practice, the greater part—and certainly the most remunerative—was in the personal-injury field. This was natural enough. In the first place, it's about the only one in which a young lawyer can make any money.

Not that this type of litigation was a soft touch—it wasn't. The hardest part of it was getting the cases. Competition was keen. Many attorneys employed runners to gather them in. The fact that this was forbidden by both law and the canons of the Bar Association wasn't much of a hindrance. At most it required a small amount of circumspection.

The most capable solicitors were employed by the most respectable firms. These also had deals with hospital stewards, police officers and others who could supply leads. Speed was the principal requirement. More than one person learned of the death or injury of a dear one from an attorney's runner soliciting the case.

Those lawyers who had pre-empted the market gathered a rich harvest from it. Their capital investments were sometimes quite large. They guaranteed medical and hospital bills, and frequently carried an injured person's family over his disability period.

Naturally, those who could afford such risks captured the lion's share of the business. A beginner like myself, poor and unknown, had to be content with culls and rejects and an occasional sleeper which had escaped their diligence.

At that time the chief defendant in such cases was the Market Street Railway Company, which owned most of the city's street-car lines. Most of the others were against automobile and truck drivers, who were represented by one of another of a small group of law offices, actually employed by the insurance companies indemnifying the defendants.

These litigants had wealth and influence on their side, and only the most bemused would expect a judge to return a judgment against one of them. Therefore, those plaintiffs' lawyers who knew the least thing about their business demanded jury trials in all such cases. The defendants then got around this device by taking over the jury. This was not too difficult, since they already had the judges in their pockets and the juries were selected from a list compiled by a jury commissioner appointed by the judges. The Market Street Railway Company simply put its own man in as jury commissioner—James Coffroth.

When Mulvey replaced Coffroth, who had been involved in the original bribes which obtained the Market Street Railway Company its initial franchise, the change in personnel did not alter the relationship which had existed between the goddesses of Justice and Chance in San Francisco. Mulvey procured a partner to run the betting joint, while he moved into the lordlier offices in the city hall. In these latter he made one new installation which aided the purposes for which they were being run. This was the appointment as his chief assistant of one William Lynch, an employee of the Market Street Railway Company. Lynch was to remain on that company's payroll during all the years he served as an officer of the courts.

These two racketeers, Mulvey and Lynch, selected all jurors

for the trial of criminal and civil cases in San Francisco. The lists from which these were chosen were furnished by the Market Street Railway, insurance indemnity firms, trucking companies, taxicab owners, bankers and others having interest in the litigations which would come before them. There was a directness about the process which almost amounted to honesty. For example: in a case which I tried against the Market Street Railway Company, the prospective jurors included the brother of William Abbott, its chief counsel, and the mother and sister of Cyril Appel, the attorney against whom I was trying the case.

Needless to say, it was almost impossible to recover a verdict for the plaintiff in a death or injury case. The few which were allowed were for inadequate amounts—usually less than the defendant had offered in settlement.

Besides being jury commissioner, Mulvey was secretary of the Superior Court, and as such had control of the court calendar. In addition to planting jurors for his principals, he saw that their cases were assigned to favorable judges. Of course, he would never have been appointed—let alone given such a free hand—if the majority of the judges were not dishonest themselves. He controlled them with the usual metal. He managed their election campaigns and collected the funds to finance them. The favored litigants were the chief contributors. In addition, they procured elevation to the Appellate Courts of judges who had earned their favor by long subservience.

This carried a triple benefit. It rewarded the faithful, seduced the waverers, and provided an extra check on possible adverse judgments. If they got past the Superior Court, the Appellate department could be counted on to dump them. I hadn't tried many cases before I knew that there was something awfully fishy about the San Francisco jury system.

On the other hand, I had no special reason for doing anything about it personally. However poorly the other plaintiff lawyers were making out, I had an imposing string of wins. This was due to two factors: I was a hell of a hard worker, and some accidental arrangement of genes and chromosomes had given me The Touch.

The Touch is easy to recognize, but not so easy to define. It involves a combination of qualities which just happen to fit one for a particular field. Without it, an actor remains mediocre after years on the stage; a writer never really clicks. I've seen lots of athletes who had speed, stamina, courage—everything that would apparently make for greatness—and the first time I saw them each in action I knew they'd never quite make it. You may say: "This guy has plenty of self-confidence!" That's right. That is an indispensable ingredient of just what we're talking about.

I had no fraternal bonds with the other lawyers which would excite me to correct their wrongs. They all operated on a strictly dog-eat-dog principle. Its motto, actual if unexpressed, was: "To hell with you, Jack; I've got mine." I would probably never have belted into Tom Mulvey's racket and the Pandora's box of troubles in which it involved me, if it hadn't been for what happened to Mike Riordan.

Mike was a fabulous character. I first met him when we were both freshmen at Saint Ignatius Law School. It was a night school, and many of the students worked during the daytime. At that time Riordan was a sergeant on the San Francisco police force. He was a real Irishman, big, burly, with a wide Celtic face, gray eyes, and a brogue as broad as his back. He also had a fine mind and a capacity for work bordering on genius. He never stopped working. He carried one of the legal codes of the state with him at all times and studied it on the streetcars or while waiting to be served his meals.

He had emigrated from Ireland not many years before and had worked his way across the country in various laboring jobs, finally coming to port in the local constabulary. He didn't stay put very long. As fast as he became eligible, he took the promotional examinations in the department. They were duck soup to Mike. He was the only man in the history of the force to take first place in all three examinations for sergeant, lieutenant and captain. Ultimately he became chief of police.

Having some hours to waste in the evenings, he invested them in law school, breezed through the courses, and passed the bar examinations with ease. Some years later he took a leave of absence from the police department, formed a partnership with me, and plunged into practice. Here he learned some quirks of civil procedure that were to be found neither in law school nor in his beloved codes.

Mike was an immediate success. You could be sure that in every case he tried he had the facts and the law down cold. In court he was sharp, direct and persuasive. He was elated by his initial victories and aspired to bigger game. A good case was coming up against the Market Street Railway Company, and he wanted to try it. I warned him of the jury complications and turned him loose on it. I knew he would not leave a fact undiscovered or a legal point unexplored. In addition, his honesty and directness canceled out his inexperience.

The case was assigned for trial to the department of Judge Daniel Deasy, with whom Mike had friendly relations, both from official contacts and joint activities in certain Irish-American societies. After several days of trial, Riordan won a substantial verdict. On motion for a new trial, the judge set it aside upon the ground that the evidence had been insufficient to justify it. The law gives the judge this right. It means that he can substitute his judgment for that of the jury, and grant a new trial.

An appeal from this ruling is practically worthless, since the Appellate Courts will not interfere with the decision if there is any conflict in the evidence. It is another anchor to windward for defendants in damage suits, and is often employed in their favor. I have never heard of a verdict for a defendant being set aside on this ground.

Riordan took the blow philosophically and reset the case for trial. This time it found its way into the department of Judge Timothy Fitzpatrick. His relations with Mike were almost exactly the same as Deasy's. So were the results of the trial. The jury gave the plaintiff an even larger award, and Fitzpatrick granted a new trial on the grounds of the insufficiency of the evidence.

This time Riordan wasn't quite so philosophical. In fact, he was blazing mad. He was ready to break with two eminent Irish Catholic magistrates. "Take it easy, Miehal Og," I advised him. "According to what I'm told, that kind of thing has been going on for a long time in our Temple of Justice. Let's look the ground over before we get in too far to back out."

I went to the county clerk's office and ran down the trial record of the Market Street Railway for several years past. The company's tie-up with Judges Deasy and Fitzpatrick became obvious. Between them they had tried more than half of all the cases against it, although there were twelve departments in the Superior Court, to any of which they might have been assigned.

In addition, three other cases had fared exactly as Riordan's had. That is, the plaintiff had won a verdict before either Deasy or Fitzpatrick and the judge had granted the defendant a new trial for insufficiency of evidence. The retrial went before the other of the duo. Again the jury had given its decision for the plaintiff, and again the judge had set it aside—insufficiency of evidence.

Moreover, neither had ever permitted a verdict against the Market Street Railway to get out of his court. If the plaintiff succeeded in getting past the roadblocks set up by the bench, his good fortune lasted only until the defendant asked for a new trial. Having gone that far, I decided to go somewhat further. I hired a man to make a run-down of the jury list. After a couple of weeks' work he handed in his report.

"Do you know," he inquired, "that more than half the people in this city work for the Market Street Railway Company or an insurance company—or else someone in their family does?"

I took the report to George Ford, one of the best-known trial lawyers in the state. He was now past his prime, but still one of the most active members of the bar. He was a tall, good-looking man, and his almost invariable good nature had etched mementos around his eyes and the corners of his mouth. He listened in silence to what I had to say, and then sat gazing out the window for some moments. Finally he said, "Vincent, I want you to promise that you won't repeat what I tell you."

I assured him that I would not, and he continued, "I've lost thirty straight plaintiff cases in the San Francisco Superior Court. I would have concluded that I had lost my touch, but I've been trying them in Alameda—San Mateo—Marin—and winning my usual proportion.

"We all know that there is something crooked about the jury system in city hall. Maybe if I were starting out—like you—I'd try to do something about it; now I'm past the point where it matters that much to me. Then too I represent the Northwestern Railroad, and once in awhile I try a case for an insurance company, so I'm not in a position to kick. You see, sometimes I'm the one who gets the advantage of the packed juries.

"I don't know if anything can be done about it. That's a pretty tough combination, with almost all the judges head over heels in it. I'm the last one to urge another fellow to tackle something I'd be afraid to take on myself.

"I'll give you one piece of information that may help you decide what to do. I know the lawyers in this city, and there isn't one of them will lift a finger to help you. We're a lot of cowards. If you start something and miss, we'll stand by and watch you get smashed. If you win, we'll grab the profit."

To be frank, I didn't understand Ford's position. His warning of possible danger puzzled me. Where could there be any danger? Surely everybody was interested in protecting the integrity of the courts. Then there were the newspapers. If it were shown that the jury was rigged, wouldn't they all rush to put a stop to it?

I took my statistics to another prominent plaintiff lawyer. He too listened carefully and thoughtfully. His judgment of the situation was similar. Then he gave me some additional information, prefaced by an admonition that I was to hear twenty times over— "But don't use my name!"

That phrase was the theme song of my interviews. I finally came to the bleak conclusion that if anything was going to be done about the jury-planting in city hall, I'd have to do it and I'd have to do it by myself.

I sat down and punched out a long letter to the San Francisco Bar Association, setting out the situation and asking its help. In a few days I received a reply stating that it had appointed a committee to investigate the charges. McKenzie had been named chairman, and a date and place fixed for a hearing. I was immensely gratified. If I could get this powerful body behind the movement, we would make short work of Tom Mulvey's racket.

This feeling was somewhat dampened when I entered the bar meeting. It was packed with traction and insurance lawyers. The atmosphere was downright chilly. The committee members stared at me with open hostility. I looked around for a friendly face. Seated quietly in the back of the room were several of the attorneys who had furnished me information under the obligation not to use their names. They avoided my glances. No nods, no smiles. George Ford slipped in quietly and took a seat among them. He did not look in my direction.

Three of the Superior Court judges were in attendance. I was on friendly terms with them, but you'd never have suspected it then.

McKenzie started off with brusque directness: "Mr. Hallinan, you've made some very serious charges against our courts and judges. We want to hear what you have to back up these accusations."

The form of the statement and the manner in which it was made dispelled any remaining illusions as to the purpose of the gathering. Not Thomas Mulvey nor the jury system nor the corrupt judges were to be tried. I was to be the target. If that was the way they wanted it—all right.

I snapped back at the chairman, "Very well! Just sit back and listen, and you'll hear plenty."

McKenzie smiled a bit feebly and said, "We're listening."

I spread out my charts and other data and proceeded to outline the methods by which the trial juries were packed. Names, addresses, occupations, relationships, rolled out in unanswerable succession. The evidence was conclusive. More than 50 percent of the jury lists were persons working at occupations which actually engaged only a small fraction of one percent of the city's population.

I concluded and sat back triumphantly, waiting for a challenge of my statistics. I had brought along Jim Lascelles, who had done the investigation for me, and was prepared to have him sworn and examined on them. The challenge never came.

Instead, one of the committee members asked me coldly, "What's behind this move of yours? Who's putting you up to it?"

I felt my face flush with anger. "I'll tell you what's behind it. I'm not going to walk my clients into a court where the cards are stacked in advance. Even you insurance lawyers should think more of your profession than to see it corrupted as it is in the city hall."

Before he could reply, another member interrupted. "Who do you think you are, making accusations like that against other members of the bar?"

In an instant the session degenerated into a shouting contest. Anyone who has witnessed a couple of lawyers roaring at each other in court can form an idea of how it sounded with six or eight storming at the same time.

Suddenly there was a denouement. In a lull in the storm Judge Michael Roche said calmly and loudly, "Why do we pretend that there is nothing wrong, when we all know that there is?"

His statement was a bombshell. Abruptly, everyone fell silent. Roche lifted himself slowly from his chair, looked around with a sarcastic smile, and said, "Let's not be hypocrites."

If he had expected cooperation from the spectators, he was disappointed. He waited a few moments with the same look on his face. "Good night, gentlemen," he concluded, and walked quietly out of the room.

He had scarcely gotten out of the door when I realized that I had missed a golden chance. McKenzie, wiser in such procedures, closed the gap. "Mr. Hallinan," he suggested, "if you will withdraw your charges of fraud, I will recommend to the Bar Association that it make a further study of this situation."

I refused to make the concession.

"Very well," he said, "we will consider the matter submitted and will file a report later."

The committee recommended that nothing further be done in the matter, and the Bar Association hastily dropped it.

A few days later I received a phone call from Superior Judge Edward P. Shortall. He asked me to come to his home that evening. I had a sinking feeling that he was going to ask me to lay off Tom Mulvey. I liked Ed Shortall. He had the reputation of being the most humane and honest of the local judges. In addition, he had displayed real friendship toward me from my first appearance before him, when I had excited his interest and amusement.

Dan Ryan had sent me out to argue a demurrer which had been filed against a complaint of his. The opposing lawyer came up with a point which seemed completely valid. However, in presenting it, he said, "Your Honor, this point is so obvious that it requires the citation of no authorities."

When it came my turn to argue, the judge said to me, "Don't you think that the point is good? It seems to me to be so."

I answered, "While this gentleman was arguing the point is seemed to me also to be good, and I was about ready to concede it. However, when he ended by saying, 'It requires no citation of authorities,' I became suspicious that that may not be so. Baron Bulwer-Lytton has written an essay entitled, 'Professor Tomlinson's Advice to His Pupils'—his pupils being scoundrels and thieves—and among other things, he instructed them: 'Whenever you wish to assert something completely false, always preface it with the statement: "There can be no possible doubt" or "It is universally admitted that." '

"Now, when a lawyer says: 'It requires no authorities to prove, etc.' I get suspicious that there may be no such authorities. I would be grateful if this matter could be continued one week to permit me to see what the authorities actually hold on this point."

Shortall laughed heartily. "Counsel," he said, "I didn't think anyone read Bulwer-Lytton any more. I have had some experiences which bear out what you say. I'm going to continue this matter one week, so that you may satisfy yourself on the particular point involved."

The following week I showed up, armed with a decision of the Supreme Court which completely demolished my opponent's "unanswerable" point. The judge heard me through with great amusement and overruled the demurrer, upon which the other lawyer strode sulkily from the court, apparently finding nothing funny about the matter.

Shortall was the only judge in the city who could be counted on to give a fair trial to the plaintiff in a personal-injury case. He had an extremely sympathetic nature and disliked to see anyone hurt or disappointed. Indeed, he carried this to the point that when he was required to make an adverse ruling he did so in the most apologetic fashion. He would shake his head with an air of great concern, and explain the necessity he was under to rule correctly. Some of the less understanding had fastened upon him the sobriquet of "Crying Eddie," in derision of this habit.

Now, for all my regard for him, if he should ask me to drop my inquiry on the courts and juries, I was going to turn him down. However, this was far from his intention. He received me with his characteristic expression of solicitude, regarding me as though I had just emerged from a dangerous operation.

"How are you?" he inquired anxiously.

"Never felt better," I assured him. It was true. All my life I have suffered from chronic good health, and in those days I was brimming over with energy.

"Vincent," he said abruptly, "you are absolutely right in what you are doing. Mulvey is a complete crook, and the courts are being run for the benefit of the Market Street Railway Company and the insurance companies. Several of the judges are hand in glove with them, and the rest are afraid to open their mouths. If I say anything, they'll put a candidate against me at the next election. They control the newspapers, and they'll spend money to defeat me. Meanwhile, I don't want to see you standing out alone when everybody should be helping you. If you ask me to do it, I'll take my chances and come out openly against Mulvey."

I was relieved and pleased to hear him say it. I thought it out for a few moments and then advised him to do nothing. In the first place, I didn't want to take the chance of sacrificing Shortall. One honest judge off the bench, and we'd all be the worse for it. I also wanted to first present my proofs in a more important forum than the Bar Association.

When I left the judge's home that night, I was in possession of all the inside information on the city hall setup. I knew which judges to avoid and which would be secret allies. I was also greatly pleased to know that I had misjudged neither Edward Shortall nor Thomas Mulvey.

One of my cases was coming on for trial, and I used it to make my next move. I filed a challenge to the panel of jurors upon the same basis which I had employed before the San Francisco Bar Association. That body then showed just how impartial it had been and just what chance I had had of getting it to help reform the system. It appointed two lawyers to defend it and to resist my challenge.

One was McKenzie. The other was Maurice Harrison, Dean of Hastings Law College, the legal school of the University of California. They presented an interesting contrast. McKenzie was of medium height, sturdy of build, and brusque in approach. Harrison had a singular homeliness. He was tall—over six feet— but thin, stooped, sunken chested, with long, gangling arms and legs. His sallow face was extended laterally by a pair of prominent ears, and his large, loose mouth opened to disclose an uneven set of teeth. But he had fine eyes and a dignity and character of expression which actually canceled out these bizarre features. He had great poise and address, and the respect of the judges. This was not diminished by the fact that he numbered among his clients some of the wealthiest and most powerful organizations in the city.

Ordinarily he was a most courteous opponent, but on this occasion he had evidently been inspired to ruder tactics by McKenzie. He astounded me by opening his appearance with the statement: "Your Honor, I'd like to warn the court in advance that this is nothing but a publicity stunt by counsel for the plaintiff."

This would be like seeking publicity by getting into a fist fight with Jack Dempsey. The courtroom was crowded with lawyers interested in the proceedings. The rigged juries touched all of them, but those most affected still stayed in the background. The contest did not promise to be close. On one side was the lone troublemaker, absolutely in the right but without the prestige to carry it himself, nor the supporters to carry it for him. On the other were a predetermined judge and two of the bar's most imposing ornaments.

I had expected little more than an opportunity to expose the facts to public view and educate the lawyers as to how the system was working. That's all I got out of it too. My motion was denied.

Next I hired a lawyer who had some legislative experience, and sent him to the state capitol to lobby for a bill which I had prepared. It required that all juries be drawn by chance from the register of voters. Mulvey sent a representative to oppose it. The San Francisco legislators informed us that it would not support a measure which did not have his approval, and we could not find anyone to present our bill.

Mulvey's machine had powers which extended outside the porticoes of the city hall. He was singularly bold. One would have expected him to avoid occasions for attack. Instead, he seemed to welcome them. One of my best cases against the Market Street Railway Company was coming up for trial, and he calmly jockeyed it into Judge Daniel Deasy's department. This was one of the duo which had dealt so badly with Mike Riordan.

He probably thought that I would not want to tackle this aspect of the fix while immersed in another phase of it. If so, he was mistaken. I filed a motion to disqualify Deasy from trying the case, on the grounds that a fair trial could not be had before him in any case involving the traction company. I supported this with an affidavit setting out his record in actions involving it.

A judge from another county was appointed to try the charge. We had a long and acrimonious hearing. The railroad attorneys testified that in every case in which Deasy had granted them a new trial the plaintiff's claim had been without merit and the juries had been extremely remiss in thinking otherwise. The plaintiffs' lawyers preferred not to be involved in the controversy.

Deasy testified and made an elaborate defense of his rulings. I gave him a rough time on cross-examination. To my surprise, he treated me most respectfully. If Mulvey was bold, the judge certainly was not. He had a reputation for ragging parties, witnesses and attorneys when endeavoring to swing a jury against them. Now, under attack, he displayed only timidity. I checked that away for future use.

Of course, his colleague on the bench exonerated him from the charge of prejudice. I have never heard of one judge disqualifying another. We went to trial in Deasy's department.

I had guessed by this time that he would lean over backward to be fair, and that is what he did. No one would have suspected his customary sharpness and sarcasm toward plaintiff lawyers. Finally he carried the reform to embarrassing lengths. He had taken a legal point under submission, and during the examination of witnesses was poring over volumes. He descended from the bench with two of these in his hands, came over to the counsel table, spread them out before me, and indicating some passages with his finger, whispered, "Here's how the Supreme Court has held on that point." Then, with a wan smile, he retreated to his post on the bench.

Cyril Appel, trying the case for the defendant, regarded this performance with open mouth. The jury gave us a very large verdict, and the railroad moved for a new trial. Appel argued especially that the award was excessive and that there was insufficient evidence to justify the verdict.

As Deasy was obviously pretty well intimidated, I determined to use some psychology to prevent him from granting a new trial, or at least reducing the judgment.

When it came my turn to speak I said, "I'm not going to argue this motion. We will not accept any reduction in the verdict, and if a new trial is granted, I'll make a banner of it that will sweep the Market Street Railway and its hatchetmen out of the superior court." Upon which I slammed my papers into my brief bag.

"Very well," said the judge, "the matter is submitted."

He denied the motion for a new trial. It was the first time he had permitted a verdict against the railroad to leave his court.

I do not wish to convey the impression that this finished the case. The defendant had pals on the Appellate Court also. They reversed the judgment, and I had to win it all over again.

For awhile the situation remained static under an uneasy truce.

The Mulvey ring had apparently decided not to force the issue and to confine its machinations to less combative victims. Then it ran into a dilemma which required it to act positively. Another of my cases against the Market Street Railway came up for trial. It was a difficult one to win, but dangerous to the defendant. An eleven-year-old boy had had both feet cut off by a cable car. If he won a verdict, it would necessarily be large.

The company took no chances. On the day set for trial only two departments were free. One was Daniel Deasy's and the other Timothy Fitzpatrick's. The case was called for assignment in the presiding judge's department. I presented an affidavit and a motion to disqualify both available judges. Together with the allegations of their bias, I charged that the case was being jockeyed into one of their departments.

Louis F. Ward was the presiding judge. He was a small, quiet man of personable appearance. He could deliver a most damaging cut with apparent disinterestedness. In the present instance he heard my objection, and without waiting for my opponent to answer, stated: "Mr. Hallinan, I consider the charge that cases are jockeyed into particular courts constitute a charge of dishonesty against the presiding judge and is contempt of court. I will give you an opportunity to withdraw that portion of the affidavit."

I felt myself flush with anger. By this time I could recognize the technique. It was to attack the attacker. By putting him on the defensive, it was possible to push his charges into the background. I was to encounter this device many times thereafter. It was not new. Historically, it has been employed to block many reforms and to destroy their champions.

I protested that the judge should not fasten upon my statements the interpretation he was giving them. I said, "Until the cases enter your department for assignment, you cannot know what cases are to be tried, nor the departments which are vacant. The jockeying is done in the jury commissioner's office, and I have no thought of suggesting that Your Honor has anything to do with it."

He insisted that I amend the affidavit, and I refused to do so.

"Very well," said Ward, "I adjudge you in contempt of court and sentence you to a day in jail. Meanwhile, this case will be dropped from the calendar. Mr. Clerk, what are the next two cases available for trial?"

I procured a stay of execution of the sentence and a writ of *habeas corpus* from the District Court of Appeals. The presiding judge of that court had been elevated from the San Francisco Superior Court, where he had distinguished himself as an invariable friend of the Market Street Railway Company, and indeed of all the corporations which came before him. He carried this disposition onto the Appellate bench, and the department over which he presided was known as the "bad department" to lawyers representing injured persons on appeals.

True to its colors, the San Francisco Bar Association sent a lawyer to oppose my writ. This time it was Bartley Crum. He later became better known as the author of a book on British intrigue in Palestine entitled, *Behind the Silken Curtain,* but suffered some diminution of fame when he was sued for services by the man who had ghost-written it for him. His clothing was in the flamboyant style of those young lawyers who, having read Gene Fowler's account of William Fallon, and Adela St. John's of her father Earl Rogers, suppose that they can duplicate their positions by imitating their raiment. For this occasion Crum wore a cream-colored suit, and a shirt with pink stripes; a long gold pin, stretched beneath a lavendar tie, secured its collar ends.

To this apparition I opposed an old associate, Carey Van Fleet. He was a rugged and able veteran of the bar, a member of a socially prominent San Francisco family, and his father had been a federal judge. Carey had been chief deputy attorney general of the State of California for many years, but had fallen on evil days. He drank too much, worked too little, and had no money. He drifted into my office and remained there until his death.

Carey was a homely man. He had a heavy jaw and a hangdog look. His lower lids fell away from his eyes, giving him an expression of perpetual lugubriousness. He was a real lawyer and knew more tricks and angles than a sackful of foxes.

Now he surveyed his opponent's satorial magnificence with a baleful eye. He was sure of our legal position, and heard his opponent's argument through with a look of sour contempt.

The only point Crum could make to urge affirmance of the commitment was that in it Ward had stated that I had presented my motion "in a contemptuous manner." Here we were safe. A few years before Samuel Shortridge, afterwards United States Senator, had been adjudged in contempt, and the same phrase had been used in his commitment. The Appellate Court had reversed the conviction, holding that where the language used is not contemptuous it cannot be made such by the addition of a qualifying description. The respondent's words, and not the judge's subjective reaction to them, must be the basis of the charge. The decision in *"ex parte* Shortridge" was now firmly embedded in the law of the state. Certainly the Appellate Court could not hold that the mere effort to disqualify a judge would constitute contempt. To do so, it would have to throw out all the code sections providing procedures for that purpose.

At this juncture the presiding justice tossed our opponent an additional argument. He suddenly interjected, "Why was the motion to disqualify made before the presiding judge? It seems to me that proper procedure would have been to wait until the case was assigned and then present the objection in the trial department. Suppose he had gone down and thrown this thing around in the probate department, wouldn't anyone think he was doing so to blacken the courts?"

We were taken aback by the hostility of the statement and its lack of logic. Certainly the time to interpose a challenge of this kind was at the first available opportunity; to wait might be construed as a waiver of the objection. One might expect that a representative of the Bar Association would decline to avail himself of such an opening.

Instead, Crum, who had probably never thought of the point, jumped to his feet and said with fervor, "Your Honor, that's precisely our point."

After some acrimonious discussion by Van Fleet, the matter was submitted and we filed out. I waited half an hour in the

corridor, to take a punch at Crum, but he remained in the courtroom until I had cooled off and left.

Some days later we were notified that the court had affirmed
my conviction. We hurried to procure a copy of its decision, curious to discover by what perversion of logic it could have sustained
the judgment on the narrow premise suggested by the presiding
justice. It would have a hard time making that grade.

It hadn't tried to. Instead, it had taken a new look at the
phrase, "in a contemptuous manner." It discussed its previous
opinion in "*ex parte* Shortridge." It decided that it had been in
error in that case. It held that it was really bound by the lower
court's finding as to the respondent's demeanor and manner.
It threw out "*ex parte* Shortridge" as the leading authority on
contempt of court, and installed "*ex parte* Hallinan" in its stead.
This meant that any lawyer who wished to disqualify a judge
would be in real danger. The members of the bar were seriously
concerned.

They needn't have been. The very next time the point came
before the Appellate Court it pulled a complete switch. It decided
that it had been right in its first appraisal of "*ex parte* Shortridge"
and wrong in its second. It threw out "*ex parte* Hallinan" and
reinstalled "*ex parte* Shortridge." This was a most practical solution of the problems involved. It took care of everything—the
eternal principles and the immediate emergency.

When the decision became final, I prepared to put in the
prescribed stint in the county jail.

One day I found Van Fleet in the library. He was reading a
volume and chuckling audibly. "I thought that was it," he
exclaimed and turned to me, laughing with the lower part of his
face and sorrowing with the upper.

"How long are you going to stay in that hoosegow?" he asked.

"Twenty-four hours," I answered. "What did you think?"

"Twenty-four minutes!" he replied vigorously. "Look. You
didn't get twenty-four hours; you got one day. How long is a day?"

"Twenty-four hours," I ventured, now somewhat puzzled.
"Isn't it?"

"Not by a damn sight. In law a day is any part of a day.

You're going to show up at that jail at twenty minutes to midnight and walk out at midnight."

He shoved a copy of a Supreme Court decision toward me. "Read the syllabus," he said.

That was it, all right. We showed up at the booking desk at twenty minutes to midnight, and the deputy sheriff duly booked me. He started to usher me toward a cell.

"No use bothering with that," I told him, "I'm leaving here in ten minutes."

The deputy hurried into his office, and we could see him through its window, frantically dialing and then speaking over the phone. As he talked the worried look left his face and he broke into a grin. He emerged smiling.

"You're dead right," he admitted, "the sheriff says you should have given Ward a few hours, anyhow. He'll be sore as hell."

"Tell him for me," I answered, "that we wouldn't have come in until five minutes to twelve except that we were afraid you could delay booking me until after midnight and hold me for the whole twenty-four hours."

"Oh, by the way," said the deputy a bit shamefacedly, "I've got something for you."

He reached under the counter and came up with a large white-frosted cake. In red letters across the top was the one word: WELCOME.

"Who dreamed that up?" I asked.

"Mulvey," he confided. "I wasn't here, but they tell me he waited a couple of hours here this morning with a flock of reporters. Then they figured you wouldn't come until tomorrow."

"It's probably sweetened with cyanide," Van Fleet growled.

"Spread it around where Tom's cousins can enjoy it," I suggested. "You know—give it to the rats."

CHAPTER 4

Victory Over Corruption

RADICALS and reformers are not the darlings of their own times. Future generations may regard them with respect, but their own considers them cranks and pests. This should not be surprising. They are attacking some segment of the *status quo,* and after all, what is that but the system under which the most powerful and influential elements of the population desire to live?

These elements may constitute only a small minority, but they control the media of communication, particularly the newspapers, and they keep the majority educated to the belief that what is good for them is good for everybody. In this way, what starts as a racket becomes a vested interest. It acquires respectability, becomes part of "our way of life," and partakes of that concept's aura of sanctity.

When some conscientious soul finds it intolerable and undertakes to root it out, he runs into unexpected consequences. His motives may be unselfish and disinterested; they are examined closely, and it will be suggested—if not openly charged—that they are evil and personal. His antics, first regarded with amusement, are now surveyed with indignation. He is built up as a chronic malcontent, a troublemaker, and eventually, a clown. He finds himself assailed by the most powerful forces in the community, and what is worse, avoided by the ones he thought he could count on for support.

As Anatole France once put it: "The bitterest penalty a martyr must endure is to gaze out through the flames which are consuming him at the complacent faces of those he is dying to defend."

This sort of reaction didn't particularly bother me. I was pretty thoroughly disgusted with the lawyers. They had chickened out and let me carry their fight alone. I wasn't surprised when most of them avoided me, especially in the city hall. They were afraid to be seen talking with me, and would hurry by with bent heads, apparently lost in thought. Almost all the judges stopped speaking to me. Most of them considered me a personal enemy. The rest were afraid they would be considered friendly, or even neutral.

Newspaper accounts of the various developments were in a derisive vein. The reporters assigned to City Hall knew what was going on and were generally sympathetic. They sometimes gave me confidential information, but the rewrite men doctored the news so as to put me in the worst possible light.

None of these things caused me any concern. I had learned during the preliminary investigation that the other attorneys would not involve themselves, and I supposed that the judges would support their jury commissioner.

Recognizing the danger, I became extremely prudent. I checked every item carefully before including it in an affidavit. I couched all my charges against the judges in respectful language, and presented them courteously. It would be most difficult to maintain an accusation of perjury or contempt against me. Unfortunately, my precautions didn't cover all the fronts. I made the mistake of underestimating Mulvey. This was inexcusable. Long before, I had memorized Gibbon's account of the assassination of Alp Arslan: "The wound was mortal, and the dying sultan bequeathed an admonition to the pride of kings. 'In my youth,' said Alp Arslan, 'I was admonished by a sage to humble myself before God, to mistrust my own strength, and never to despise the most contemptible enemy. This advice I have neglected, and for that neglect I am now paying with my life.' "

I had overlooked the strongest weapon in Mulvey's arsenal. That weapon was the Grand Jury. Looking back, it seems incredible that I should not have suspected that he could use it to get me. Its members were selected by the Superior Court judges, and they were completely under the control of Mulvey, as jury commissioner. William Lynch, the Market Street Railway Company agent, was specially assigned to it as "Grand-Jury expert," whatever that meant, and its general comfort was in the hands of David Supple, another Mulvey appointee.

I suppose that my oversight in this regard arose from the traditions concerning grand juries, in which we have all been steeped. They have been glorified from the days of the Magna Charta. They are supposed to be shields between the people and the tyranny of government, and swords with which to reach those who would otherwise be above the law. I imagine that sometimes they are. In the present case I found that they could also be used as hatchetmen by a racketeer.

Since then I have had little reason to regard them with respect. Customarily, they exactly reverse the historic role ascribed to them. They act as shields to protect false accusers against actions for malicious prosecution, and they are used by state and federal attorneys to conceal evidence from the accused and to procure indictments where the evidence is insufficient to get a holding from a magistrate.

The San Francisco Grand Jury entered the battle on behalf of Mulvey by an oblique maneuver. Its first fire was directed, not at me, but at my clients and associates. This was sound strategy. My own position was fairly secure. The others were more vulnerable, if only because they did not anticipate danger. This is standard practice. I have encountered it many times since. One becomes involved in a fight with some powerful and ruthless interest. He expects reprisals. What he does not forsee is the injury which will be done to others about him, some of whom may have no interest in the matter.

In my own case I was like a man whom gangsters had marked for death. It was even dangerous for others to be on the same side of the street. This phase of the battle started when one of my associates, Emmet Burns, won a verdict for a woman who had been injured while a passenger on a Greyhound bus.

When a motion for a new trial came on, the judge before whom it had been tried was absent from the case. Somehow Donald Geary, a Superior Court judge in nearby Sonoma County was appointed to hear it in his stead. Since he had not been present at the trial, he was required to learn the facts from a typewritten transcript of the evidence.

He made the remarkable finding that the witnesses for the plaintiff had testified falsely, although the jury had heard them in person, had a far better opportunity to judge between the conflicting accounts of the accident, and had accepted our witnesses' testimonies. He granted the defendants a new trial. Mulvey then dispatched a copy of his decision to the Grand Jury, and got that body to indict our two witnesses for perjury. Burns defended them on the criminal trial, and got a speedy acquittal. Now, two juries had accepted their version of the accident as true.

No one could believe that Geary had based his judgment on the facts in the transcript. I made an investigation of his connections with the defendant. He, his brother, and an attorney named Tauzer, had been partners at the time he was appointed to the bench. Their principal client was the Northwestern Pacific Railway Company. Both this railroad and the Greyhound Bus Lines were owned by the Southern Pacific Company. I filed a motion to set aside the order granting the new trial, on the ground that Geary had fraudulently concealed his relationship with the defendant.

Another outside judge was appointed to hear this proceeding. On the witness stand Geary swore that he did not know that the Southern Pacific Company owned the Northwestern Pacific Railway Company, although his firm had handled the transaction under which it had acquired ownership. He also claimed that he did not know that the Southern Pacific Company owned the Greyhound Bus Lines, although almost every other person in the state did.

Of course, the judge who heard the motion found Geary innocent of fraud and refused to set aside his order. The bus company then settled the case.

Some months later another young associate represented a child who had been molested sexually. A criminal charge was pending against the accused man, who was represented by Roland Becsey, a former deputy district attorney, and one of Mulvey's buddies. The younger lawyer imprudently suggested to Becsey that if he would get his client to settle the civil liability, it might be possible to dispose of the criminal prosecution also.

The defendant's counsel hastened with this morsel to his friend the jury commissioner, and my youthful associate was horrified to find that the Grand Jury had indicted him on a charge of "Attempt to compound a felony." A mere offer of the kind involved here, if unaccompanied by any overt act, is not a crime. I moved to dismiss the indictment, and the court promptly granted the motion.

Next, a juror who had served on a jury which gave me a verdict was indicted for an alleged false answer on his *voir dire*. My office represented him, and he was acquitted easily.

All the time this was going on I kept up the pressure on the stacked juries. As each of my cases was called for trial I challenged the panel and filed a copy of the affidavit I had used on the prior motions. I was so involved in this end of the affair that I did not pay enough attention to the countermoves of the enemy.

I was like one of those characters in a motion picture who pursues some object, unconscious of knives flashing past him and trap doors snapping in his wake. Abruptly, I was yanked into reality. The Grand Jury indicted *me*.

The fact that I was astounded and outraged by this shows that I was still rather naive. I did not yet understand the true situation into which I had barged with such abandon.

The new development commenced when Burns, the associate who had been involved in the Greyhound case, was engaged in another damage action. The morning this went to trial he came to my office and confided, "I have a couple of witnesses outside who don't sound just right. Wade dug them up, and they act strangely."

Wade was an investigator whom he sometimes employed.

"What's wrong with them, Emmet?" I asked. "Were they eye-witnesses to the accident?"

"They say they were," he replied, "but they're pretty vague about how they happened to be at the scene." He laughed. "I wouldn't put it past Wade to ring in a couple of phony pals on me. Have a talk with them, and let me know at noontime whether I should use them."

He ushered the men into my office. They were disreputable in appearance and furtive in manner. I asked them, "How did you happen to get in touch with Wade?"

They glanced at each other and the older replied, "We saw a notice on a bulletin board that he was looking for witnesses to that accident."

This was obviously nonsense.

"Where was the bulletin board?" I asked.

"In a hotel we stayed at in Los Angeles."

"What was the name of the hotel?"

"I forget."

I smiled. "Listen, fellows," I said, "you didn't see that accident. If Wade put you up to say you did, he's crazy. They'd catch you on cross-examination in a minute."

They looked at each other confusedly. Then the older man leaned forward and said confidentially, "We'll make good witnesses. You tell us what to say and we'll say it."

"Forget it," I answered. "In the first place, it wouldn't work. Do you want to get indicted for perjury? There may be cases worth it, but this isn't one of them."

I gave them a few dollars and sent them away.

Early next morning my phone rang. It was a reporter from one of the afternoon papers. He wanted my side of the story.

"What story?"

"The morning papers have a front-page article about you and

Emmet Burns. Last night two fellows testified before the Grand Jury that you both tried to bribe them to commit perjury in a damage suit."

These two men had been planted on us by the insurance company defending the action. Their scheme was to have them take the stand as our witnesses and then denounce us. This device having been thwarted by their dismissal, Mulvey brought them before the Grand Jury, where they testified that Burns and I had both offered them money to tell a false story in the damage action.

It was a pretty feeble invention, and a few well-directed questions would have exposed it quickly. I phoned the district attorney and asked to appear and give my side of the story to the Grand Jury. Next night Burns and I went before that body and explained the entire transaction. Incidentally, guilty persons do not voluntarily testify before grand juries investigating their conduct; they wait until they have read the prosecution's evidence before committing themselves to a story.

We expected to convince the jurors that the tale told by the disreputable duo was an obvious invention. However, this particular group wasn't concerned with such matters. It had other considerations than the truth or falsity of the charge. Among these was religious bigotry.

As I have said, the Grand Jury was in the hands of two of Mulvey's appointees, William Lynch and David Supple. The latter was Grand Knight of the Knights of Columbus, the Roman Catholic fraternal organization. Several of its members were grand jurors. It was part of Supple's duties to tip these off that I was a renegade Catholic. To an Irish Catholic this is the unpardonable sin.

The deputy district attorney assigned to the Grand Jury was also a trial lawyer for insurance companies. I had once unselfishly done him a considerable favor. He now repaid it by urging the jury to indict. Between these factors and Mulvey's friends on the inquisitorial body, we hadn't a chance. We were indicted on a charge of conspiracy to procure perjury.

Among the emotions most perilous to oneself is indignation. It combines two reactions: one is a protest against injustice, real or fancied; the other is anger. If tempered by moderation, the first may carry on safely; the second is always a dangerous guide to conduct. To recognize the foregoing is one thing; to manage oneself accordingly is another. With regard to the latter process, I must confess a constitutional infirmity which has kept me picking myself up in territory unmarked by the footprints of angels.

Consistent with this, my reaction to the Grand Jury's proceedings was outraged indignation. I was much more concerned with exposing the fraud through which it had arrived at the indictment than in guarding against its possible consequences.

I did take the precaution to retain Edward Cunha to defend Burns and me in the criminal court. He worked up a great hatred for the two witnesses who were against us. He said, with wishful emphasis, "The gangsters have the right idea on these goddamn stool pigeons. I'd sure like to figure someway to get those two sons of bitches knocked off."

I had different ideas. I was plotting how to get them over on our side. As usual, I got so immersed in my own schemes that it didn't occur to me that the other side might be doing some additional plotting on its own. I wasn't the least afraid of the pending prosecution. I was sure that no jury would convict on the evidence presented before the Grand Jury. The trouble was that the Mulvey gang figured the same way. They weren't quite satisfied with their situation and were out to sweeten it.

They prepared a new frame-up and set a trap for me. I dashed right into it. One evening I received a phone call. "Mr. Hallinan," said the voice at the other end, "this is Curtis Cox." It was the older of the two witnesses. "I don't like what's happening here," he continued. "I'd like to have a talk with you."

This was down my alley. "Come to my office tomorrow morning," I urged him. "I'd like to talk with you too."

"No," he answered guardedly, "I can't do that; I don't want to get in trouble with these people. Why can't you come over to see me?"

"All right," I agreed, "where are you living?"

He gave me an address in the East Bay, and I promised to meet him there the following afternoon.

I phoned Cunha immediately. He didn't share my enthusiasm. "We'd better look out," he warned. "This might be some sort of trap they're setting. We'd better think it out overnight, and I'll see you in my office in the morning."

What he thought out was disturbing. "Here's something you'll have to consider," he advised. "Right now you're away out on the side in this. Burns and Wade are in the center. You're the fellow they want to get, and so far they haven't got you. We may come to the position where we'll have to advise Emmet Burns to get his own attorney and watch out for Number One."

I protested vigorously. "It's just the other way around," I informed him. "I'm certain that Burns is entirely innocent in this thing. The only reason he's involved is because he's in my office. I wouldn't do the least thing toward protecting myself at his expense."

"Well," Cunha conceded somewhat grudgingly, "we probably won't ever have to come to that. Meanwhile, I'm watching out for you first."

We finally evolved a plan which we supposed would insure against another double cross. We would send an experienced investigator to talk with Cox and open the way for further discussions. I had just the man for the job, Ed Garrett, who had done investigating work for my office.

He was a wiry, hard-bitten little fellow, energetic and self-reliant. He was shrewd and discerning, but commonplace in speech and appearance. I felt that he was the right man to win the confidence of the two rogues. He accepted the commission eagerly.

Next night he phoned me at my home. He was excited and elated. "Vince," he said, "I've got these boys right in my hand. I've been with them all day. They're ready to retract their testimony, but they want to speak to you personally."

"Can you get them to come to Cunha's office tomorrow?" I asked.

"No!" he exclaimed fervently. "Look! I've got them in the right mood, and I'm afraid to let go of them for a minute. We've got to tie them up right now. They won't go to anybody's office.

They're afraid of being dictagraphed. I made a date for you and me to meet them at eight thirty tonight at the corner of Seventh and Broadway in Oakland. I think that if you talk to them for awhile you can get them to sign an affidavit, but they won't talk to anyone else."

I was unable to contact Cunha. He was in the country for the weekend. But, like a fool, I went.

I drove up to the appointed spot—one of the brightest-lighted corners in the East Bay city. Garrett was waiting with the two men. He greeted me effusively. "Vince," he declaimed, "these boys are a hundred percent. They didn't understand what they were being used for. I've told them the whole story, and they're willing to help."

To tell the truth, the "boys" looked neither one hundred percent nor willing to help. They shifted about uneasily while I wasted half an hour on the same arguments with which Garrett had undoubtedly belabored them.

At the end of this effort Cox broke in. "We changed our minds. If we sign any kind of an affidavit now, they'll charge us with perjury. We don't want to get mixed up in nothing. We'll be caught in the middle. You give us enough to get to Nevada and carry us for a few days, and we'll light out of here. They won't have any witnesses against you, and they'll have to drop the trial."

I would have left right then, but Garrett had to try again. He argued and fumed while I edged farther away from them. I had no fear of the impending prosecution. Paying these two to decamp would be to exchange a real crime for a fictitious one.

Finally I called to Garrett, "Come on, Ed. We'll talk this over. We'll see you fellows later. Just let things ride for the present."

The two men went shambling down to a saloon on the corner, and Garrett and I, after a few comments, prepared to enter our cars.

As I opened the door of mine a large, burly man approached me rapidly. "Don't get into that car, Hallinan," he said. "You're under arrest." He held out his hand, displaying a policeman's badge.

I glanced toward Garrett's automobile. A similar scene was being enacted beside it.

"What's this about?" I demanded angrily. "What's the charge?"

"Tampering with witnesses," replied the officer.

"There isn't any such crime," I informed him. "Nobody owns a witness. We're entitled to talk to anyone we want to. Where do you get the authority to interfere with us?"

"I'm not going to argue with you," he answered. "We're under orders to arrest you, if you talk with these two men."

"Who gave you those orders?"

"The chief."

He motioned toward the saloon, from the doorway of which we could see the two witnesses, peering out. "I want to talk to these fellows," he said.

"Well, go ahead and talk to them," I said disgustedly. "What the hell do you think we're going to do? Run away?"

He smiled awkwardly and disappeared within the doorway while we waited, annoyed, a considerable time. He re-emerged, looking somewhat thoughtful.

By now I had recovered my equanimity. After all, if these officers were acting under orders, they had no choice but to arrest us. There was no reason for any rancor against them. I said this to the man in whose car I was being driven to San Francisco.

"I'm glad you feel that way," he replied. "To be perfectly frank, I'm not a bit happy about this entire assignment."

"What's your name?" I asked.

"Frank Lucey."

"And who's the other man?"

"Jesse Ayers."

I had heard of both men. Lucey was a sergeant, and Ayers an inspector, on the homicide detail.

"How does it happen that two men are taken off an important detail like that to handle this job?" I inquired.

"It's worse than that," he answered. "We've been in charge of those two birds ever since you were indicted. I don't understand it myself."

I told him of the events leading up to the indictment. He knew of my struggles with the jury setup, generally. After a period of silence he said, "I'm not supposed to discuss this case with you, but I'm going to disobey orders. Those fellows say you gave each of them a hundred dollars to leave the state."

I almost went through the roof of the car. "Sergeant Lucey," I assured him, "they're a couple of goddamn liars. They asked for money to leave the state, and we told them we weren't interested in that. We were trying to get them to retract their testimony against us."

"Well, I'll tell you something more," he replied. "We were watching you through glasses all the time you were talking with them. Those glasses brought you up within ten feet of us. If you had given them anything, we'd have seen it, because that is what we were looking for, and nothing like that took place.

"I talked to Ayers, and he says the same thing. As a matter of fact, you never got closer to them than three feet."

I whistled with relief. "Sergeant Lucey," I said, "I'm very grateful, and I am also very lucky that they put a couple of honest men on that job."

"If they think that either Ayers or I are going to be in on a frame-up, they have another guess coming," he assured me. "I'm sure you didn't give them any money, and I'm not going to book you on that charge. I have to charge you with a misdemeanor, but if they try to hang a felony rap on you, I'll testify that those two birds are lying."

That was it. We were duly booked, bailed out by a friendly bail-bond broker, and went home to bed and some salutary conclusions.

The principal one was this: when you are under the paw of the lion, don't bite or scratch. If you just lie still, he may go away.

Next morning I phoned Cunha. He had already read the accounts in the newspapers.

"Ed," I informed him, "I'm right in the middle; right in there with Burns and Wade."

He laughed wryly. "How bad is it?" he inquired.

"Not too bad," I assured him. "I'm back to believing in guardian angels."

Lucey's position did not interfere with the Mulvey gang's program. The Grand Jury heard the two turncoat witnesses, did not call either of the police officers, and indicted Garrett and me of felony; namely, bribing witnesses to leave the state. We weren't worried. If Lucey and Ayers would testify as they had stated, there was no possibility of conviction. Meanwhile, the indictment itself satisfied the ring's immediate purposes. It kept the attacker backed to the wall, defending himself.

About a week after this affair I received another phone call. A voice which I did not recognize said, "Vince, I'm not going to tell you my name, because I can't afford to get mixed up in anything, but I have some information that can be of help to you. There's a private detective named Joe Manning who hangs out at a bookie joint,"—and he gave me the address. "Yesterday he told a couple of people there that he knows you're being framed, that he was right in the inside of it, and that he would testify for you. You can catch him there at two o'clock any afternoon."

By this time I should have been allergic to such phone calls, but the voice seemed friendly and sincere. I thanked him and hastened to discuss the message with Cunha. He barely waited to hear me through. Then, "Nothing doing!" he exploded. "For Christ Jesus' sake, are you going to walk into another one of those?"

I suggested that we get someone else to check the story.

"Garrett?" he enquired, sarcastically.

"No," he concluded after further discussion. "If this isn't phony, it means that Manning has something to sell and used that way to open negotiations. Leave it alone, and he'll make the contact himself."

I agreed completely with his judgment, promised solemnly to avoid the danger, left his office and hastened to the bookie joint. It was shortly after two o'clock. Leaning over the cigar counter which formed a front for the betting establishment, I whispered to the clerk, "I'm Vincent Hallinan. I want to talk to Joe Manning."

He pressed a button and a peephole opened in an adjoining door. I repeated my message to the eyes which looked through the opening, the door opened, and I entered. The attendant indicated a short, stocky man who turned as I approached, smiled, and said, "Let's go somewhere else and talk."

As we stepped out on the sidewalk he said, directly, "This thing they're pulling on you and Burns is a pretty raw frame-up. I've been with those two bums, Cox and Patterson, ever since they contacted the insurance company. Wade knew they were phonies, but they both told me that neither you nor Burns did. Somebody fixed them up since."

I had expected considerable maneuvering and a request for compensation from the man, but he spoke out with surprising frankness and readiness. I asked if he would go to Cunha's office and repeat his story.

"Sure I will," he answered. "Let's go right now."

I phoned Cunha, but he had not relinquished his customary wariness. He also scolded me vigorously for my disobedience of his orders. "Get Manning to stand by for a day. There's another development I want to talk about with you," he finally said.

This development was that he had consulted John Taafe, probably the leading trial lawyer then active in San Francisco, about trying the cases.

Taafe was brilliant and a hard worker. He was young, slight of build, wiry and aggressive, and would fight a buzz saw. On cross-examination he had the tactics and tenacity of a bulldog; he would fasten upon a weak part of the witness' testimony and rag it until he had torn the story to pieces.

He was a devout Roman Catholic and had once been a Christian Brother. Cunha warned me that if he learned that I was anti-Church, he would probably reject our employment.

Ed was an atheist, or—as is more fashionably said—a freethinker. He hated everything ecclesiastical, but carefully concealed his animus from all but a few chosen confidants. He once showed me a pair of rosary beads which he always carried in his pocket. "Whenever I get a few of these mealymouthed mushheaded bastards on a jury," he had said, "I contrive to pull these out with my handkerchief, and let them fall on the floor. One of them is sure to call my attention to them, and I pick them up with the most upset look I can get on my face."

Taafe almost immediately swung the conversation over to religion. "You'll have to watch out for the juries in this city," he told me. "There are a lot of Catholics on them, and you have the reputation of being anti-Catholic."

"Why, that's a lot of damn nonsense—" I began.

But Cunha cut in. "One of Vin's sisters is a nun," he expostulated.

"That might only make it worse," replied Taafe grimly. Then he gave a short illustration of proper cross-examination. He suddenly shot at me, "Have you had your children baptized?"

I grimaced, as though even asking the question was ridiculous. "Of course I have," I lied vigorously.

He relaxed, obviously satisfied. "That should take care of that," he said.

He agreed to take the case. We gave him a brief run-down of the facts and informed him of my interview with Manning. He had none of Cunha's caution. He wanted to see the detective as soon as possible. I made an appointment to bring him to Taafe's office the following day.

I contacted Manning and appeared with him next morning at our new counsel's, where he repeated his story. Unknown to both of us, Taafe dictagraphed the conversation.

Some days later John received an additional tip from Frank Lucey. The policeman informed him disgustedly, "I don't know what makes them think I'm in on this frame-up. One of these punk D.A.'s got ahold of me yesterday and wanted me to testify that Hallinan or Garrett were in a position where they could have slipped those bums some money without us seeing it. I told him nothing doing. That was just what we were looking for, and it didn't happen. Another thing—both cases are set for the same day. They intend to try the second one first. They'll answer 'ready' on it and expect to catch you unprepared. You'd better get set for both."

Sure enough, when the trial day arrived, the deputy district attorney informed the court: "We are ready in the case of *People versus Hallinan and Garrett*. We ask that *People versus Hallinan, Burns and Wade* stand over one week."

The judge was one of Mulvey's pals. He turned toward the defense table, expecting a protest and prepared to reject it.

Both he and the prosecutor looked nonplussed when Taafe announced quietly, "Ready for the defendants."

John massacred the two turncoat witnesses. The police officers and Manning flatly contradicted them. If they had been testifying for the defense, they would have been arrested for perjury the moment they left the stand. The jury quickly returned a verdict of Not guilty. The court then dismissed the other case on motion of the district attorney.

Sometime after this Taafe began to lose his reputation as the city's leading criminal advocate. He was absent from his office and neglected his cases. He was said to have taken to drink.

When friends sought to reason with him, he excused his conduct on the basis of an unexplained illness. He complained of nervousness, dizziness and constant headaches. Doctors whom he consulted found nothing to cause these conditions, and they were accepted as excuses for his continued alcoholism.

Finally, a neurosurgeon took them seriously and opened a hole in his skull. Inside was a large and deadly tumor. The skill of the physician was powerless to excise it. Somewhere in the course of the operation Johnny Taafe's brilliant mind departed his tormented brain, and his brave heart was stilled forever.

I continued to try damage cases in this atmosphere, but it was somewhat wearing. Fixed judges and juries were bad enough, but they were nothing compared to the strain of seeing a possible plant in every potential witness.

As far as the cases themselves were concerned, I was far better off than any of the other plaintiff lawyers. The "fixed" magistrates avoided open clashes which might lead to adverse publicity, and I had learned how to identify a juror subject to pressures. The verdicts were relatively small and hard to win, but everyone else was faring much worse. The Market Street Railway Company was a sort of testing ground. A verdict against it conferred real distinction. I tried about thirty jury cases against it, and lost only one.

The company had three trial lawyers on its staff. Cyril Appel, youngest of the trio, was its principal work horse. He was a big, handsome man, six feet two or more in height, with curly hair graying at the temples. He was always thoroughly prepared and tried his cases in a straight line, refusing to rise to the barbed shafts which I frequently threw for the purpose of confusing an opponent.

He sedulously ignored cracks which would make other opponents bristle and bark back, thereby involving them in exchanges which rarely worked to their advantage. At most, he would assume a hurt look and appeal to the court in injured tones for protection from such untoward remarks. Women jurors liked him, and it was difficult to get a large verdict when he represented the defendant.

Where the going promised to be tougher, William Cannon entered the fray in his stead. He and William Abbott were chief counsel for the company. Abbott was one of the fixers who had been indicted with Coffroth and many others when the railroad bought up the whole San Francisco board of supervisors, back in 1906.

Cannon once had the reputation of being the best civil-jury trial lawyer in the city. He was now well past his prime, but if he had lost any of his fire it must have been quite a blaze in his youth. He was vigorous and bad-tempered, and had the boldness of a man who knows that the court is fairly in his pocket. He wore a goatee which with his white hair, thunderous declamation and flowing gestures, added drama to his appearance.

I had gotten several verdicts against the railroad when they had sent Cannon against me in one damage case. He had obviously keyed himself up for a Donnybrook. He was hair-triggered and testy. He ignored my first small needling, but finally roared, "I'm not here to be insulted by a whippersnapper like you!"

I looked at the jury as though astounded by the outburst.

Finally he was assigning almost everything I said as "Misconduct." After one such stricture I remarked wearily, "By the time this case is through I'm going to be awfully tired of two people—Mr. Cannon and his sweetheart, Miss Conduct."

The jurors and spectators laughed, heightening Cannon's rancor. When it came his time to argue the case, he shouted his entire presentation.

I started off in reply, "Cannon to right of them, cannon to left of them—Cannon in front of them volley'd and thunder'd. . . ."

He jumped up, literally screaming. By this time he had become fairly ridiculous. I had been warring with his company for several years, and the exasperations of the struggle had nullified the instructions of experience. In blowing his top, he blew his case, and we won a large verdict.

When a case promised to be a bit tough for even the Olympian Cannon, the railroad rang in Walter Linforth. He was both rich and socially prominent. He was a first-class trial lawyer and extremely sly and crafty. He covered the latter qualities with an air of perpetual righteousness. In the courtroom he displayed a condescending assurance which overawed judges, juries and even opponents.

He was of medium size and build, wore a mustache and an air of great dignity. When he wished to utter a particularly profound phrase, he did so through his nose. His sonorous pronouncements, together with the high assurance with which they were uttered, supplied an apparent validity to the most arrant nonsense. Under his urbane exterior he was a real fighter, and when stung, would drop his pompous demeanor and storm like a fury.

Linforth hated me. He was friendly with the Mulvey ring of judges and took my assaults upon them as a personal affront. In addition, I had wounded his vanity so often that, like Cannon, he lost his perspective.

We were once engaged in the third trial of an action involving serious injuries to the leg of a four-year-old girl. That is to say, she was four years old when we started. She was fourteen when the Appellate Court finally permitted an award to stand.

I had first tried the case against Appel and gotten a verdict of $5,000. It was reversed on appeal, and on the retrial I took

Cannon for $10,000. It was reversed again. Linforth was then sent in to stop the carnage.

He had his motorman on the stand and wanted to build him up with the jury. The man was a veteran of World War I, and Linforth wanted—improperly—to get this before them.

He asked, "By the way, were you with the American forces in France during the recent unpleasantness?" The sentence rang sonorously through his nasal passages.

On argument, he belittled the child's injuries.

In rebuttal, I asked, "What can you expect from a man who describes the cataclysmic tragedy of the World War as 'the recent unpleasantness'?" I uttered the last phrase in an imitation of Linforth's nasal twang.

He got to his feet, his face flushed with anger, started to speak, couldn't find the words, glared at me for a moment and resumed his seat.

On this trial the jury gave us $14,000.

The next time I went against him he outdid Cannon in touchiness. By the time we reached argument he was fuming. He started his shouting and went up from there. After a few minutes I pretended to ruffle through my papers, and then strolled out of the courtroom. I waited in the corridor until I judged he was about exhausted, and casually returned to the counsel table.

On rebuttal, I spoke in the most moderate tones. I said to the jury, "You can't convert falsehood into truth by screaming it like a madman."

In this one I caught the Market Street Railway Company with a solid punch. The verdict was for $50,000. It was the highest ever recovered against that defendant and the second highest in the country for the same injury. In addition—and much more surprising—it was affirmed on appeal.

Meanwhile the jury planting had gone on apace. The other plaintiff lawyers were becoming desperate. I was faring better than any of them. This was upon a well-known principle: "He is oftenest whipped who is easiest whipped."

These gentlemen were not yet prepared to join in the raucous campaign which I had been waging singlehanded. They wanted to remain "respectable." Very quietly, a delegation from among them called on the presiding judge, imploring relief. This was like telling Al Capone that his gangsters were misbehaving. The magistrate heard them briefly and dismissed them without encouragement.

This effort was not publicized. I heard of it through the grapevine. In treating it so cavalierly, the presiding judge had been guilty of a serious tactical error. The attorneys who had presented their humble petition were themselves influential. Now their vanity was wounded. For years they had suffered under a system which robbed them and their clients, dishonored their profession, and defamed their community.

These things they resented, but none of them had the spur of injured pride. A man may forgive the theft of his goods or the seduction of his wife; he may excuse treason and infidelity. Outraged vanity must be placated by revenge.

In the present case the magistrate should have expressed the gravest concern for the purity of the courts; he should have felicitated the delegates for their roles in protecting it; he should have promised an immediate and searching inquiry and assured them of a forthwith correction of the situation; he should have dismissed them with encomiums and encouragements. Then he could have done nothing, and the protestors would have shrugged their shoulders and let it slide for a couple of more years.

But now they had to act; they had to vindicate their dignities.

George Ford phoned me. Could he and a half-dozen other plaintiff lawyers have a half hour or so to talk with me? We made an appointment for that afternoon, and I sat back to await the disgruntled delegation with mixed emotions.

For several years I had been fighting their fight. True, they had sometimes timidly supplied me with some of the information which helped me wage the fight in their behalf. But time and time again Mulvey and his aides—when caught up in a situation— would take the witness stand and swear under oath that some accusation which I knew perfectly well to be true was a lie. Meanwhile, listening to them, would be the lawyers who could prove that the gang was lying, but would not do so; and I could not call them as witnesses because I had given them my word to protect them when they gave me the information. It was the classic difficulty of proving what everybody knew was true.

In due time the delegation of lawyers arrived. It contained the *crème de la crème* of the independent trial attorneys.

Ford, as their spokesman, wasted no time. "Vincent," he said, "we're pretty ashamed of ourselves, and we all owe you an apology for the way we've let you carry this fight over the last several years. I suppose you know about our visit to the presiding judge a few days ago?"

"Yes," I answered, "I've heard all about it. I could have warned you that you were wasting your efforts."

"As a matter of fact," he replied, "we didn't expect much else, but we thought we owed him that courtesy before taking other steps. To come to the point, would you be willing to institute a new challenge to the jury panel, if we agree to join in it? By that I mean that all of us will sign your motion and furnish affidavits or testify, as the case may be, that a plaintiff can't get a fair trial in a damage case before the jury panel as it is now selected. We've been working on this for some time, and we have about twenty lawyers lined up to go along with us."

Between Ford's phone call and this visit I had smothered some malicious impulses. For instance, I had relinquished the temptation to say: "Finally, I can use your names."

After all, my purpose throughout had been to end the corrupt jury system. I had undergone dangers and disadvantages to accomplish it; now I didn't propose to lose an opportunity for final victory for the satisfaction of reproaching these gentlemen. They needed me and I needed them. With their aid, I believed I could push the rock of Sisyphus over the rim.

I agreed to go along with their program. The mechanics were easy. By this time I had mimeographed copies of motions and affidavits applicable to any damage case. I had only to insert the appropriate titles and file them.

My new allies demonstrated their value at the outset of the proceedings. They got the judicial council of the state bar to appoint three outside judges to pass on my new challenge to the panel. We would not have to submit it to one of Mulvey's pals.

The hearing took place before a packed courtroom. Again I submitted my charts and statistics. More important, about twenty of the city's leading lawyers testified in favor of my motion. They were unanimous in their opinion that the panels were packed in favor of the traction and insurance companies. After three days of such testimony the judges gave a "Scotch verdict." They held that "no conscious fraud had been proven." They denied the motion to dismiss the panel.

This was a face-saver for the San Francisco courts. Immediately after their decision, the three judges who heard the matter got together with the local Superior Court magistrates. Behind closed doors they formulated a set of rules for selecting the trial juries—they were to be chosen by lot from the great register of voters.

This was the exact method which I had tried to get the legislature to enact years before. So finally, after many lost battles, the war was won. Mulvey's wings had been clipped, but he still had spurs to strike and a beak to crow with. He boasted that the judges had exonerated him. Even those who should have known better suggested that he had not been actuated by personal interest. I had to wait a couple of more years before Thomas Mulvey went to his eternal reward and this position collapsed.

On the jury challenge hearing I had been permitted to question him as to his assets, to determine whether he was enriching himself by bribery. He testified that he had no money except that on his person, no stocks, bonds or other real or personal property, and that so far as he knew, neither did his wife.

On his death his safe-deposit box was opened in the presence of the state treasurer. It contained $200,000 in currency.

CHAPTER 5

Time to Grow Up?

WHILE the court corruption fight was going on I did not take time out to assess its cost to me. It was probably mere pugnacity which prevented me from doing so. The struggle being over, I examined the cost. My office organization had been disrupted; my ablest associates, justly concerned for their own safety, had gotten out of the line of fire; I had lost clients and revenues; a host of powerful enemies, still strongly entrenched, awaited any opportunity for revenge.

Even credit for what I had accomplished was short-lived. Some few years after the campaign was over I received an invitation to join an organization of lawyers. Among the achievements which it listed as an inducement to new members was that of having brought about the reform of the trial-jury system in San Francisco. Until I read its circular, I had been unaware of this secret ally's efforts. They had probably been confined to prayer.

As for Thomas Mulvey and his crew, they were no better nor worse than thousands of others similarly situated. Our peculiar economic and political system has permitted favored persons and groups to acquire certain prerogatives. These have become practically vested rights. Among them is the control of the instruments of government, including the courts.

Customarily, this is exercised with discretion. Its processes are rarely as raw as those in San Francisco, but the end sought is the same. There is no use getting heated up over one small segment of this universal condition. During my campaign I received a lesson in a more urbane approach to it.

This occurred on a visit to my office by a lawyer from a neighboring county where a system similar to that in my own existed. There, the Superior Court was controlled by a group known as "The Ring." This consisted of a number of magistrates, the district attorney, the jury commissioner, and a small coterie of law firms, most of whom represented banks, insurance companies and similar clients. The presiding judge, an ancient veteran of the bench, was its titular head.

The jury commissioner interviewed all prospective jurors personally. They were questioned on their attitudes toward personal-injury litigation, their social and fraternal connections, and their religious affiliations. Regularity of attendance at divine services was deemed a proper subject of inquiry.

In this way a triple benefit was subserved. Damage-case verdicts would be held to a minimum, conviction was assured in criminal prosecutions—especially if sex were involved—and The Ring had information which would enable it to reach and influence individual jurors.

My visitor described the losses and frustrations which he and the other lawyers outside the favored group suffered through its activities. I suggested, "Why don't you get the Bar Association to start an investigation and put an end to it?"

He recoiled in horror. "Oh no!" he exclaimed, "I'm trying to get into The Ring!"

As I discovered, a radical or reformist policy makes few useful friends and many dangerous enemies. In my case the latter included judges and other public officials who were in a position to injure me. Opposing lawyers frequently sought to exploit this hostility so as to gain an advantage over me. I was constantly assailed as "attacking the courts," "casting discredit on the judges," or even "making a mockery of the law."

Those who made such statements had more practical purposes than sustaining the dignity of the bench. They had participated in its corruption or stood by not daring to peep, but did not hesitate to attack anyone who sought to restore its integriy. They were like those described by Julius Stein, who prate about the sacredness of the Flag, yet love not the land nor the people.

The same spirit is widespread through the country today. Those who urge that our economic system has exhausted its possibilities and must be replaced by one better suited to our technological advancement are denounced as "un-American." It should be expected that those whose privileges are threatened by the radical or reformer should dislike them. It is difficult to understand how they can get others to share their feeling.

George Bernard Shaw once said: "A reasonable man adjusts himself to his environment; an unreasonable man tries to adjust his environment to himself. Therefore, all progress depends upon the unreasonable man."

The average person should have an unwavering policy in such matters. For his own, and the general advantage, he should follow one rule, namely: "Protect the gadfly." There have always been radicals among lawyers. The trouble is that there are not enough of them. The great majority subscribes to the general conservatism.

The profession may be roughly divided into three categories. First come the attorneys for big corporations. They are an integral portion of the nation's "Power Elite." They are rich in their own right, have graduated from the correct schools and have the family connections to place them in the lofty positions they occupy. They help select the legislators who pass the laws and the judges who interpret them. In their choice they are only concerned with the interests of their clients. They also show the latter how to evade such statutes as might be to their detriment. They rarely appear in court. Their cases are not of the type to bring their names before the public. If they appear in the press, it is on the society page where they are seen in white ties and tails, opening the opera season or escorting debutante daughters to their coming-out parties. Occasionally they take Sabbaticals in the President's Cabinet or on State Supreme benches. They have squires and men-at-arms who do their detail work. These have usually been so submerged in the folklore and personalities of their superiors that they have lost any perspectives they may ever have had.

I once had a client who had been defrauded by one of these nobles of the bar. An attempt to settle the claim was rejected by the latter with disdain. Anything which even faintly implied wrongdoing on his part could not be considered. We went to trial. It was a rather plain case of fraud, and we recovered a substantial verdict.

Some days later a young lawyer in the defendant's office discussed the case with a friend. He said, "I am so disgusted and upset that I feel like quitting law." His friend was about to advise him that he should not feel such disillusion at the revelation that prominent persons occasionally descend to fraud. Fortunately he had said nothing, when the other continued, "To think that they could do a thing like that to Mr. [the defendant]."

Next we come to the ordinary practitioners. They form the great majority of the profession. Among the decisions, they diligently seek the golden thread which will guide them through the labyrinthine ways. They hurry to court with their brief bags crammed with papers. They are entirely unaware of the hidden influences which will really decide their cases. They return to their offices puzzled and vexed, having never sensed the invisible Minotaur.

The third group is a sort of light-armed contingent which dashes in and out of the slaughter. By courage, cunning and dexterity, they escape with much booty, sometimes seizing rich prizes from under the very vizors of the Elite.

To do so with consistency, however, they must learn certain harsh fundamentals.

The first of these is that the law is no stately dispenser of justice; no disinterested philosophers direct its administration. It was enacted originally for the benefit of specific interests, and its operations continue that purpose. In all jurisdictions there are persons and organizations against whom an ordinary individual can never possibly win a case, regardless of its merit.

Next, it must be understood that these interests are not only individually powerful. They are closely coordinated. They stick together and make common front against assault. Their tactics of defense and reprisal are ruthless.

These statements may appear extravagant. If the reader will be patient he will see that they are not. I have frequently heard the representatives of these favored litigants address Bar Association banquets and other such affairs. Their speeches are so full of morals and ethics that one would suppose their makers resurrected Solons. Threaten the prerogatives of their principles, and they will cut you down with complete cynicism. They are like one of those Stuart cavaliers, elegant and courtly, who, for all their frills and laces, would run a yard of steel through a man with the utmost coolness. They prescribe lofty ideals for their opponents; for themselves it's a matter of "No holds barred."

If one is to compete successfully in such a milieu, he needs more than a certificate of admission to the bar and a knowledge of what is going on. There are certain qualities requisite for any considerable advancement. For one thing, it is no field for the faint of heart.

Timidity is one of the most disqualifying defects a lawyer can have. Yet an enormous number of frightened people practice law. They are bullied by judges and trampled down by prosecutors and other representatives of the Elite. It is strange that they should permit this. They are paid to defend those unable to protect themselves. The goods they vend should not be adulterated with cowardice. The profession does not condone such shortchanging. Whatever its practices, its traditions are in the heroic mood. Courage is commended in its history, and the decisions of the courts justify its exercise.

Judges and public opinion are the most formidable bugaboos. There is really nothing to be dreaded about either of them. One has more to lose by yielding to his fears than either of these can cost.

Part of an ode by the Roman poet Horace has been described by Voltaire as being the noblest words penned by man. It says: "When a man is just and constant in his purpose, then neither the passion of his fellow citizens urging him to the wrong, nor the glare of the approaching tyrant can daunt his firm purpose; nay, not the South Wind, restless leader of stormy Adriatic, nor the mighty hand of thundering Jupiter. Should the broken orb of Heaven fall to pieces, its ruins would strike him still undismayed."

Courage is a glowing and infectious virtue. Danger is an exhilarating experience to the man who is not afraid. Moreover, the penalties for boldness in court are small; its sensations can be enjoyed at a low cost.

A lawyer cannot be asked to risk his own liberty merely because he has been hired to protect that of another. It is quite a different thing when he allows himself to be bullied and insulted and his client robbed of his rights by some petty tyrant on the bench, rather than take the inconsequential hazard of being adjudged in contempt or of incurring the displeasure of a magistrate whose goodwill is no compliment.

As a rule, judges follow the pattern of all politicians; they are extremely sensitive to adverse publicity. They dread involvement in controversies which will make them appear to favor one litigant over another. Accordingly, they rarely carry quarrels with attorneys to extremes.

There are two instances, however, in which they become dangerous. In both they have the news agencies, and presumptively, public opinion with them. The less menacing of these is in those instances where a powerful newspaper sets out to get an accused person convicted. The other, and more formidable, is in political prosecutions. I shall have more to say on these later.

Except in these two instances, you can usually count on the ordinary rules. It is wise to learn them in advance, so that you may know how far you can go. Within their protection there is considerable space for vigorous action. You can make quite a brave show without transgressing them.

Some of these have been cited in numerous decisions. Sir James Stephen, in his *History of the Criminal Law,* says:

> The barrister's province is singularly well defined. It is to say for his client whatever, upon the evidence, it is by law open to him to say and which he thinks likely to be advantageous. The judge's province is equally well defined. It is to prevent misstatements of law and of fact and attempts to intimidate and mislead the jury. Again, though the form of the law is clumsy, its substance is, on almost every subject, so minute and complete that there can be little doubt as to the point at which a barrister begins to misstate it or to ask the jury to transgress it.
>
> Finally, the whole legal profession is pre-eminently a manly one. It is a calling in which success is impossible to the weak or timid, and in which everyone, judge or barrister, is expected to do his duty without fear or favor to the best of his ability and judgment.
>
> A decision of the California Supreme Court on the subject asserts: Attorneys must be given a substantial freedom of expression in representing their clients . . . The public interest in an independent bar would be subverted if judges were allowed to punish attorneys summarily for contempt on purely subjective reactions to their conduct or statements. . . . An attorney has the duty to protect the interests of his client. He has a right to press legitimate argument and to protest an erroneous ruling.

Strange things can happen to these precedents when the courts resolve to get around them. However, many lawyers have taken brave stands without injury. Yet few lawyers dare provoke magistrates, and sycophancy toward judges is the rule.

William B. Cleary of Washington, D. C., who was once kidnapped and ridden out of Bisbee, Arizona, for defending striking members of the Western Federation of Miners, attended a bar banquet at the Palace Hotel in San Francisco and wagered that he could point out the judges who entered the room. He picked out eight or ten without a mistake. Most of them looked and acted just about like the other diners, and Cleary's table companions were mystified as to how he did it. He explained:

There is a story of an Arabian emir who heard that a judge in one of his provinces was remarkable both for his justice and for his acuteness in determining the truth. Wishing to verify the reports, he disguised himself as a Bedouin, mounted his horse, and rode to the city where this judge was holding court.

As he entered the gate a man hobbled up to him and asked for a lift to the market place. The emir let him climb up behind him, but when they got to their destination the fellow refused to dismount. He said: "Get off yourself; I've ridden you far enough."

"What's this?" demanded the emir, "It's my horse you're riding."

"Why you thief," said the fellow, "I've been good enough to give you a ride, and now you want to steal my horse!"

A crowd gathered, and the police took them both before the famous judge. The emir stated what had happened, but the other man swore that it was he who owned the horse and that the stranger had worked a trick on him to get on its back and then claim it.

The judge heard them both through and then said, "Leave the horse here; come back in the morning and I'll give my decision."

The next morning when the two claimants appeared, he took the emir to the stable where several horses were tethered, and asked him to identify his, which of course he did at once. Then he put the other man to the test, but he picked out the disputed horse just as readily as had its real owner.

"This man is lying," said the judge. "Take him out and give him fifty lashes." Then, turning to the emir, "Take your horse and go."

The emir now revealed his identity and the reason for his visit. "But," he asked, "how did you know that the horse was mine? The other man picked him out as readily as I did myself."

"I didn't care what you or he did," answered the judge, "it was the horse I watched. When you came into the stable, he lifted his head and looked around at you, but when the thief came in he did nothing."

Now [continued Cleary] the way I knew that each of those men was a judge was that he had not come ten feet into the room before someone rose and fawned on him.

When elevated to the bench, judges are apt to forget the twists and tricks they employed in their former trade, and to be highly critical of the lawyers who continue to use them.

Most judges regard with hostility those who would use the courts to injure the wealthy and powerful. Sometimes there is added a peculiar psychological twist which operates when the magistrate himself feels that his decision might not be acceptable to that final judge whom he believes he will confront on the Day of General Judgment, when—as Charles II put it—"The good Lord will know whose 'erse is blackest." He may then develop a guilt complex. Any competent psychologist will explain the mechanism. To fall into it, the jurist must have a weakness of character which prevents him from complete acceptance of the established mores and which requires him to compensate the remnants of his conscience.

He feels that he must admit to himself that he had done an injustice, unless he can discover in the victim some hateful quality which merited the ill-treatment. The latter's misfortune is then enlarged because the judge will not stop with the matter at hand. His complex will hurry him into further mistreatments. He does not reflect that his own invention has created the distasteful parts which he professes to see in the object of his malice.

I once experienced a classic example of this curious phenomenon. It will serve as a guide to lawyers and a possible case history in elemental psychology.

Mae Pierce was a widow who had been defrauded of all her possessions. She had been left by her husband, an Alameda County official, in comfortable circumstances. Her natural simplicity had been augmented by senility. She fell into the hands of a group of swindlers which in a few months reduced her to poverty. She owned some real estate which the gang was not equipped to handle, as its forte was oil stocks. It therefore divided that part of the loot with persons more experienced in this type of property.

As part of this procedure, she traded a building from which she was receiving some income, together with her home, for an equity in an apartment house owned by a rich and influential

San Francisco lawyer. The apartment house was encumbered for more than its value, and the bank which held the first mortgage had notified the owner that upon the expiration of the note secured by it he would have to make a substantial payment. The transaction was accomplished by the use of misrepresentations and promises which should not have deceived a child. The poor silly old woman was scarcely ensconced in her new possession when the bank took it away from her.

I attempted to procure a criminal prosecution of the conspirators, but, as they included persons of wealth and influence, never succeeded in getting the district attorney's office to do more than give the matter a casual inquiry.

Then I filed a series of actions for fraud, and at length brought the one involving the lawyer above mentioned to trial before a jury. The case was assigned to a judge who—I know not why—had a reputation for honesty and ability. He was a long-legged, homely fellow, who fancied that he resembled Abraham Lincoln and kept a picture of the rail-splitter hanging in his court so that spectators might remark the resemblance.

As the trial progressed I lost whatever preconceptions I may have had as to his ability. On questions which appeared to have been clearly decided by the Appellate Courts of the state, he allowed the defense attorneys to spend long hours, citing rulings from other jurisdictions, and driving me to researches which would have been unnecessary to convince a small-town justice of the peace. I finally guided the case past a thousand roadblocks, and the jury was allowed to pass on the issue. It returned a verdict against all the defendants in the sum of $50,000.

I was quite worn out trying to educate the judge, but I did him the charity of concluding that he was only overconscientious. He had resolved every doubt in favor of the defendants; there could be no errors in the judgment; and it was certain to stand up on appeal.

The defendants made motions for a new trial and for a judgment, notwithstanding the verdict. These were based upon points which had been argued at length during the trial and which had been ruled upon, I had supposed, for keeps. However, His

Honor permitted them to be reargued. This consumed several days. He then granted a new trial to all the defendants except a couple of impecunious salesmen from whom a judgment for fifty cents couldn't be collected, and he granted a judgment notwithstanding verdict to the lawyer defendant.

I was sufficiently casehardened by this time not to be shocked or upset. If the honest judge saw it that way, he was entitled to so rule, even though I now thought him an extremely stupid man. Moreover, I neither did or said anything which could be construed as offensive to him, and I accepted the rulings with good grace, but filing a notice of appeal from his orders.

Up to this time the judge and I had been on good terms. I had appeared before him on numerous motions and had visited with him in his chambers for the purpose of having papers signed and other formalities. Our relationship was apparently quite cordial.

The first time I met him after the ruin of my verdict he barely nodded to me. The next time he passed without even doing that. Thereafter his attitude toward me continued to degenerate. It was obvious that he had formed a strong dislike for me. I was puzzled, but not resentful. If the judge knew, or thought he knew, something about me which barred me from his friendship, it was his privilege. If I had had cause to dislike him, I would have made no apology for passing him in the corridors without notice.

Meanwhile, the defendants stole a march on me. They declared Mae Pierce incompetent, in a neighboring county, and had a relative appointed her guardian. They then settled her claims with the guardian for $7,500.

Some years later another jury trial in which I represented the plaintiff was assigned to the court of this same magistrate. On the first day of the trial the defense attorney made a perfunctory motion for a mistrial, which—as much to his surprise as mine—the judge indicated he was inclined to grant. The law on the point was clear and had been fixed in numerous decisions. I so informed him and asked him to reserve his ruling until after the noon recess so that I could present authorities which would demonstrate that the motion was without merit.

The authorities were never presented. While I was collecting them, a lawyer friend called on me. "I understand," he said, "that you are trying a jury case before judge So-and-So?"

"Yes."

"Do you know that he has been a close, personal friend of Attorney—?" He named the lawyer defendant in the Mae Pierce fraud case.

I almost choked.

"While that case was in progress," he continued, "the judge and that defendant spent every evening at the home of one of them, going over the facts and the law. I was friendly with both of them and helped them on several occasions. The only reason the judge didn't grant his friend a directed verdict was that he hoped the jury would find in his favor. You never had a chance of holding him. I have often thought of telling you this, but you can understand why I kept putting it off. Now I would not like to see the same thing happen to you."

At the commencement of the afternoon session I confronted the judge with what I had just heard.

He replied coolly, "Mr. [naming the lawyer defendant] and I have been intimate friends for twenty years."

"And you thought it proper to sit through a trial in which he was a defendant and not acquaint the plaintiff's lawyer with that fact?" I demanded.

"I felt," he retorted, "that I was under no obligation to do so."

The remainder of the colloquy is not for delicate ears. He did not dare invite publicity to his conduct by citing me for contempt, even when I suggested that the resemblance which he fancied he bore to Abraham Lincoln was the same which an ape bears to a man.

A couple of years later he was elevated to the Appellate Court. I wrote a letter to the Judicial Council, the body charged with examining the qualifications of nominees to that august body. I also appeared before it and presented the foregoing narrative. Of course nothing came of it, and he was duly enrolled in the higher court.

The psychologist will draw from this incident the following conclusion: The judge was so sacrosanct that he could not admit to himself that he had done anything dishonest in aiding his friend to escape the consequences of his own wrongdoing—while charged with the duty of securing equal and exact justice for him and the old woman. It was impossible to attribute any fault other than the weakness of senility to her, yet he had to justify his conduct to himself. He invented some sufficient reason why her attorney was unworthy of fair treatment, and he built this into such a system that he could not even bring himself to be courteous to me.

I have known confidence men who smoothed whatever tiny segments may have remained tender in their consciences by saying of a victim: "Nature never intended him to have that kind of money."

This episode ended a difficult phase of my life. It is said that African natives believe that: "A man knows fear three times in his life. The first is when he sees the track of the lion; the second is when he hears the lion roar; and the third is when he meets the lion face to face."

I had encountered all three in the course of my crusading career, without being deterred from pursuing it. Finally I learned wisdom, not from fear, but from a remarkable spiritual experience. This converted me to more sensible activities. I abandoned the profitless search for justice and concentrated upon the quest of wealth. For many years I gathered money, respectability and the appearance of stature. I was invited to fashionable functions; I addressed cultured audiences on mildly controversial issues.

I was solicited to enter the political arena; a Democratic party boss assured me of an ultimate seat in the United States Senate if I would put myself under his tutelage. Unhappily, events followed which collapsed this seemingly solid structure. The defects of character which had precipitated me into so many mishaps in my youth proved constitutional. Perhaps the advance of age weakened those guards which I had erected against them. We will consider this matter later.

In any case, I did experience an interior illumination which impelled me to end my unprofitable career as a reformer and to pass a long and comfortable period of remunerative conformity.

Part II

The Law in Action

CHAPTER **6**

Laughter in Hallowed Halls

JURIES—despite the grumblings of most lawyers—are only human. The light touch and touches of wit are almost always gratefully received as refreshing breaks to the tedium of trials.

My one-time employer, Daniel Ryan, was an artist at developing an opening when an amusing comment was in order. Once when defending an action brought by a doctor's wife for personal injuries, the lady's physician was on the stand, testifying to the extent of her injuries and pointing out that the brevity of her stay in the hospital was certainly no indication that the injuries were not severe. He concluded: "Doctors' wives are difficult to handle."

Ryan replied, "Why do you limit it to doctors' wives?"

By the time the trial neared completion the jury was hanging on every remark Ryan made, hoping for further entertainment. Meanwhile, if his opponent got off a funny remark, Ryan— though bursting to laugh—would say sternly, "That would be very amusing if this were not a serious matter." He won his case.

Carey Van Fleet was another San Francisco attorney who had a talent for wit at the opportune moment. Once when he was trying a case in Nevada, a spectator tied a mule to a nearby hitching post. While his opponent was addressing the jury the animal began to bray. Van Fleet, feigning annoyance, stood up. "If the court please, I think we should have argument from only one of the gentlemen at a time." The other attorney had to sit down amidst the laughter.

Stanislaus Riley, a tall, serious San Francisco attorney, was defending a conspiracy felony case. He had tried time and again to have a mass of testimony which was injurious to his client struck from the record. Time and again the jurist had replied, "Motion denied."

In midafternoon an earthquake struck. The chandeliers swayed, tables slid, books dropped to the floor, while jurors and spectators froze in fear.

Riley stood calmly. "Did your honor deny that motion too?" he inquired.

Porter Ashe, another San Francisco attorney, was once so annoyed with a client that he couldn't resist a sardonic remark. He was defending a mayhem case, his defendant having been charged with biting off the ear of a waiter in a fashionable restaurant. It had been a tense morning. Only the nonchalant client seemed relaxed, watching the clock, twisting anxiously in his chair.

Finally he turned to Ashe at the table and whispered, "It's lunchtime."

Ashe turned to him with scorn. "Shall I call a waiter?"

Just as humor will turn the tide in court, so will a dramatic or amusing character command attention if he is not too bizarre.

One of the most striking San Francisco lawyers was Harry Stafford, a man noted for his wit and vast insolence. Harry was five feet eight inches tall; weighed 300 pounds; was bald, with a fringe of light hair clipped as closely as possible; and affected large glasses rimmed in tortoise shell. With his small features, his head resembled a shining billiard ball. In court, he was so striking a figure that his easy flippancy—which would have annoyed a jury, coming from a less picturesque man—was accepted as innocence. Stafford was a *bon vivant* and an intimate of the more sportive elements of the profession, including many judges. If the occasion presented, he would turn the case he was engaged in into a hippodrome, diverting harmful evidence or comments with his ready wit.

He was once defending a criminal case, and while a witness was on the stand was engaged in a whispered colloquy with his associate. The judge said to him, "Mr. Stafford, I would advise you to pay some attention to the testimony. Did you hear what this witness just said?"

"I am sorry, Your Honor," answered Stafford, "I did not."

"Well, she just testified that you have attempted to bribe her to testify falsely in this case."

"That is ridiculous," retorted Stafford, "Your Honor knows my principles. Whenever I do any bribing, I figure one juror is worth ten witnesses."

Another time, he was trying a contested divorce action against Harry Young. Stafford's client was a difficult witness, and he kept asking her leading questions over the protests of his opponent.

Finally Young said to him in exasperation: "Mr. Stafford, if you're going to be sufficiently indecent to tell the witness what to testify to, at least be sufficiently discreet to do it in the corridor and not when the witness is on the stand."

To which Stafford replied coolly, "That's what I did, but she's so dumb she forgets what I told her."

On a jury trial, when he was in a somewhat similar predicament, the judge attempted to help him out by asking the witness some questions, but with such ill effect that Stafford finally interrupted him by saying, "Well, Judge, if you're going to try it for me, don't lose it for me."

Defending an action for alienation of affections, he cross-examined a detective who claimed to have observed certain intimacies between the defendant and the plaintiff's spouse. These, the witness said, had taken place in a country cottage, and he had spied upon the couple from a privy near the bedroom window. To facilitate his espionage, he had been compelled to stand upon the toilet seat.

Stafford seized upon this with avidity. His cross-examination ran along such questions as the following: "All right, you've gotten yourself into the privy and up on the seat. Now, how long were you on the seat before you got off?" "Now you're looking through the hole in the door. Are you still on the toilet seat or have you finished with that?" "Tell us what you're doing now. Do you stay on the toilet seat or do you get off?" He kept this up until the whole courtroom was howling. During a recess his opponent settled the case to avoid further embarrassment.

He was once awarded $50 as a fee in an uncontested divorce case and complained that the amount was too low, upon which the judge observed, "There are lots of lawyers who would be glad to get a fifty-dollar fee in an uncontested divorce."

"Yes," answered Stafford, "but they're all on the bench."

He once had the tables turned on him by crusty, irascible old Judge Frank Dunne, who fixed his compensation in a probate matter at an amount which Stafford considered inadequate.

"I consider the amount sufficient for the few hours' work consumed in this matter," said Dunne.

"That might be correct," replied Stafford, "if Your Honor considers only the actual time employed in this particular transaction. However, I point out to you that there should also be taken into account the long preparation necessary to prepare a lawyer for practice. Your Honor will understand that, in addition to the few hours consumed on this matter, I spent four years in college and three more in law school. I believe that the time and expense involved in that preparation should be considered by the court."

Dunne listened to this facetious statement and then inquired acidly, "Why don't you send your father out to collect the fee?"

Stafford's excessive indulgence in food and drink brought his career to an early end. His partner Edward Cunha was notified that he could not live for many more days, and called upon his friend for the last time. He thought he detected a tardy penitence in the dying man.

"If I come out of this, Ed," whispered Stafford—and Cunha

bent to hear what reforms in conduct he contemplated—"I'm going to throw the biggest party this town ever saw."

The minor criminal courts of a large city usually have one or two strange advocates who practice only in them. They often lack formal educations; they may have only sketchy notions of the law; but they often have a certain efficiency from the knowledge of two principles. These are: that a witness is worth more than an argument; and that the surest way to get rid of a criminal misdemeanor is to bribe a cop.

The grand exponent of this tradition in my time was Jimmy Carroll, a legendary figure, who died during the 1930's. He had been a lightweight professional pugilist, and bore the marks of that trade in a flattened nose and thickened ears. He suffered from myopia, and peered at the world through thick lenses. I once asked how he had done so well in the ring with the handicap of poor vision.

"I could see the length of my arms. That's all I needed. The other guy was right there," he replied.

Carroll was intelligent, honest within the rules of his code, affable and witty.

He had a set technique. When a fellow attorney with a misdemeanant in tow consulted Jimmy in the corridor of the Hall of Justice, he would listen carefully to the facts involved, and then ask, "How much money have you on you?"

Being told, he would say, "Give it to me."

Let us assume that the client had $200 and the charge was driving an automobile while intoxicated. Carroll would find the arresting officer and put the matter directly to him. "I'm representing this fellow So-and-So. He has two hundred dollars. You take a hundred and say he was out of the car when you first saw him, and the court will have to dismiss the case."

If accepted, the matter was forthwith concluded. If the cop declined the offer, Carroll returned to the client, handed him back the entire amount, and advised him to get a continuance and another lawyer.

It was always difficult to get Jimmy off the second floor where the police courts were housed. Occasionally, of course, he would handle cases on straight issues and would have to appear in one of the Superior Courts held on the third floor of the Hall of Justice.

A client of his had been held to answer to the Superior Court. Carroll failed to appear at the arraignment. The judge dispatched the bailiff to fetch him. When Jimmy appeared under such duress, he was sternly lectured upon his obligations with respect to the two tribunals. The dignity of the Superior Court, he was informed, was not to be sacrificed to the convenience of the police courts. It was the duty of the attorney to consult the wishes of the higher tribunal.

"Yeah, yeah, Judge, I know," retorted Carroll impatiently. "But the groceries are down there on the second floor."

When a magistrate fined his client $25, he asked him, "Couldn't you make it fifteen? All he has is twenty-five, and you could leave ten for Jimmy."

At one time Police Captain Charles Goff was testifying against a culprit whom he represented. Goff was rigidly honest, but— like many of his description—inclined to fanaticism. In this instance his testimony, which was vigorous and damaging, was interrupted by Carroll.

"Can't you take it a little easy, Captain?" he inquired. "And I'll cut you in on my fee."

When an argument on a legal point arose, he would glibly run off a string of citations, inventing the titles as he went along: "Your Honor, that point has been decided by the Supreme Court in *People* vs. *Mulligan* in 176 California, and *People* vs. *Smith* in 186 California."

One of the deputy district attorneys decided to trap him in this device. Carroll had rattled off three or four titles when the deputy produced a pad and pencil and said, "Just a minute, Mr. Carroll. Will you kindly repeat those citations? I wish to make a note of them and check to see if they hold as you say."

"Never mind, son, never mind," Jimmy admonished him. "It won't do you no good to look at those books. There are no pictures in them."

A number of us were once standing in the corridor of the Hall of Justice when two men were brought in by the police. They had apparently been in an automobile accident or a shooting affray. Both were bandaged about the head and arms, and clots of blood showed through the bandages. Somebody said, "I wonder what happened to them?"

"Oh," said Jimmy nonchalantly, "they just made a free and voluntary confession."

His myopic eyes failed him in a grim moment. While he was swimming a motor launch backed into him and fatally injured him.

Contemporary with Carroll was John Greely, a small, dapper man. His manner of citing authorities was even more cynical than Jimmy's. He would furnish the court with such recondite information as: "There is a case somewhere and I don't know what it holds but . . ."

When cross-examining a witness, he would habitually turn and regard the entrance to the courtroom as though he expected someone to enter at any moment, and in default of more pertinent inquiries, he would ask questions as: "How old are you?" "Do you shave?" "What with?"

Another attorney who frequented the same sacred halls was deaf and utterly incompetent, but nevertheless maintained a reasonably lucrative practice. When he found himself in any difficulty, his deafness became so acute as to offer a complete barrier to the reception of whatever he chose not to hear. I once saw him pretend oblivion to a statement which a judge was making to one of his clients while granting him a new trial: "I want to tell you now that if you had been represented by any other attorney, or even if you had represented yourself, you would have been acquitted, and I advise you to go out and hire some lawyer who knows at least a little."

Until his death in 1947, Carey Van Fleet had been a partner of mine for many years. He was erudite and well-read, and had been chief deputy attorney general of the State of California for a long time. He had a most solemn appearance which was completely belied by a great sense of humor and even an inclination to mischief. He was inclined to drink too much, and on such occasions became most expansive and happy. He and a fellow attorney were once locked up in a small-town jail, for disorderly conduct. Next morning Carey suggested that each defend the other. His case came on first, and his friend performed so ably that he was acquitted.

When his friend's case was called, Van Fleet solemnly stated to the court: "Your Honor, the defendant desires to enter a plea of guilty and to throw himself on the mercy of the court."

In order to avoid arguments, many judges refrain from making rulings from the bench, preferring to mark the matter under discussion "submitted" and then decide it in chambers. Judge Frank Muraskey, of the San Francisco Superior Court, became notorious for this practice. It was said that he would not decide even the most obvious point in court.

Van Fleet had filed an action on a promissory note to which his opponent entered a general demurrer, merely to procure delay. It appeared on Muraskey's court.

The other lawyer said to Carey, "I will bet you ten dollars right now that, even if I submit my demurrer without argument, Muraskey won't rule on it from the bench."

Van Fleet accepted the bet.

When the case was called, the defendant's attorney said simply, "I will submit the demurrer without argument."

Whereupon Carey stated: "Your Honor, in looking over my complaint, I see that I have made an important omission. The defendant's demurrer is good and should be sustained."

"Very well," said the judge. "The demurrer is sustained."

Edwin McKenzie once procured the acquittal of a man named Lococo who had shot and killed his employer, Harry Gray. The defendant, who was very poor and had several children, had been defrauded of his wages by the deceased. It was shown that Gray habitually used the device of inventing controversies as to the amounts which had been earned by the poor and ignorant laborers who worked in his contracting company, and settling with them for less than they were entitled to. Lococo had taken every legal means to collect what was due him. He had charged Gray before the state labor commission and had attempted to procure a warrant for his arrest.

In his closing argument the district attorney endeavored to rescue the slain man's reputation. Disclaiming any intention to justify these oppressions which had been proved against him, he nevertheless called the jury's attention to the surviving family of the victim. He led the jury to a consideration of how much the deceased had meant to them; that among them there had been only love and consideration; that his friends mourned the loss of his help and companionship; that the hard demands of a complicated business might have led him on occasion into some injustice, but that such things as had been recounted could be ascribed to error rather than to malice or greed. Harry Gray, he suggested, was probably like any one of the jurors—or even like the prosecutor himself—in that he had the usual admixture of faults and virtues. "Indeed," he declaimed, "I think that we can conclude that this dead man was neither entirely white nor entirely black."

"No," interrupted McKenzie, "he was Gray."

For several years James Brennan was chief deputy district attorney in San Francisco and handled the most important criminal cases. He had been an amateur boxer and football player, and was of formidable appearance. With considerable ability and shrewdness, he combined the tenacity and aggressiveness of a bulldog; in fact, he thrust his jaw into the faces of hostile witnesses so much that he finally came to possess some of the physiognomy of that animal.

McKenzie had great faith in visual display. Whenever possible, he used photostatic enlargements of exhibits and even of excerpts from testimony on his argument. He was also accustomed to write out the chief points of his argument on the courtroom blackboard and to leave them thus displayed to the jury during the rebuttal of the prosecution and the reading of the instructions.

Brennan was prosecuting a case against him and undertook to neutralize this blackboard technique. Accordingly, after McKenzie had used one side to impress his points, Brennan took advantage of a recess to set out his own outline on the other. He then pinned over his handiwork a large map which formed one of the exhibits in the case. This was not large enough to cover the entire board, and the beginnings and ends of the sentences extended beyond its borders.

At an appropriate place in his rebuttal he growled, ". . . and he used a blackboard to show what he means. Well, that's a game that two can play at. I'll show you what it can say on our side."

He swung the board around, showing the map, from under the edges of which the beginnings and ends of his sentences were visible. With a dramatic motion, he ripped the map from its position.

There was a moment of surprise, and then a gale of laughter roared through the courtroom.

The blackboard under the map was entirely blank.

McKenzie regarded it with a look of innocence.

Nathan Coghlan was compelled, on several occasions, to dodge and cut before Brennan's frontal assaults. In one case, the latter had fairly well cornered a defense witness and was pressing his examination within a yard of the man's face. When he deemed a respite useful, Nate rose and gravely instructed him, "Mr. Witness, the assistant district attorney is not going to assault you. He does appear as though he is about to strike you, but you need not be in the least afraid that he will. Just you relax and assure yourself that you are safe from any physical violence."

The witness looked relieved. The jury laughed, and Brennan withdrew in some confusion to a farther position.

Brennan had worked up a number of parables and illustrations which he was accustomed to use in argument. One of these was on the subject of circumstantial evidence. "This morning," he would say, "as I descended from the streetcar I saw a piece of string lying on the ground. I picked it up and brought it with me to show you what I mean by the strength of the combined pieces of evidence which constitute the circumstantial proof in this case." Producing a piece of cord from his pocket, he continued, "You can see how each separate thread of this string is weak and can easily be snapped"—he would break one of them —"but bound together, it is impossible to break it."

Coghlan had heard him use this figure before he finally opposed him. When Brennan, in his argument, began his descent from the streetcar, Nate interrupted. "Mr. Brennan, I got off that streetcar before you did and picked up your piece of string, so you will have to use some other illustration today."

Maxwell McNutt was one of the defense attorneys in the famed Tom Mooney case. Actually a witty man, he looked like an undertaker, and his long, solemn face seldom broke into a frosty smile.

Fickert, the district attorney, conducted the prosecution in person, as the case was widely publicized and was supposed to have political value. Apparently the Russians were as good whipping boys in 1918 as they are today, and Fickert attempted to bring them into the affair. He undertook to trace a connection between the defendant and an alleged anarchistic organization. To color the allusion, he introduced one or two Russian terms. One of these was the word "ukase," meaning an order or directive. He had neglected to learn its proper pronunciation. In his argument to the jury, he declaimed, ". . . and this organization issued to Thomas Mooney its ukeskee—"

"It's whatskee?" demanded McNutt's sepulchral voice. "What was that term you used, Mr. District Attorney?"

On another of the trials arising from this outrage, Tom O'Connor cross-examined a wierd little old woman, a Miss Edau. She explained a discrepancy in locations by stating that her physical body had been in one place and her astral body in another. She had had numerous interviews with Draper Hand, the police officer charged with the preparation of the case.

O'Connor turned to the jury. "The voice is the voice of Edau," he said, "but the hand is Draper Hand."

CHAPTER 7

Juries Can't Be Trusted

MANY lawyers, particularly those representing wealthy interests, claim to distrust and despise the jury system. They are probably justified. I have seen judges who will do everything but deliver the verdict, to aid some wealthy interest—only to be repudiated by the jury. "Juries can't be trusted," goes the old saw.

Indeed, sometimes a jury will even refuse an instruction to return a given verdict. I recall one celebrated case in San Mateo County, south of San Francisco. The matter involved the estate of James Flood, a gold-rush pioneer who had become a millionaire. A woman, Constance Gavin, stepped up to claim a portion of the Flood inheritance, claiming she was an illegitimate daughter, but legitimized by acceptance into the Flood family.

The judge who heard the case could hardly be objective. As a boy he'd worked in the Flood stables, and the family had paid his way through law school. It was open talk that he had turned down retirement only to repay his debt to the family.

The Flood estate was represented by the influential Gavin McEnerney, an able lawyer who recalled William Jennings Bryan in appearance, and—among other affluent clients—claimed the Roman Catholic Archbishop in San Francisco.

McEnerney had an assurance consistent with his power. I recall hearing him argue an appeal before the state Supreme Court. The chief justice at one point interrupted to ask a question. McEnerney made no effort to hide the contempt in his voice. "I'm surprised to hear the chief justice ask such a question!" he began in disdain, then went on to deliver a lecture on the point involved. The chief justice sat meekly back, seemingly pleased to escape with nothing more than a tongue-lashing.

McEnerney had with him in the Flood case Theodore Roche, one-time partner of the late Hiram Johnson, U. S. Senator and Governor of California. They made an impressive team.

Constance Gavin was represented at first by George Ford, attorney for the Western Pacific Railroad. He soon knew he was dealing with rough foes. He told me that private detectives had been assigned to follow him day and night. One, whom he managed to befriend, told him their mission was to find something which could lead to Ford's disbarment.

Meanwhile the woman had to establish three things in order to have the case submitted to the jury: she had to show that she was indeed James Flood's child; that she had been accepted into his home; and that his wife had consented to this with knowledge of the relationship between her husband and the child. Flood's widow had died many years before.

Mrs. Gavin, by this time, had one Eugene Aureguy as her attorney. He was an astute artisan, if also a monumental cynic. He'd established the first two requisites soon enough, and found an ancient dame who had once been a nurse in the Flood household. She testified that, when Constance Gavin was a child, Mrs. Flood had once told her that, "you know she's Mr. Flood's."

This should have clearly taken the case to jury. But the one-time Flood stableboy, now sitting on the bench, guessed that the jury was in sympathy with the woman. He granted a motion made by McEnerney for a directed verdict. Despite cries of rage, he convened the jury and explained his ruling, directing them to return a verdict for the estate.

Despite his reputation as a courtroom tyrant, when the jury filed back and announced that it refused to follow his instructions, he simply ordered the clerk to enter the judgment. On appeal, the Supreme Court held that the evidence entered by Mrs. Gavin's attorney was sufficient to take the case to jury. Before a new trial started, the claim was settled for a large amount.

My own experiences with civil juries were almost always in cases where I represented the poor and obscure against wealthy defendants. Most were damage cases for personal injury or death. In selecting a jury, I was generally concerned with two questions. Were—or could—the prospective juror's interests be involved in the trial? Were his vanity or prejudices involved? If he did not have to overcome one of these, I usually accepted him.

Personal-injury cases cover many facets of one's life, occupation, business and personal relationships, and it's foolish to keep a juror whose vote may be affected by one or more of them. One must question closely to uncover dangerous ties; the juror's assurances of fairness mean nothing. Of course, one should not keep anyone who is related to the opposite party or to his attorney, to a witness, or to another participant.

If a juror's occupation is connected with that of one's opponent, it is wise to let him go. One must always keep in mind that an effort will be made to reach the jurors. Any business relationship facilitates the approach. If, for example, one's action is against a trucking company and a prospective juror is employed by someone in a related line, it is probable that avenues exist through which the defendant can contact his employer and have a good word put in for him. This type of influence is almost conclusive; the juror cannot be expected to jeopardize his job to be fair to a stranger, and he should not be asked to do so.

Some concerns which are subject to many claims spread their patronage around with the direct object of creating liens through which they can control juries. They carry accounts in several banks. If a clerk from one of these is selected on a case in which they are engaged, they contact his superior and have him either put the fix directly on the employee, or feed him propaganda which will affect his vote.

Such favors become valuable means of increasing business.

Most large firms are quite willing to have their employees serve on juries, and they cooperate with the jury commissioners in their selection. Traction and insurance companies encourage this practice. Where the juries are rigged, such companies assign their own people for service on them.

It goes without saying that you will not retain anyone who is subject to the same sort of claim as you are pressing. I know of no lawyer who would keep a doctor's wife on a medical malpractice case.

Personal relationships are as dangerous as business connections. Naturally, friends of the party or of his attorney will be eliminated at once. In doing this, it is advisable to suggest to your opponent that he consent to the juror's discharge. You should do this before inquiring of the juror whether his friendship will influence his verdict. People almost always deny that it will, and a challenge for cause will not lie. You must get rid of him, but you do not want to use up your peremptory challenges. Asking your opponent, in the presence of the other prospective jurors, to consent to his release, puts him in the position of almost having to agree. Otherwise he will appear to be seeking an unfair advantage.

A more deceptive situation exists where the prospect states that he has met your opponent or his attorney but has had no further acquaintance with him. Here is where you must be careful. You inquire as to the circumstances of the meeting. Let us say that it was at the home of a mutual friend. "Are your relations with him still friendly?" "Yes." Then a telephone call may suffice to swing that vote.

The mere fact that the meeting is remembered is cause for concern. We humans are more than our individual selves. Things which are associated with us become extensions of our personalities. Our vanity vests them with worth. We are as much offended by reflections upon our family, our homes, our cars or our clothing, as by those upon ourselves. "Love me, love my dog." We like to think that the people we associate with are superior. We retain agreeable recollections of chance acquaintances. We meet some celebrity for whom we have conceived a dislike. He chats amiably with us for a few moments, and forever after we defend him from the same charges we once leveled at him.

In addition, these chance acquaintances may be renewed. Unless you have reduced your peremptory challenges to the danger point and there are worse prospects waiting, get rid of the chance acquaintance.

When I was about twenty-five, I had a friend who was a student in a Dominican college for girls. One afternoon I attended a tea dance at the convent. I was introduced to a beautiful and charming girl. We exchanged small talk.

From time to time I encountered her picture on the society pages where I eventually read of her marriage. Years after our meeting I had a damage case, and her name appeared on the jury list. With it was that of another young woman, prominent in San Francisco society.

At first blush these two wealthy women would seem to be among the least desirable of jurors for the plaintiff in a death case against a big corporation.

The insurance company was represented by Jewell Alexander, an adroit, persistent and persuasive advocate. He had a complete report on the panel of prospective jurors, and manipulated his challenges deftly so as to procure those with a defendant bias. On his first effort he drew the other society woman and beamed contentedly. She was, presumably, just what he wanted.

Then he started fishing for her partner of the upper crust. He excused two more of somewhat innocuous complexion, and then exercised his fourth and last challenge. Up popped my charmer from the convent. Alexander's complacency with his success was short-lived.

The judge asked a preliminary question: "Do you know **any** of the people whose names have been mentioned here?"

"I met Mr. Hallinan once," replied the juror, "but it was so long ago he probably doesn't even remember it."

The defendant's last challenge had been used up, and I could capitalize on the opportunity without danger. "Indeed I do remember!" I interjected, and turned to the defense table. "You will hardly believe this, Mr. Alexander, but it was at a tea dance in the Dominican convent in San Rafael."

The lady smiled brightly. "Yes, that is so," she confirmed.

Alexander almost had a stroke. He strove mightily to establish something which would justify a challenge for cause. He insisted there was probably some remaining impression or sentiment which might color the lady's verdict, but she steadfastly repulsed his efforts. She remained in the box, and the defense counsel looked increasingly gloomy as the two society girls consorted intimately throughout the trial. On the argument, I asked for a verdict of $70,000. The jury returned one for $40,000, at that time a record for the state. Afterward the two young women came up to me in the corridor. They were almost in tears. "Oh, Vincent," said my lovely acquaintance, "we are so sorry! We tried to get you the $70,000, but they just wouldn't give it."

Find out, if possible, whether the juror belongs to any fraternal organization, club or other society of which your opponent or his counsel is a member. Not only are there opportunities for reaching him through such connections, but the juror may not want to be curtly treated when he meets his confrere in the steam room.

In actions against public bodies such as the state, city or other political subdivision, do not keep employees of other agencies. This is not a matter of bias alone. It will surprise you how far attorneys for public bodies will go to win. Ex-employees are also suspect, as are retired military officers and others who have been inculcated in the sanctity of the state. In criminal cases they are almost invariably poison for the defense.

In making your selection, do not be influenced by the juror's estimate of his own integrity. Few admit, even to themselves, their prejudices and biases.

In 1934, I defended a man named Andrew Yates. Late at night he had driven his automobile into the back of a streetcar, striking the conductor, who was switching the trolley pole. He was arrested at the scene. The arresting officers, several witnesses who were present, and a city doctor who examined Yates, charged that he was profoundly intoxicated. When one of my associates bailed him out next day, he did not know what had happened, nor why he was in jail.

The unfortunate conductor's right leg was so badly mangled that it had to be amputated. He was an officer of his union and had influence with the district attorney's office. His brother also had political liens. Yates was indicted on two felony counts.

The defendant and his wife were natives of Scotland. So were most of his friends. They all spoke with a wonderful collection of burrs. On the jury list were three thoroughly Scotch names. I manipulated the challenge so that all their owners were in the box when the jury was sworn. All were obviously immigrants from the banks and braes o' bonny Doon. The district attorney didn't notice anything until it was too late.

When his automobile had collided with the streetcar, Yates had fortunately been thrown against the windshield, and had sustained a cut on his forehead which was described in the police and hospital reports. The witnesses for the prosecution testified, with considerable unanimity, that in their opinion the defendant had been very drunk at the time of the accident. They stated that he had staggered when he walked, spoken incoherently, and that his breath had smelled strongly of alcohol. I confined their cross-examinations to a description of the cut on his forehead and the length of time the car had been in darkness while the trolley pole was being changed.

Yates testified that there had been a gathering of friends at his home that evening and that he had driven some of his guests to their homes and was returning when the car loomed suddenly in front of him. He claimed to have been completely sober, but to have struck the windshield with such force that he was thereafter unaware of what was going on.

I then called a doctor as an expert witness. He stated that one suffering from a brain concussion displays precisely the same symptoms as the witnesses had attributed to the defendant, and that when one has a head injury and a breath smelling of alcohol, it is impossible to determine whether these symptoms have been caused by a concussion, or by intoxication without knowing how much alcohol has been taken.

The defendant's wife and friends followed, either to corroborate his story or to attest his reputation. I had advised them that it was unnecessary to make any extreme effort to alter their native speech patterns. By the time the last one left the stand we had bluebells and heather blowing all over the courtroom. I spent much of my argument extolling the land of the thistle and the morality and veracity of its children, and we got a quick acquittal.

Of course, when the shoe is on the other foot, you must devise a method of neutralizing the disadvantage.

In 1933, when I represented Mae Pierce, I filed several damage suits against the racketeers and certain "respectable" persons who had deliberately sold her worthless securities. On the trial of one of these a German grocer was on the jury. He was big and vigorous, the most imposing man on the panel.

The head of the defendant brokerage firm was a handsome persuasive fellow and a glib witness. He put special emphasis upon one incident in the various transactions which had covered a period of three years or so.

The reason for accenting this phase became apparent when his lawyer asked, "Now, were you even in San Francisco at that time?"

To which the witness answered, with scarcely concealed enthusiasm, "No, sir. I was in Germany studying music."

A series of questions followed, identifying the German cities in which he had studied and his length of residence in each.

On argument, I called attention to the undue emphasis which had been placed on this one incident, and suggested that it had been done to influence someone of German origin on the jury.

I continued. "While he was in Germany he might better have devoted himself to acquiring some of the morality and philosophy of the German people. I recommend him especially to a poem of Heinrich Heine, directed to people exactly like him. It speaks of the grand persons, with their fine clothes and elegant manners, and ends: *'Ach, wenn sie nur Hertzen hätten!*—Ah, if you only had hearts!'"

The German grocer was foreman of the jury. He looked at me

with triumph when the clerk read out its verdict, which was for $50,000.

Relying on "hunches" and other psychic impulses is an idle and foolish procedure when selecting a jury. As I mentioned, while in law school I was employed as a clerk by Daniel A. Ryan, the brilliant trial lawyer. He was a great orator, and while still very young had been the Republican Party's candidate for mayor of San Francisco. He affected a theatrical appearance, wearing a cutaway coat and wing collars. His garb belied an earthy and humorous nature; he was extremely witty and was given to salty comments and explosive epithets.

He had me sit with him throughout the first jury case he tried after my arrival in his office. He was representing an old man who had been struck by an automobile, and was suing for $25,000. Among the first twelve jurors drawn was a man named Taylor, a solemn-looking fellow who resembled Woodrow Wilson.

When it came time to exercise his first peremptory challange, Ryan whispered to me, "What do you think of that fellow, Taylor?"

I frantically disclaimed any judgment in the matter.

"I don't like his looks," he said, and pondered dismissing the juror, but finally changed his mind and kept him.

Throughout the trial Taylor displayed slight attention. He appeared to have about as much emotional capacity as an eel. Ryan's uneasiness concerning him increased as the case progressed. "I know," he cogitated, "that I've helped hang that son of a bitch's father!"

The jury returned a verdict for $15,000. The jury was polled, and when Taylor was asked if that was his verdict, he answered with an emphatic *No*.

Ryan nudged me furiously. "You see! I told you so. The son of a bitch!" he growled.

When the jurors left the box, Taylor came up to Dan and began, "Mr. Ryan, I couldn't vote for that verdict . . ."

Without rising from his chair, Ryan retorted stiffly, "That was your privilege, sir."

Taylor continued. "That man was entitled to the whole twenty-five thousand dollars, and I wouldn't come down a cent."

It is not uncommon for jurors to conceal relationships and pre-dilections which will affect their verdicts. They usually do so with the direct purpose of aiding one side, even when the chances of detection are great. Needless to say, this can be highly dangerous, not only to themselves but to those they are attempting to help.

I once examined a jury upon which there was an old friend whom I had also represented in litigation. As the questioning approached him I became convinced that he intended to disclaim any acquaintance with me. Not only was there a good probability that our relationship would be discovered, but the case did not warrant the risk.

When the examination of the man preceding him had been completed, I turned to the opposing attorney and said, "The next juror is an old and dear friend of mine. If he says that he will not be prejudiced in my favor, don't believe him. Isn't that correct, Mr.—?"

The juror looked startled, then smiled and nodded.

"I'll stipulate that he may be excused," I added.

My friend's confused air as he stepped from the jury box helped confirm my suspicion of his intentions. I got up, shook hands with him, and sent him away—in this action avoiding a danger and establishing my fairness with the remaining members of the venire.

Somewhat franker was a juror whom Leo Friedman examined on a sex case in a rural community. The action, as might be expected, had excited great interest, and there was even a considerable amount of betting on its outcome.

When asked if he knew of any reason why he could not be a fair juror, this man replied, "No. However, I think it is only fair to tell you that I have made a substantial bet on the outcome of this case."

Of course, juries often base their verdicts on matters which have no relation to the law or the facts. I once knew a woman juror who refused to convict on a clear case, only because the defendant had been held in jail for almost six months awaiting trial. She conceded that he was guilty, but asserted that he had been sufficiently punished. The other jurors argued that the judge would take this into consideration in fixing the sentence, but she declined to afford him that discretion.

She had some well-known precedents for her position. A Welsh jury once returned a verdict: "Not guilty, but we recommend him not to do it again."

An eighteenth-century English jury, having before it a culprit charged with burglary—then a capital offense—wished not to destroy the man, since no element of violence was involved. It returned the safe verdict: "Guilty of getting out of the window."

It remained, however, for an Irish jury to arrive at the limits of such discretion. The defendant had pleaded guilty, but had been permitted to withdraw his plea. The jury acquitted him.

The judge, in surprise, exclaimed, "Why, he has confessed his crime."

To which the foreman responded, "Yes, My lord, but you do not know the fellow, and we do. He is the most notorious liar in the whole county, and no twelve men who know this character would believe a word he says."

The jury adhered to its verdict, and the prisoner escaped punishment.

On the other hand, jurors will sometimes follow the law very closely. Walter McGovern once had a difficult case in which one juror held out for acquittal. Some days later he happened to pass a shop owned by this man, and dropped in to talk with him. Assuming that he had been convinced of the defendant's innocence, McGovern suggested that he would have his client come in and thank him personally.

The juror exploded. "Don't have that goddamn crook come in here. I took an oath to acquit on a reasonable doubt, but the doubt isn't reasonable enough to trust the bastard in my store."

Lawyers frequently fall into the error of supposing that when a man takes his seat on a jury, he leaves his common sense outside with his hat, and that he will surrender his judgment to the most vigorous speaker. They explain every detail as though the jurors lacked the ordinary powers of observation and would miss anything omitted from the argument. As a matter of fact, jurors are often offended by meticulous discussions of points which they should be credited with having noticed. It is well to leave something to them.

Frank Murphy, who died when his ability as a criminal lawyer was coming to wide recognition, used to illustrate this principle with an experience of his own. During a trial he noticed that one juror made frequent notes. He jotted down the matters which the man seemed to be observing, and on his argument, avoided mentioning them. When the cause was submitted, the notetaker produced his memoranda and argued them to his fellow jurors. After they had returned a verdict freeing Murphy's client, this man expressed contempt for the lawyer's talents.

"Why," he said, "the big dummy missed all the important points. If I hadn't made notes of them, the jury would never have remembered them."

Sometimes too a juror will take a position quite at variance with that which his profession or position might lead one to expect. Ed Cunha once tried a difficult rape case, and feared that he had offended one of the jurors, an ex-minister, by Elizabethan language and quarrels with the judge. But after the verdict the man congratulated him precisely on those two things.

In another action, involving alienation of affections, the squeaking of a bed was enlarged on as evidence of guilt. When it was mentioned in the jury room, an old maid member commented scornfully: "Oh, pish! Many a night my own has squeaked, and it didn't mean a damn thing."

It is advisable to keep in mind the possibility of chance encounters with jurors outside the courtroom. Quite frequently verdicts result from disclosures in the jury room of facts learned by a member from such sources. I once tried a damage case for a woman who limped visibly and carried a cane throughout the trial. It resulted in a very moderate verdict. Later I learned that on a weekend recess one of the jurors had seen the plaintiff on the street without a cane, and had followed her for several blocks, during which she walked without limping. The juror disclosed this information during the deliberations, and greatly reduced the amount of the verdict.

Less pertinent discoveries may produce bad results. I know of an instance in which a woman juror held out for conviction, for the sole reason that she had seen the defendant and his wife walking down the sidewalk and the wife was on the outside.

When jury-stacking was at its height in San Francisco, it was customary for persons entitled to patronage to place their super-annuated relatives on the criminal trial-jury panel. These would serve for long periods and constituted a sort of professional jury. Many were not only senile, but desirous of adding to the fee of two dollars a day by selling their votes. One of these jurors had been bribed to vote for acquittal in a case on which he was serving. He was so stupid that he was strongly cautioned to never vote anything but Not guilty.

The jury received the case late in the afternoon. It had been deliberating only half an hour when it was proposed that the court be requested to send it to dinner. The foreman called for a vote on the motion and collected the twelve written ballots. Eleven read: "Dinner"; the twelfth: "Not guilty."

There is a story of a juryman who was bribed, in a dangerous murder case, to hold out for manslaughter. The deliberations of the jury consumed two full days, at the end of which the weary members consented to a verdict of manslaughter.

When the opportunity afforded, the defense counsel sought out his juror, and after felicitating him on his success, inquired about the difficulty of his task. The juror assured him that it had been hard indeed. "Why," he said, "the other eleven wanted to acquit him."

It is hardly necessary to advise that jurors be treated with the utmost consideration. In fact, it would be a very nice world if we acted toward everybody as though, next day, he was to sit as a juror in a case we were trying.

I am referring to real consideration. This is something quite different from fawning and flattery. It implies recognition that the jurors have common sense and self-respect. Many lawyers attempt to win their goodwill by procedures which are nothing but cheap tricks and fraudulent devices. Such advocates will memorize the names of the jurors and take care to address each by name before the trial has finished. At close of day they will open the gate between the sections of the courtroom, bidding each juror an affectionate good night as he passes through it. They will be solicitous for their comfort, and will ask the judge whether a window might not be opened or a shade drawn, or something else which will contribute to it. This is usually done with a worried air and apologetic smile, as though the gentleman was consulting the jury's welfare at some unexpressed peril to his own.

The remedy for all devices of this sort is based upon the fact that people do not like to be imposed upon. Jurors, no more than anyone else, relish being tricked. Once they catch on to the fact that they are being hoosiered, they are apt to give a chill reception to the confidence man.

I tried a damage case in Alameda County, against Elliot Johnson, one of the ablest trial lawyers in the state. My client's husband had engaged in a controversy with a bus driver, in the course of which he was punched and knocked to the curb, striking his head with fatal results. It was a difficult case, and the defendants had refused any settlement.

Johnson was riding high in the East Bay. He was continuously in court and had gotten to know many of the jury panel; he was not backward in warming the acquaintanceship. He had developed a dual-personality technique. He treated the opposing clients and lawyers as if they were pickpockets, and the jury as if they were his sweethearts.

I deliberately let him get away with everything he tried. I didn't respond to his discourtesies. He was all but kissing the jurors, and I pretended not to notice.

On the closing argument, however, I took both matters up quite thoroughly:

There are different ways [I told the jury] by which lawyers win cases. They may devote their efforts to learning the facts and presenting them in a straightforward way. Another method is to bribe the jury. The direct payment of money for this purpose is expensive and dangerous. There is a safer and cheaper way. It consists in fawning upon and flattering its members. It acts upon the basic assumption that the people who constitute the jury have no sense of the dignity and responsibility of their office; that they are vain and foolish; that, in return for an ungraceful condescension, they will forget their oaths and their duties; and that they are susceptible to an open and oily flattery.

This system involves much less work than is required to collect and present evidence in a decent and honest manner. To be sure, it takes some effort. For instance, you must memorize the names of the jurors. This is made easy by long practice. After several years, one acquires the trick. He prepares a list with the names corresponding to the position of the jurors in the box. At evening, he hurries to hold open the gate—a task which the bailiff would be glad to perform. [I walked to the gate, held it open, and imitated Johnson's voice and manner.] "Good night, Mrs. Jones." "Good night, Mr. Jackson." "Good night, Mrs. Smith," and so on for a half dozen more. [I returned to the table.] I don't know [I continued] how much any one of you would demand if he wished to sell his verdict in this case for cash. I imagine that it could not be less than a thousand dollars. I do not know what value Mr. Johnson puts on the shabby bribery by flattery which he is attempting to foist upon you; I would put thirty cents as the extreme upper figure. I haven't the slightest notion that he will get away with it; if he does, it will be the cheapest bribe in history.

Another indication of the poor respect in which he holds you is the manner in which he treats the unhappy woman who has come before you, asking justice for the murder of her husband. [I picked up a portion of the transcript and read off several questions and answers, snarling and growling in Elliot's best style.] She is entitled to just treatment at your hands. That includes that, in presenting her case before you, she shall be treated with courtesy and respect. In denying her that right, Mr. Johnson is being equally insulting and discourteous to you. His contempt for this jury is as much illustrated by his mistreatment of us, who have come before you seeking justice, as by his shabby efforts to win you over by a course of unprincipled flattery.

We recovered an unanimous verdict.

Some lawyers have formulas which they habitually employ in arguments to juries. One of these is the "chummy approach." I have seen it recommended by respectable authority, and it is much used. It consists in discussing the case as though the jury and lawyer were on the same side. A friendly, confidential manner is assumed, and the whole thing is talked over on a broad, homey sort of basis. Our advocate invites himself into a chat with the jurors, and from that vantage point tries to wheedle them into agreement with him.

One of the least amiable characters at the San Francisco bar had this technique. His practice was confined to defending insurance companies. He was well fitted for this type of litigation. He had all the warm sympathy of a crocodile.

He was arguing a case against me and said to the jury, "Do not think because I represent the defendant that I have not the same sympathy for the plaintiff as you must have. When I saw this boy's injuries on the stand, I felt the tears come into my eyes."

I interrupted and suggested to the court that it might be advisable that we stand for a few moments in silence, since we had apparently witnessed the greatest miracle since Moses smote the rock.

When I first tried a case against him, on the argument he launched into his specialty. Its basic formula was the repeated use of the phrase "You and I." As, for example: "The plaintiff claims thus and so; but *you and I* know that that simply can't be true."

On rebuttal, I handled the device about as follows:

> You ladies and gentlemen of the jury are unbiased, neutral judges, sworn to decide this case on an impartial basis. My opponent, the lawyer who has just addressed you, is a hired partisan, paid to win for the side which has employed him. I have the same position on the opposite side.
>
> Now will someone tell me, by what right does he undertake to climb into the jury box, sit down on your laps, and pretend to act as a sort of thirteenth juror—your friend and confidant—who can tell you what "you and I" are thinking?

I would like to hear him make an argument like that to a judge. The first time he said to him: "Your Honor, you and I know better than that," he would be rebuked for his presumption; the second time, he would be in contempt of court. But he has the effrontery to employ it on you, who are the judges in this instance, not once or twice, but eleven times.

CHAPTER 8

The Fine Art
of Winning Verdicts

IN A criminal case the battle is over and the victory won with an acquittal. In a civil action, however, there is no such finality. A money judgment comes under the pruning knife of the trial judge. And, past him, the Appellate and the Supreme Court each get a whack at it. If the award is against one of the powers which have helped any of these judges to the bench, it has to be of an extraordinary nature to survive the gantlet.

I have had meritorious cases which have been tried three or four times over periods up to ten years. In each, successive juries have returned large verdicts which were finally annulled by either trial or Appellate courts, so that the persons recovering them never collected a nickel.

But getting such verdicts remains important. The defendant often fears that a retrial might bring a larger award, and settles the claim. And even when nothing is recovered, the defense lawyers gain respect for the winning counsel, which makes settlement more likely in future cases.

Winning verdicts involves many elements of character and personality. In a city like San Francisco, which can count probably 3,000 lawyers in active practice, there will be found only a handful—10 or 12—first-class advocates. In addition, there will be a score of men sufficiently capable in defending damage suits to be retained permanently by the insurance companies. Another score can represent plaintiffs in such actions with reasonable success, or obtain acquittals in easy criminal cases. The rest usually stay away from jury cases, or hire one of the more gifted to try them.

Thomas Erskine, the eighteenth-century English barrister, was once asked what talents he considered requisite for success as a trial lawyer. He replied that he believed that success in any department of life depended more upon accident and certain physical advantages than upon the most brilliant talents and the most profound erudition.

Personally, I think that the primary essentials are self-discipline and hard work. Everybody suffers from stage fright, and nobody likes to work, but if you're going to surrender to laziness or nervousness, you'll be out of place in a tough trial. Undisciplined talents are a drug on the market. I have seen brilliant men badly cut down by mediocre opponents who took the trouble to read a few decisions before appearing in court.

Daniel Webster once said: "Accuracy and diligence are much more necessary than great comprehension of mind or brilliancy of talent. [A lawyer's] . . . business is to refine, define, split hairs, look into authorities, and compare cases. A man can never gallop over the fields of law on Pegasus, nor fly across on the wings of oratory. If he would stand on terra firma, he must first descend. If he would be a great trial lawyer, he must first consent to be a great drudge."

All around us we see apparent—but only apparent—contradictions of the adage. The attorney hero of television or movies consistently wins by some flamboyant twist which has little to do with struggling over lawbooks. In most novels, and for that matter in nonfiction, authors attribute every talent to the protagonist except hard work. The reader is left with the illusion that the "Golden Touch" has worked again and that the colorful attorney, in eccentric raiment or awash with bourbon, has conquered by sheer cleverness and intuition.

These stories have a strong influence on young barristers. Many embraced the profession because of the glamor portrayed in them. They try to possess themselves of the mystic charm by copying Earl Rogers' sartorial splendor or William Fallon's intemperate living.

I believe that James Martin MacInnis, one of my associates, was influenced to become a lawyer by such romances. His first case, in the late 1930's, was a criminal misdemeanor, and he proceeded to follow the prescribed pattern. He equipped himself in the dark gray cutaway coat, striped trousers, yellow gloves and derby hat, which he understood to have been the uniform of the Great Mouthpiece. He then thrust a flower in his lapel, possessed himself of a large lawbook, and headed for San Francisco's Hall of Justice.

At an earlier time he would not have made it. Thus accoutered, he could have traversed Market Street to Kearney and thence to Sutter, without molestation. From that point, the chances against him would have increased geometrically. By the time he got to Bush Street, he would have been perceptibly glowered at. In the next block to Pine Street, he would have been jeered at and cat-called. By California Street, he would have been jostled at least twice, and from there on you could write your own ticket.

In the more effete day in which he essayed his venture he tacked safely into the grimy portals of the Hall of Justice. Unruffled by the critical survey of its habitués, he crossed its lobby. Near the elevator he was called aside by Harvey Wing, veteran reporter of an evening paper.

The newspaperman examined him with a questioning, although not unfriendly, eye and then gave him a solemn admonition. "Jim," he said, "let me give you a piece of serious advice: *Never*"—and he stressed the word—"never again come into the Hall of Justice with a lawbook in your hand."

Another Jim—Governor James Folsom of Alabama—excited comment by his election tactics. He traveled the state with a hillbilly band, and illustrated his cleanup campaign with bucket and mop. He finally invaded the north, displaying his props and kissing the girls. An exasperated hometown paper commented: "Jim can't help being a fool, but he *could* stay home."

Similarly, a lawyer may lack special talents but he *can* work. He should not wait until he is arguing his case to find out that a statute he is relying on has been repealed, or was not enacted until after the circumstances involved in his action arose. Many times the decisions of Appellate Courts construe laws in a way one would never expect from reading the statutes. Where reliance is placed on such enactments, the opinions construing them should be read in advance of the hearings.

Edwin McKenzie confesses that he once cited as a "leading case" a decision of the State Supreme Court, upon which his opponent stated, "If it is a leader, it is without followers," and proceeded to show that the decision had been overruled in a subsequent opinion of the same court. On another occasion, an attorney for a title insurance company cited against him a case from South Carolina which had been overruled in that state seven times.

Laziness or carelessness in ascertaining facts has cost many a verdict. It is inexcusable to proceed to trial without having inspected the scene involved.

Some years ago I represented a boy who had been struck by a truck after alighting from the tailboard of another on which he was stealing a ride. There was a good defense of contributory negligence, lost to the defendants because I went to the scene of the accident and inspected it and their lawyer did not.

The accident had occurred at the intersection of Potrero Avenue and 25th Street in San Francisco. They do not run directly across each other, the westerly side of 25th Street being about 150 feet south of the easterly side. There was a carline on Potrero Avenue, and a safety zone for passengers alongside the tracks. This was about 60 feet in length. Its southerly end was opposite the north property line on the west side of 25th Street.

I took the deposition of the defendant truck driver, a husky young man, as soon as possible after filing the complaint. He was mixed up on topography. He did not know, or had forgotten, about the jog in the intersection. He said that the boy jumped off when the truck on which he had been riding made a left-hand turn to go east on 25th Street. He gave his own speed at that time as 25 miles an hour, and said that at that speed he could stop in about 40 feet. He claimed to have brought his vehicle to a halt so quickly that when he did so its cab was over the buttons on the south end of the safety zone.

If I could hold him to that story we had a win. If his cab was where he said it was after the accident, then his truck had gone over 200 feet from the time he saw the boy dismounting until he brought it to a stop. By his own statement, he could have done it in 40 feet.

This would bring the case within the "last clear chance" rule and offset the defense of contributory negligence. Ordinarily, if a person sustains injury through the carelessness of another, he cannot recover damages if his own negligence contributed to it. However, if one sees another in a position of danger and has a "last clear chance" to avoid hurting him and fails to do so, the contributory negligence of the injured person is no longer a defense.

I gave him plenty of opportunity to enlarge his story. Most witnesses like to sweeten their testimonies. By being a bit offensive, I set him off. I knew he wanted to belt me. But he held back, taking out his anger in more and more positive assertions. "You're quite an observing young man," I would remark with sarcasm. He bristled, then elaborated in more positive terms what he had said before. He was sure of the other truck's left-hand turn into 25th Street, because he remembered the hand signal preceding it, and other such circumstances. He was sure that he had stopped opposite the safety zone buttons, because when he descended from his cab, he had stepped on them.

The lawyer for the insurance company sat calmly through all this testimony. It was obvious that he too was unaware of the irregularity in the intersection.

When we went to trial, his case was in such poor shape that he did not even put the truck driver on the stand, and we won an easy verdict in what would have been ordinarily a difficult case.

George Ford told me that he once defended an action involving the collision of a train and an automobile. The plaintiff testified that his vision had been obstructed by a large tree at the crossing. Ford had been at the scene and knew that no such tree existed. In questioning the witness, he was careful not to warn him of this circumstance, but couched his inquiries in such a way as seemed to agree with his description of the location. The witnesses who followed were led into accepting the error, and all included the tree in their statements. He later requested permission of the court for the jury to inspect the crossing. The jurors were astonished to discover that there was no tree in the vicinity.

The earlier the preparation starts, the better. I once represented a woman who had sustained some slight injuries in an automobile accident near a small town in Central California. She had been taken to the local hospital where she was treated by a physician. As part of the treatment, her thigh was subjected to heat from an infrared lamp. This was improperly adjusted, and she suffered a severe burn.

I filed an action against the hospital and doctor, and we went to trial. What would seem an easy case was completely frustrated when the plaintiff, who had no other witness, was contradicted by the defendant physician and all the members of the hospital staff. They swore positively that no lamp had been used at all and that the deep scar on her thigh had been caused by the automobile accident.

Some years later a man appeared at my office with almost identical facts involving a doctor and hospital in Yreka, a town in the northern part of the state. Mindful of the previous experience, I asked my brother Jerry, who did investigative work for our office, to see if he could foreclose against a similar deception.

He phoned the doctor at Yreka, and giving a fictitious name, said, "Doctor, I'm an investigator for the Aetna Casualty Company, and I've been asked to look into a claim against you. I can't find your name in our file. Are you insured with us?"

"No," answered the physician, and gave the name of the indemnity company with which he was insured.

"Oh!" said Jerry. "That explains it—they're a subsidiary of ours. Wait a moment, will you? Yes, here it is."

"What's the claim about?" asked the other.

Jerry gave the name of the claimant. "He says he was burned by a lamp in your hospital."

"He's lying," retorted the doctor immediately. "There wasn't any lamp used on him."

My brother laughed. "Listen, Doc," he said, "we're on the same side. We're not admitting anything to him, but we've got to have the true story for our files. That's confidential between you and me, you know. If this bum has a claim, we can get rid of him for a few hundred dollars. Will you send me right away a full report of everything that happened—just what injuries he had, the treatment and so forth? If a lamp was used, let me know the make, how long it was on him, how far away, how often it was changed—you know. If there's anything you can think of that might constitute contributory negligence—like leaving too soon or not taking orders—put that in too."

A couple of days later he received a full report from the doctor, describing the lamp, the manner in which it had been used, and the burns caused by it. It stated that these were due to the fact that an inexperienced nurse had failed to move the lamp at proper intervals.

Sometime later we filed a suit and associated local counsel to handle the trial. The doctor was called as a hostile witness and swore that no lamp had been used in treating the plaintiff, nor had the latter suffered any burn in the hospital.

He was then confronted with his letter. We recovered a large verdict, and the defendant, out of embarrassment and possibly fear of criminal prosecution, moved from the town.

It is a mistake to employ an attorney who has a practice larger than he can handle efficiently. Many lawyers are too busy to prepare their cases properly, and go into court scarcely knowing what issues are involved.

I was once called upon to fish out of the fire a most pathetic case. A twenty-year-old boy had been terribly injured. His parents hired an attorney with limited personal injury experience to handle his claim. Sometime before the trial, this man employed one of the most brilliant jury lawyers in San Francisco. The latter's reputation had procured him a great deal of business. In this instance he met his injured client for the first time in the courtroom a few minutes before the trial started. He made a bad mess of it and seemed certain to lose. In order to get a second chance, he introduced proof that the defendants were insured. The judge, who was sympathetic to the plaintiff and who sensed which way the wind was blowing, promptly declared a mistrial.

The case was then transferred to me, and on the retrial the jury gave us an enormous verdict—in fact, the full amount sued for.

It is not to be supposed that mere man hours of labor and research will result in the proper presentation of a case. You must know what you are looking for, or at least have a sufficient understanding of the scope of your inquiry to recognize what is important when you see it. Remember Plato's, "The mind alone sees and hears; all else is deaf and blind."

Where expert evidence is to be introduced against you, you will be at a great disadvantage unless you have prepared to cross-examine the adverse witnesses along technical lines. If a case is worth trying, it is worth this preparation. By confining his research to the portion of the science involved which directly bears upon the problem, the lawyer can go into court knowing at least as much as the expert whom he will face. There are few experiences on the trial of a case so satisfying as that of completely discrediting such a witness, who has relied upon the presumed mysteries of his trade to perpetuate a deception on the jury.

In 1930, I was presented with a difficult case. A man named Lincoln Weaver had been burned to death in a filling station to which a truck of the Shell Oil Company was delivering gasoline. The only witness was the driver of the truck. I had the problem of determining whether any negligence on his part or on that of his employer had caused the fire, and if so, to prove it by circumstantial evidence.

I read a number of books which I procured from the Mechanic's Library, and came to the conclusion that there had been such negligence. The logical explanation of the tragedy appeared to be that static electricity had been generated by the gasoline running through the hose; that the nozzle of the latter was not firmly inserted in the filling stem of the underground tank, so that a small gap existed between them; and that a spark had leaped across this gap at a moment when the mixture of air and gasoline vapor was just right for an explosion.

The defendants challenged this theory and produced the professors of physics and chemistry from the University of California, as expert witnesses. The physics professor took the stand first and gave testimony which, if believed, would completely destroy my theory of the accident. He had an imposing list of qualifications and a schoolmaster's approach. Unless I could destroy his credit with the jury, the case was surely lost.

I procured the courtroom blackboard and questioned him about the constituents of gasoline and their properties, writing down his answers as he gave them. He knew that gasoline consists of a mechanical mixture of the saturated hydrocarbons of the paraffin series, but he did not know how many of them were contained in it. He guessed very badly on the molecular weight and boiling point of each.

I had carefully memorized all of these matters and everything else on which I questioned him. He made his worst estimates on the proportion of gasoline vapor and air necessary for an explosive mixture and the lowest temperature which would ignite it. He also guessed badly at the temperature of a lighted cigarette, a match, a blowtorch and an electric spark.

He had testified, on direct examination, that he had investigated many gasoline fires and had never found one which he could ascribe to static electricity, and that most of those which had come to his attention had been caused by smoking.

I asked him if a person were standing ten or twelve feet from a closed gasoline tank, smoking a cigarette—no match or other flame being present and the gasoline tank uncovered—would it be possible for sufficient vapor to come from the tank to be ignited by the cigarette in the smoker's mouth. He answered emphatically that it could, and that he had known of several fires caused in exactly that way.

This was just the answer I had been hoping for. Previously, I had placed in a drawer of the counsel table a small bottle of gasoline, a bowl, a pack of cigarettes and some matches. I took out the cigarettes, lit one, and proceeded to smoke it. Then I poured part of the gasoline into the bowl, and holding the same within an inch of the cigarette, continued to puff vigorously. Several people in the courtroom, including some jurors, emitted little squeals and cries of apprehension. The defendants' attorney protested the danger of the experiment, and the judge expressed concern, but I assured everybody that there was nothing to fear.

I then produced another cigarette, lit it off the first, and extinguished it by slowly immersing it in the gasoline.

"Why won't it light?" I asked the witness.

"It isn't gasoline."

"Oh, yes it is; and it's Shell gasoline."

I lit a match and held it a couple of inches over the surface of the liquid. A flame shot up several feet into the air and burned fiercely until the contents of the bowl were consumed.

"Now," I said to the witness, "I'll tell you why it didn't burn: the lowest temperature necessary to ignite gasoline is about one thousand, four hundred and thirty-six degrees Fahrenheit, and a lighted cigar or cigarette is only about eight hundred degrees Fahrenheit. Under no circumstances can you ignite it with one."

At the noon recess I made a trip to the Mechanics' Library on a hunch. Sure enough, there was a book by the same gentleman on the very subject we were discussing. At the next session I confronted him with a passage in it warning of the danger of explosions in oil fields from static electricity generated by belts operating machinery. I also brought with me a small machine of the sort used for generating static in high-school physics laboratories. I wound a piece of cotton on a wire, dipped it in gasoline, and was able to ignite it repeatedly by a tiny static spark generated by only a quarter turn of the device.

The chemistry professor had not been present during any of his colleague's testimony, and obviously had not been warned of his discomfiture, for he followed him to the stand and testified at great length along the same lines as his associate.

On cross-examination I asked him only one question. "If one

were standing, smoking a cigarette, ten or twelve feet from a closed gasoline tank—no lighted match or other flame being present—and the tank were uncovered, could the vapors from the tank be ignited by sparks from the cigarette?"

The witness answered emphatically. "Certainly! And I know of several fires caused exactly in that way."

The jurors and spectators roared with laughter. The witness regarded them with amusing bewilderment.

"That is all," I said. He left the courtroom still casting puzzled glances at its occupants.

We recovered a verdict which was then the record for death cases in the state.

This type of examination is especially valuable in dealing with hostile medical witnesses. Insurance and traction companies usually have a string of physicians upon whom they call for expert testimony. Customarily, these are selected on the basis of their glibness and persuasiveness. Really competent doctors who take pride in their profession are unlikely to accept this type of employment, and most of the "experts" are charlatans. Old Judge John Hunt, of the San Francisco Superior Court, said of them: "They're like a man in bed; they lie on one side and then turn over and lie on the other."

Charm of manner and confidence of opinion are their chief assets. After many appearances they become proficient witnesses. They get chummy with the jury and patronize the opposing counsel.

Their remuneration is high. They can earn much more on the witness stand than in their offices. Continued employment depends on their ability to hold down verdicts. Most of them get quite unconscionable and will say anything to help the side which is paying them.

They are usually vulnerable to close inquiry on the subjects concerning which they testify. Their glibness vanishes when they are called upon to remember parts of the anatomy involved in the opinions they have given on direct examination. Effective use of this technique requires intelligent work on the lawyer's part. He must study a standard work on anatomy, such as Gray's or

Cunningham's, which contains detailed drawings of the separate parts of the body. Proper application will enable him to memorize the names and relationships of the various bones, muscles, vessels and nerves. By copying the relevant portions of the drawings several times, he will fix them in his memory. More must be learned than will be used. The cross-examination must be directed to some purpose beside that of confusing the doctor on anatomy. It must be such that the jury can follow the designs sought to be created.

A good example of these suggestions in practice occurred in a case which I once tried against the Market Street Railway Company. One of their cars had struck a small girl, the wheel gouging away the flesh from the back of her leg. Her physician testified that, when he first saw her after the accident, the bones were visible at the bottom of the wound. The defendants produced an expert witness, who—among other things—gave his opinion that this was not possible, since such an injury would have severed both the main artery and nerve in the leg, and that if she had not bled to death, her leg would have been permanently shrunken and deformed.

The expert was handsome, dark haired, in his late thirties. He had the polished, courteous air common to the breed of physicians who set out to become legal experts. His easy mannerisms and disarming friendliness to the jury and the other lawyer marked him as a dangerous witness.

On cross-examination I asked him to draw on the blackboard a picture of the bones as they would appear viewed from the rear. He did so, laughingly disclaiming much skill as an artist. When he had finished, I asked him, "Now, if we were looking at the back of this child's leg and if all the muscles and other overlying structures were removed, the bones would appear approximately as you have drawn them. Is that correct?"

"Making allowances for my defects as an artist, yes."

"What are the names of those two bones?"

"This is the tibia, and this is the fibula."

"This child has a peculiarity of her bone structure, is that correct?"

"I don't understand what you mean."

"In most people the fibula is outside the tibia. I notice that you have drawn hers on the inside."

"Oh. Oh that is a mistake. I was confused. I thought we were looking at her from in front."

He changed the sketch so as to put the smaller bone outside.

"Let us agree to this, Doctor: that, hereafter, when you answer a question, you will use the correct medical term to describe the part of the body involved. I do not want you to use what you doctors sometimes call 'layman's language,' or what a part 'is sometimes called.' Do you understand?"

This is to prevent the witness from covering up his errors by using the excluded devices. If he is held to the technical terms, he can be contradicted by standard medical works.

"Will you please name the muscles of the leg?"

"You mean all of them? There are quite a lot."

"We have time. Go ahead."

"Well, let me see. There's the sartorius muscle—"

"Pardon me, Doctor, is the sartorius muscle in the leg?"

"Why, yes. It is right here"—indicating his thigh.

"That is not part of the leg. Is it?"

"Oh, I see what you mean. Medically, that is the thigh. The leg is the portion below the knee. I was using the ordinary term."

"We agreed not to do that, didn't we?"

"Very well, I'll try to avoid that. There's the gastrocnemius." He spells it out for the reporter. This is the mark of the experienced medical witness. "That is the big muscle lying directly under the skin. Under that is the soleus. Then there's the peroneus, and the two muscles which flex the toes and the large toe. They are separate muscles. I forget their Latin names at the moment."

"You mean the *flexor hallucis longus* and *flexor digitorum longus*."

"Thank you; you have a better memory than I. Then there are the muscles which extend the toes."

"What are they called?"

"You just substitute extensor for flexor in the names you just used."

Here the witness put himself in second place very early in the game. The previous compliment on his opponent's memory was a plaint for mercy. The witness could sense what was in store and was preparing to get off the hook at any cost.

"Are there other muscles in the leg?"

"Not at the place where this injury occurred. That is about all."

"The injury was in the upper third of the leg, was it not?"

"Yes, that is right."

"Did you ever hear of a muscle in that region called the plantaris?"

"Oh yes. I had forgotten that one. However, it is a very small muscle, relatively. It is not a strong muscle. It doesn't have any important function."

"Doctor, I dare say that whatever power designed the human body had a purpose in providing it with a plantaris muscle. At any rate, let's not omit any merely because we are not sure of the function they subserve."

Feeling that his conciliatory motions had not accomplished any good, the witness became testy. He blurted out, "I might say, Counsel, that I did not come here prepared for a memory test in anatomy. I haven't looked into an anatomy book since medical school. If I had known this was to be a quiz, I could easily have brushed up on it last night—just as you have probably done."

"Doctor, you come here, posing as an expert on the particular injury involved in this case. You do not consider it too much that you should be asked to name the very parts concerning which you are testifying as an expert, do you?"

"No. Certainly not. Go right ahead. As I say, though, I am somewhat rusty on my anatomy."

"Can you tell us the name of the artery which you have described in your direct examination as the main artery, and which you say would be severed by an injury deep enough to expose the bones?"

"I believe that it is called the tibial artery."

"That is close enough. It is called the posterior tibial artery. Will you tell us its location in the leg?"

"Well, it starts from branches in the foot—down around here —and runs up the leg to the popliteal space—here behind the knee where it joins another artery—I believe, the popliteal."

"Aren't you falling into the same difficulty as you did with the bones? You are not suggesting that there is some anomaly in this child's blood vessels, are you?"

"What do you mean?"

"I have never heard of an artery *starting* in an extremity and flowing toward the heart."

"That's being pretty technical. Technically, you are correct. An artery starts at the part nearest the heart, and flows to the extremity. But that's pretty technical."

"What is the correct name of the nerve which you have described in your direct examination as the main nerve, and which you say would be severed by an injury deep enough to expose the bones?"

"It is probably called the tibial nerve also. I am not sure."

"The posterior tibial nerve and the posterior tibial artery run side by side throughout the length of the leg. Do they not?"

"Yes; I believe they do."

"At the point of this injury, where do they lie with regard to the muscles we have talked about?"

"I believe that they are under the gastrocnemius, but I am not sure whether they are above or below the soleus muscle."

"Where are they in regard to the plantaris?"

"I am not sure just where that muscle is—as I say, it is a very small muscle. I have forgotten."

"The plantaris lies between the gastrocnemius and soleus muscles."

"All right. If you say so, I will accept your statement."

"In brushing up on anatomy last night, as you suggest I have done, Doctor, I learned something which I will ask you now to confirm: that in the lower part of the leg this artery and nerve —the posterior tibial—lie between the two big muscles, the gastrocnemius and soleus, but in the lower third of the leg they both bend inward, penetrate through the soleus, and thereafter lie below that muscle also and between the bones of the leg. Will you kindly tell us if that statement is correct?"

"I cannot say that that is not so. I had not supposed so, but it may be as you state."

"Who was the author of the anatomy book which you say you looked into in medical school?"

"Gray, I believe—or Cunningham."

"Here is a copy of Gray's *Anatomy*. Please read the passage I am indicating and tell us if it refreshes your recollection that the statement I have just made is correct."

After reading the passage. "Yes, that is correct."

"So that, at the place where this child's leg was injured, the main nerve and artery lie below the muscles and between the bones of the leg. That is so, is it not?"

"Yes, I would say that is so."

"Therefore it is possible that the muscles could have been cut through and the bones exposed, without severing either the main artery or the main nerve. Isn't that so?"

"Yes, I would say that it is possible."

"You will withdraw your statement that, in this case, the bones of the leg could not have been exposed in the wound without the child either bleeding to death or having her leg permanently shrunken and deformed. Is that right?"

"Yes. I will have to amend my opinion. The situation could have been as you say."

A few weeks after this trial, and while the anatomy of the back of the leg was still in my memory, I had an unexpected windfall from having learned it. I tried a damage case involving injury to the neck. The defendant's expert was extremely aggressive. When I started to question him on the anatomy of the neck, he protested to the judge against such procedure.

When his objection was disallowed, he flared out at me. "I have a large practice and don't have time to brush up on anatomy. If I thought I were going to be questioned on it, I would have read a couple of pages of Gray's *Anatomy* last night, as you probably did."

"Oh!" I said. "Is that how it's done? Meanwhile, Doctor, will you please tell us the medical name of the structure immediately underlying the skin of the throat?"

He thought for a moment. The correct answer is the platysma, which is a broad, flat muscular band.

To my astonishment he answered: "The plantaris muscle."

In order to nail down the error and make it more apparent when developed, I had him spell the name out, and I wrote it on the blackboard as he did so.

Then I said, "Doctor, isn't it a fact that the plantaris muscle is in the back of the leg? Let me refresh your collection. The outermost muscle in the posterior of the leg is the gastrocnemius. Below that lies the plantaris muscle. Next is the soleus. Then comes the *flexor hallucis longus* and *flexor digitorum longus*. Isn't that correct?"

He almost collapsed. He probably thought he had encountered a walking anatomy book, prepared to describe any segment of the body. From then on, he was afraid to disagree with me on a single suggestion.

There can scarcely be a more striking and successful example of scientific research by a lawyer than that through which Edwin McKenzie saved the life of David Lamson.

Lamson was an instructor at Stanford University in Palo Alto. On the morning of May 30, 1933, the dead body of his wife was found in the bathroom of the couple's home. It was lying naked in the bathtub, with the lower part within and the upper part hanging outside its ledge. The back of the head was smashed in, and probably half of the blood in the woman's body had spouted or drained from the wound. Lamson was charged with her murder.

The prosecution contended that the injuries which caused her death could not have been due to an accident, such as a fall against the washbasin, but were the result of numerous blows, and that David Lamson had struck them.

It undertook to prove a criminal cause of death through the nature of the injuries, as interpreted by experts, and the presence of spattered blood a considerable distance from the body. The defendant's culpability was based upon his presence at the scene and the absence of any other suspect; the finding of the alleged lethal weapon and of a bloodstained cloth in a bonfire he had been tending; and the suspicion that he had quarreled with his wife and that he was paying attention to another woman.

The fatal injury consisted of a depressed fracture of the skull, roughly in the form of a triangle. The depressed portion comprised four fragments having a total area of about two square inches. From each apex of the triangle, a fracture line extended outward into the skull. The scalp above this was lacerated by a contused cut, some three inches long, with connecting tears along one side, the whole forming a capital E, with the upper foot extended backward.

The state's experts testified that these injuries could not possibly have been caused by a single blow—such as a fall against the washbasin—but were the result of four separate strokes, three of which were parallel and the fourth at right angles to them.

Scattered blood marks were found in and around the bathroom. Some were as much as eight feet from the dead woman's head. The same experts gave their opinions that blood would not spurt that far from a wound, and that the injuries had been inflicted where they were found and the body then transported to the tub.

In the bonfire which the defendant had been tending, the police found an iron pipe about ten inches long and a quantity of burned cloth. The state's experts asserted that tests on both were positive for blood, and that the pipe was such an instrument as could have inflicted the mortal blows. Lamson was convicted and sentenced to hang.

McKenzie was now employed to conduct an appeal. He was an advocate of great ability and of the most painstaking diligence. He was possessed of a scientific turn of mind and was familiar with the principles of physics and dynamics. He also had a considerable knowledge of chemistry.

From a reading of the trial transcript alone and without ever having spoken to the defendant, he was satisfied that in the three important instances in which they had given their opinions, the experts called by the state had been completely wrong. He believed that the nature of the fatal injury and the circumstances surrounding it demonstrated that it was due to an accident, and that there was not the slightest proof that a crime was involved.

It seemed to him a coincidence beyond belief that a series of blows could be delivered in such a way that the separate cuts and fractures resulting from them would exactly meet and end at their intersections.

He commenced a research of skull fractures and scalp lacerations. The experts whose books he consulted appeared to rely finally on Von Bergmann's *System of Surgery*. He had difficulty procuring a copy of this work. When he did so, it completely sustained his opinion. According to its author, when a single blow breaks the skull and lacerates the overlying scalp, the depressed portion of the broken bone tends to form a triangle, with the fracture lines running outward from each angle, and the scalp tends to be torn in two or more adjoining flaps.

Allene Lamson's injury was a classic illustration of the German's findings. From previous experiences, McKenzie knew that the testimony that blood will not spurt eight feet from a wound was false. He felt also that the so-called "blood tests" on the pipe and cloth found in the bonfire must be worthless. The state's experts had testified that, in order to check their findings with regard to the alleged murder weapon, they had heated an iron pipe stained with blood to a temperature of 1,000 degrees Fahrenheit, and had obtained from it a positive result for blood. McKenzie knew this to be impossible. Without research, he was aware that after blood has been heated to only 200 degrees Fahrenheit, it loses its organic structure and will no longer respond to any test for blood itself.

He reread the testimony on this subject carefully and saw that, actually, a grisly trick had been played on the defendant. The witnesses had not said that they found blood on the objects taken from the bonfire; they had only said that they had conducted tests on them which were "positive for blood."

The tests on the pipe had consisted, essentially, in placing some scrapings from it, together with a small quantity of peroxide of hydrogen, in a few drops of benzidin. The benzidin had turned blue, and on this the "positive" interpretation had been based.

McKenzie set up a small laboratory in his kitchen and proceeded to evaluate these tests. After weeks of experiment, he found that all that they showed was the presence of *oxygen*. Whenever oxygen was released into it, the benzidin turned blue. The lawyer wondered how many other substances would have given this positive result. He found a manual published by the United States Government which took three closely printed pages to list only part of them. They included iron, all vegetable substances and all animal substances.

If the lawyers who had tried the case had given proper preparation to this subject, they could have forced the state's witnesses to admit that the only thing their tests had shown was that the iron pipe contained iron.

As a matter of fact, when blood is subjected to this test, it is the iron in it which brings about the reaction. It releases one of the oxygen molecules in the peroxide of hydrogen, and this changes the color of the reagent. The iron in the hemoglobin acts as a catalyst.

This conclusion disposed, as well, of the "bloodstained" cloth. The transcript showed that it was part of a painter's discarded canvas. McKenzie reasoned that it therefore probably contained lead. Burnt lead contains more oxygen than does peroxide of hydrogen. If a molecule of that gas could be easily released from the latter so as to change the color of the reagent, burnt lead would act still more effectively.

By an order of the court, the defense had been furnished a quantity of this cloth, so as to permit experiments on it to be made. Using the benzidin test, McKenzie procured a positive reaction with a piece of this material. He did the same with burnt paint and with burnt lead. By painstaking effort, he then succeeded in extracting from a portion of the cloth a tiny pellet of lead.

To refute the contention that blood will not spurt eight feet from a wound, he filled a rubber bag with a liquid having its specific gravity. A tube with a clamp attached led from this.

He wound the sleeve of a sphygmomanometer—the device which doctor's strap around the arm to test blood pressure—around the bag, and pumped it to the pressure normal for a woman of Allene Lamson's age and build. When he released the clamp, the liquid spurted fourteen feet.

McKenzie then sat down and wrote a brief of 600 pages. The greater part was devoted to a scientific destruction of the testimony on which the defendant had been convicted. Relying on the legal principle that courts will take judicial notice of scientific facts and of the laws of nature, he set out the authorities, data and experiments which demolished the prosecution's case. His conclusions were so clearly and convincingly demonstrated that the Supreme Court reversed the conviction by unanimous opinion.

The defendant was tried twice again, but each time the jury disagreed upon the same numerical division; nine for acquittal and three for conviction. The district attorney then asked for a dismissal, and David Lamson walked out a free man. He had spent thirteen months in the death house for a crime which had never been committed.

McKenzie's 600-page brief lies forgotten in the archives of the California State Supreme Court. It should be read by those who conceive that the greatness of a lawyer depends upon those superficialities which have been stressed in recent biographies.

CHAPTER 9

Tricks Sometimes Win

IT'S A cliché that "Possession is eleven points of the law." But this is an understatement. The continued right of possession is the basis of almost all lawsuits. Still, there's an even more impressive adage not taught in law schools: *Grab the corpus and hide it.*

A famed Western gunman put it another way: "When there's one to be killed and one to be tried, I'm the one who's going to be tried."

Litigation is uncertain, consumes time, is rarely satisfactory. Many meritorious judgments expire uncollected. Hence an astute attorney never leaves the disputed object in the possession of his foe and his own client endowed with a lawsuit. It's well, of course, to use reasonable refinements. But, in the last analysis, the rule is: Get your hands on the Thing and bury it. Against a powerful adversary, this will be your client's only chance to retain what is his. Having just the object of dispute is not enough. An attorney must be able to meet any situation which unexpectedly pops up.

Typical is the common problem of the defendant who has evidence which will be harmful if revealed, but which cannot be withheld without raising dangerous inferences as to his reason for withholding it. The prosecution can construct the most damaging arguments, which—in effect—amount to the suggestion that the withheld evidence must be conclusive of guilt, since scarcely anything less would persuade the defendant not to come up with it.

Many years ago I participated in the defense of the celebrated Windmill Murder Case in Kings County, California. The chief counsel were two old-timers, Frank Pryor and Harry Brown. They were bucolic of appearance, salty of language. They were also as artful and able a duo as ever badgered a district attorney. In an interval of the case they told me of an occasion on which they found themselves confronted with a most difficult problem.

A married woman had left her home and eloped to Reno, Nevada, with another man. Her husband, learning of it almost immediately, took after the couple in his automobile. He overtook them while their car was stopped at the side of the road and the rival was changing a punctured tire. The husband shot and killed him, and was indicted for his murder.

He claimed in court that he had pursued his wife only to ask her to return, and that he had carried the gun for protection. When he approached the stalled car, he said, the deceased had attacked him with a jack handle. He had fired in self-defense.

The wife was the only other witness. It was evident that her testimony would be crucial. However, she had refused to talk with her husband's lawyers, and they believed that if she had the opportunity to do so, her love for the slain man would lead her to contradict the defendant's story.

In California a husband cannot be a witness against his wife, nor a wife against her husband, without the consent of both. The prosecution could not call her and the defense dared not. Pryor and Brown pondered how they might avoid the implications in a failure to do so. They devised a scheme to get around the difficulty.

For their last witness, they called the wife to the stand. As she passed by the defendant, however, he leaped to his feet, seized her fast, and cried out, "No! You're not going to kick her around. Hang me if you want, but you're not going to ask her a question!" He fell back into his seat, sobbing and weeping, with the woman clasped in his arms.

The jurors and spectators were visibly shaken by the spectacle. Many of them also broke into tears. Brown bent over the defendant, whispering urgently, but the man shook his head determinedly. The lawyer turned away, as though in resignation. "Your Honor," he said huskily, "The defense rests."

The coup saved the day, and the defendant was acquitted.

John F. Dore, an attorney in Seattle, once defended a man charged with attempted arson. The prosecution brought into court, as an exhibit in the case, the stove from the defendant's home. It was stuffed with oil-soaked newspapers. Dore paid no attention to this until his argument was under way, when he began to extract some of its contents casually. Suddenly he stopped in apparent astonishment and turned to the jury with a veritable roar of indignation.

"Why, what kind of frame-up is this?" he demanded. "Gentlemen of the jury, look at the date on this paper." Striding toward them, he presented one of the documents which he had taken from the stove. It bore a date subsequent to the alleged crime.

The defendant was acquitted. But he had the indiscretion to brag about the cleverness of his attorney. Disbarment proceedings were instituted against Dore. However, he was freed of the charge, and years later became mayor of Seattle.

Carey Van Fleet was once appointed in Carson City, Nevada, to defend a young woman charged with infanticide. While a passenger on a train she had given birth to an illegitimate child. Whether by accident or design, the infant's body had been dropped through the toilet and onto the roadbed. The prosecution had two witnesses, women passengers on the train who had assisted the girl.

Van Fleet learned that these two had been sent for by the district attorney and would arrive the morning before the case would go to trial. He met the two witnesses at the railroad station and took them on a tour. They were already sufficiently sympathetic, and by the time he had impressed on them the role their testimony would play in hurting his client, they were willing to do whatever he said. But they had furnished the prosecution with signed statements. They couldn't safely deviate from them. Van Fleet solved the difficulty: he put them on the train out that evening. Next morning the prosecution was forced to dismiss the indictment for lack of evidence.

On one occasion James Martin MacInnis was defending a bookmaker. It was impossible to put him on the stand; he would either have to admit facts which would be sure to convict him or lie, which would be certain to result in his indictment for perjury.

After proving what facts he could in defense, MacInnis got up and said, "The defendant desires to take the stand and testify in his own behalf. However, he knows who owns the betting paraphernalia which has been placed in evidence, and he will not become an informer against a friend. I am willing, Mr. District Attorney, to put the defendant on the stand and permit him to be asked anything you wish concerning his own connection with the matter, but not as to any other person's possible guilt. If you will agree to this, he will testify and will submit to whatever examination you wish."

The district attorney refused to make any such stipulation. MacInnis, with apparent reluctance, concluded his case without calling his client. The jury disagreed, and the prosecution dismissed the case without a further trial.

Archer Zamloch, once my partner, had an experience which he ascribes to simple chance. He was defending a young man on a charge of burglary. The defendant had an attractive wife. Zamloch believed she'd be a good witness to sustain her husband's alibi. She was about eight months pregnant, which might add to her appeal as a witness. However, the police had obtained a statement from her at the time of her husband's arrest. It was believed to contain matters which contradicted him in important details. Its use in her cross-examination would probably lead to his conviction.

On direct examination she testified fully and persuasively. Then, just as she concluded, she was seized with obvious labor pains and rushed from the courtroom. As the prosecution had been unable to cross-examine her, Zamloch was compelled to stipulate that her testimony should be stricken out and the jury directed to ignore it. But the ability of a jury to ignore what it has heard is more theoretical than practical. The defendant was acquitted.

The incident had an unfortunate sequel. About a week later Zamloch was defending an associate of that defendant, and had on the jury seven of those who had so recently acquitted him. While the trial was in progress Zamloch was horrified to observe the woman, as pregnant as ever, enter the courtroom and proceed down the aisle toward him. He made frantic signals for her to depart, but she didn't notice. She marched right up to the counsel table and handed him a note in full sight of the jury. Seven of the jurors regarded her sourly, listened skeptically to the arguments in the present case. and convicted the defendant.

One cynical associate once discussed such devices with me. "I don't believe in that sort of thing," he said. "I don't believe in overreaching your opponent, and the only time I ever did it I was heartily ashamed of my conduct. I had a felony trial on, and a policeman friend tipped me off that the prosecution's only witness was out of town, and that when the case came up the next day, they would have to ask for a continuance. So I folded up a couple of sheets of foolscap, and on the outside of it I typed the title of the cause in capital letters: Defendant's Motion for a Continuance. I went into the court the next morning, sitting opposite the district attorney. I held the paper in my hand so that he couldn't help seeing it. When the case was called, the district attorney stood up. 'The prosecution is ready,' he announced. So I just put the papers back in my pocket and said, 'The defendant is ready,' and after a few minutes the district attorney informed the court that his witness was not available, and they dismissed the proceedings. My conscience has always bothered me for having done such a thing."

When I was admitted to practice in 1921, the ablest criminal lawyer in the state was Nathan Coombs Coghlan. He had an imposing record of acquittals. A newspaper editorial once called him "A one-man repeal of the capital punishment law."

He and I represented two defendants in a murder trial which looked pretty grim for a hanging verdict. While we were preparing the case he suggested: "We must let the jury know that they can return less than a hanging verdict without making them suspect that we will be satisfied with such a result." A day or two later he said: "Here's what we will do. In examining the jury, we will explain to each one the different degrees of murder, and we will inform them that they can bring in a verdict of guilty on any one of those degrees, or that they can acquit the defendants. Then we will ask each one: 'Now, if at the end of the case, you entertain a reasonable doubt of the defendants' guilt, you will acquit them, will you not, and you will not, instead, bring in a verdict of guilty of a lesser degree just as a compromise?' "

We questioned each prospective juror along those lines. We received a compromise verdict.

Coghlan was always quick to seize upon any accidental circumstance which would afford a basis for a logical or emotional appeal. Once when he was arguing a murder case to the jury, the bells of a neighboring church suddenly rang out. Nate stopped for an instant, and then, as the chimes continued, "Mercy! Mercy! Mercy!" he cried out in unison with them. "That is what they are saying; that is what they are demanding!"

In 1945, MacInnis and I represented the defendant in a widely publicized murder trial. There were difficult circumstances in the case. The defendant was a rich woman, who—on pretty flimsy evidence—had formed a suspicion that her husband was overfriendly with a nurse. She made an appointment with the latter by telephone, and when they met on the street, invited her into her automobile to talk. While they were seated together in the car, the defendant reputedly drew a loaded revolver from her purse, shot the nurse to death, and then beat her upon the face with the butt of the gun. The victim's husband was a U. S. naval officer in the South Pacific. He procured a leave to attend the trial of his wife's slayer. We found him a most discomforting spectator as he sat near the prosecutor throughout the hearing, his breast loaded with campaign ribbons. He produced letters full of the warmest affection, which he had received from his wife almost up to the day of her death. Both in his testimony and in statements to the press, he scorned any suggestion of impropriety on her part. We contended that the killing was accidental, and at most, manslaughter.

The testimony was concluded on a Thursday afternoon, and the next morning the assistant district attorney commenced argument. He made an able exposition of the law and facts, and led logically to the conclusion that the act of the defendant was premeditated, first-degree murder. He adroitly extended his statement until 4:30 P.M. and then closed.

Here was a predicament. It was a Friday evening; there would be no court on Saturday or Sunday, and the jury would have two days in which to digest the prosecutor's arguments. Any conclusion they arrived at would be well cemented in by Monday morning.

I had prepared a statement leading as logically to the theory that the shooting had been accidental, and at worst, manslaughter. A necessary preface consisted in a close review of the law touching the degrees of murder. That alone would take at least an hour, and the court would close at 5 P.M.

Something must be done to hold the jury's judgment in suspense. I asked the court for leave to consume the remaining twenty minutes in argument, and the request was granted.

I disregarded all my prepared points. "My friends!" I cried out. "Here is no crime! Here is a poor, sick, harassed, beaten woman, striving to preserve her home by frightening another woman away from her husband! That she used a gun to do it may have been folly, but that the gun exploded was only a ghastly accident—a trick which fate played upon her, and which she never intended!"

I picked up the defendant's pistol from among the exhibits, and striding to the prosecutor, shoved my face close to his.

"What would you do," I roared, "if you found that your wife was running around with another man, neglecting you and your children for his embraces? Why, you'd take a gun and you'd go up to him and you'd jam it into his throat." I pushed the pistol against the prosecutor's neck while he stared at me in consternation, apparently certain that I had gone insane. "And you'd say to him, 'You son of a bitch! Keep away from my wife or I'll blow you to hell!'" Then I looked at the jury, which was regarding me in wide-eyed astonishment. "If the court please," I said, "I will continue the argument Monday morning."

The reporters covering the trial were shocked, and the jury probably thought I was demented—but we knew that they would wait until Monday to hear what the hell else I had to say, and that was all we wanted. On Monday I gave the argument I had prepared. A verdict of manslaughter was returned.

Cases are sometimes won, or at least jurors are influenced, by facts which are not in evidence at all, and which sometimes do not even exist.

Ingenuity is often employed to present circumstances which have no legal bearing on the controversy and which would not be admitted by the court, but which have a moral effect on the jurors. Sometimes, too, the negligence of counsel permits them to consider such matters, with disastrous consequences to the case.

An example of these is the device sometimes called the "Why did you leave Cleveland?" type of question. The name derives from a venerable chestnut known to all lawyers. (I have tried to avoid rehashing well-known tales, but I will restate this one to illustrate the point.)

In a criminal case the prosecution witness was questioned as to his prior places of residence. Among them he listed Cleveland. He was asked: "Now, will you state to this jury why you left

Cleveland?" An objection was sustained. The defendant's lawyer argued vigorously for the jury's right to hear the answer, but of course without success. Following a verdict of acquittal, one of the jurors asked the defense attorney, "Why did that fellow leave Cleveland?" The lawyer shrugged. "Damned if I know! Until he said so on the stand, I never knew he had lived in Cleveland."

Frank Murphy of San Francisco once utilized the device in a rape case. The prosecutrix had been on a night picnic at the beach with a number of friends of both sexes. She claimed that while they were returning to her home the defendant forcibly raped her.

On cross-examination Murphy asked, "During that picnic at the beach, you and a young man named Frank Avina went alone into the bushes at the edge of the park and remained there for about twenty minutes, isn't that so?"

An objection to the question was sustained.

Murphy then asked, "While you young people were seated around the fire at that picnic, this same Frank Avina sat with his hand up under your skirt, did he not?"

Again an objection was sustained.

The defendant was acquitted, and one of the jurors came up to Murphy in the corridor, exclaiming indignantly, "That was the goddamnedest injustice I ever heard of. The district attorney didn't want that girl to answer about being in the bushes with that other man, because she would have to admit it."

Murphy had had no information on which to base the two questions, and had made up the name "Frank Avina" as he went along.

Edward Cunha was arguing an action upon an insurance policy which the company had refused to pay upon the defense that the insured had committed suicide. As he finished his argument to the jury, with tears trickling down his cheeks, he said, "And when this poor man's friends and brother Masons stood around his grave down there in the Masonic Cemetery in San

Mateo County, and when they lowered him into his last resting place, no one could have told any of them that he was going to meet his God with his own blood on his hands."

When the jury returned a favorable verdict, the widow congratulated Cunha. "But," she said, "Jack wasn't a Mason and he wasn't buried. We cremated him."

"I know," he retorted, "but I saw three Masonic pins on that jury, and there's no use passing anything up."

In 1937, I procured the fastest acquittal on record in a murder case on a plea of self-defense. It was easy to convince the jury that the victim was a gangster and murderer, because he had been a long-time resident of Chicago.

On another occasion I beat an embezzlement charge because the complaining witness hailed from Reno, Nevada, and nobody saw fit to contradict a section of my opening statement that he had extracted the money in question from the prostitutes and gamblers of that sportive metropolis.

During the Prohibition Era, a San Francisco police sergeant was shot and killed by one of a trio of highjackers. They escaped without leaving a clue, and undoubtedly never would have been detected except that one of them babbled to a friend. An underworld tip put the officers on the trail. They suddenly burst into an apartment where William Rhinehart, the alleged gunman lived. In searching, they found a revolver which ballistics experts stated had fired the fatal shots. The remaining suspects were then apprehended.

During a mopping-up operation involving other activities of the gang, a client of mine was arrested. In the shadowy marches of the underworld he was known by the arresting sobriquet of Ten Grand. The police beat out of him a confession which further incriminated Rhinehart. Once out of reach of the loaded hose, however, he recanted and refused an offer of immunity for other offenses if he would help convict the sergeant's slayer. Numerous charges were then filed against him, and he was held in the county jail awaiting trial on them.

Nate Coghlan undertook the difficult defense of Rhinehart.

One day he called at my office. "I have information," he said, "that the prosecution is going to call Ten Grand as a witness in my case. Do you know what he intends to do, if they do?"

"Yes," I replied, "he's going to refuse to answer on the ground that he might incriminate himself."

"Well!" said Nate. "You'd better confirm that with him. Will you let me know if he's still of the same mind?"

I immediately visited my client and renewed the instructions he should follow if brought to court. I called Coghlan. "Don't worry," I assured him, "he's firm as a rock."

A few days later I received a request to visit my man at the county jail. He informed me that he had been taken to court that morning and placed on the witness stand, but that it was Coghlan who had required his presence and who had attempted to question him.

"What did he ask you?" I inquired.

"Why, he asked me if it wasn't true that a few days before this murder I had borrowed the pistol from Rhinehart and returned it to him a couple of days after."

"What did you answer?"

"I just said, 'I refuse to answer on the grounds that I might incriminate myself.' "

I later learned that Rhinehart had testified that he had loaned the gun to Ten Grand a few days before the murder, and had received it back the day following it. My client's refusal to answer raised enough doubt in the minds of the jurors that they spared the defendant's life.

Walter McGovern was once retained to defend an especially difficult murder case. The accused, Harry Turnello, was a native of Sicily and shared the passions and principles of that island's most violent offspring. He was estranged from his wife, and she had gone to live with her parents. In an effort to regain her, he resorted to both threats and impassioned love letters. The woman ignored him, and the only effect of his menaces was to cause her father to arm himself with a pistol and to accompany her wherever she went. Finally Turnello met his wife, accompanied by both her parents, on the street. In a blast of gunfire he killed all three. A chance for acquittal rested upon the fact that the father had managed to draw his weapon and had wounded the defendant, the bullet striking him through the testicles. The defense contended that the father had fired the first shot and that the pain and shock of the wound had so deranged the defendant that he had fired wildly, without knowing what he was doing.

The police had procured the mass of letters written by the defendant from the dead woman's effects. During the trial McGovern observed the prosecuting attorney mulling through them, seeking to find some statement which might incriminate the defendant. In the most casual way, he suggested. "Why don't you put the whole bunch in evidence, and then we can look them over, and if there is anything of value, either of us can use it?"

The district attorney accepted the suggestion and introduced the entire correspondence. Without this, McGovern could not avail himself of the portions which might aid the defendant, since they would be excluded as self-serving declarations.

He waited until the argument, and then spent an entire day reading the more impassioned epistles to the jury. He argued that a man who felt the sentiments expressed in the letters did not contemplate the killing of the person to whom they were addressed, and he procured an unexpected acquittal.

The proper spirit for jury work shows early. During his first year at the bar, Jim MacInnis was appointed by a judge of the United States District Court to defend a man accused of murder. The defendant had no money to employ counsel. His case appeared so hopeless that it was considered sufficient compliance with the constitutional requirements that an inexperienced lawyer be named to represent him.

The accused, Henry Young, while serving a life sentence in the federal penitentiary on Alcatraz Island had killed a fellow inmate. The crime appeared to be deliberate and preconceived, since considerable ingenuity was required to effect it. The victim was quartered in a separate part of the prison, and the slayer had to pass many bars and bolts to come at him; in addition, he had smuggled the weapon, a knife, past the guards by wrapping it in some castoff clothing. However, the prosecution was unable to present any motive for the crime.

At the bottom of most prison conflicts are matters relating to homosexuality or sexual perversion. Quarrels which arise from jealousy, the refusal of sexual favors, or retaliation for insults or injuries to those involved in such relationships, lead to the most violent of inmate affrays. The authorities desire to conceal the extent of these conditions within their institutions, and they pretend ignorance of the causes behind such assaults. The prisoners, of course, concur in this conspiracy of silence.

The federal prison on Alcatraz was at that time, as it still is, used to detain those whom the Government chooses to describe as desperate or dangerous criminals. The inmates are held in the closest confinement and under the strictest discipline. It is the most terrible of all the anachronisms maintained in this country for the punishment of those convicted of crime. It is an insult to the dignity of man and a reproach to the humanity of the American people.

MacInnis conceived that the best way to defend the case was to try Alcatraz Island. He contended that the prisoners there were so mistreated and that the discipline was so rigid and inhuman that Young's mind had broken under the ordeal of his imprisonment, and that he was temporarily insane at the time of the killing.

To support his position, he subpoenaed dozens of the most widely known inmates of the prison. Many of these were of national repute. The trial became a *cause célèbre,* and the courtroom was beseiged by spectators anxious to view the celebrated witnesses. The testimony as to the conditions under which they suffered played into the hands of the civic minded.

Needless to say, the prison authorities vigorously defended their administration. The United States Attorney denounced the defense as designed to divert the attention of the jury from the real issues, but MacInnis charged straight ahead.

Soon Henry Young's guilt or innocence became submerged in the graver problem of man's inhumanity to man. The upshot was that the jury found the defendant guilty of involuntary manslaughter. This carried a penalty of only one year. As it had to run concurrently with the sentence he was then serving, it was scarcely of even academic importance.

CHAPTER **10**

A Lawyer's Worst Enemy

CHINESE General Sun Tze gave, as a prescription for victory, the advice: "Know yourself and know your enemy, and you can fight a hundred battles without disaster."

When you go into a law case, you must remember that the difficulties do not only come from your opponent. Often the greatest danger is your own client. If you do not prepare your case with a view to his faults and weaknesses, you are courting trouble. It is not uncommon to see a lawyer emerge from a trial, damning his client's stupidity for losing it, when that was the one circumstance he was in the best position to guard against. He had been prepared for whatever the other side could produce, but seated beside him were the seeds of his own destruction.

Many times a party will not disclose all the facts and circumstances to his attorney. It is human to conceal what is discreditable to oneself. Indeed, subconsciously one may erect a mental barrier against unpleasant facts and be quite honest in denying or forgetting them.

The lawyer must regard with suspicion his own client's explanation of events, or he may find himself in court with a complete misconception of what actually happened.

An English chief justice once said of a barrister: "He is unable to conduct a case. He believes what his client tells him."

Considerable ingenuity may be required to win the confidence which will furnish a truthful account and enable counsel to anticipate what he will be up against.

One young attorney I know once asked a senior partner's advice on a case he was about to try. He represented two men charged with the possession of marijuana. He was satisfied that they were innocent; they had been vehement in assuring him so, and there was no reason why they should deceive him.

The senior partner asked, "Is there any reason why the police should frame them?"

The younger man confessed that he knew of none.

"Bring them in," said the other, "and let me talk with them."

After they had been introduced and told their story, he said to them, "I want you to get one thing straight. We don't give a good goddamn whether you owned the marijuana or not. I've hidden more than one body, and we'll do anything—legal or illegal—to win your case, but we have to know just what happened. If the story you just told us is true, we can go ahead on that line. But suppose they come up with your fingerprints on the package of marijuana? Then we'll have to work out something that will account for your handling it without knowing what was in it. Do you get the point?"

The men glanced at each other, and then one of them smiled at the younger lawyer in a conciliatory way.

"I'm sorry," he said. "We didn't tell you the truth. The stuff belonged to us."

George Ford told me of a case which he handled in Los Angeles, involving the estate of a wealthy industrialist. It had a value of between six and seven million dollars. After all would-be claimants had been weeded out, there remained approximately a hundred persons having some relationship to the deceased which entitled them to share in the distribution of his fortune.

The lawyers representing these persons quickly came to a settlement of their clients' rights, but a woman who claimed to be a daughter of the deceased demanded that the entire estate be distributed to her. Efforts to settle with her were unavailing, as she steadfastly refused to accept less than half a million dollars. The trial of her action consumed almost an entire year, more than fifty witnesses being brought from various parts of the country. Ford asserted that there was not the least merit to the woman's case, and the jury was out less than an hour before returning a verdict against her.

He was informed that her attorney was handling the case on a contingent basis and paying the expense of the litigation. He estimated that these could not be less than forty or fifty thousand dollars. Ford said that he knew the attorney to be a very conscientious and religious man, and believed him to be completely deceived as to the merits of the action.

Sometime ago I ran across a story by an Irish barrister which illustrates the advisability of compromising such matters before they proceed too far.

An old peddler, Sullivan, had amassed 1,800 pounds, which he'd deposited in a bank. He took sick and was received into the home of a farmer named Flanagan, where he died. A few days later a will was produced in which he left "all I die possessed of" to Flanagan.

Another farmer named Sullivan came to an attorney, with instructions to file a contest to the will, alleging that he was the next of kin of the deceased peddler. The attorney procured a barrister to try the action.

Very early in the proceedings the latter convinced himself that the will was an absolute forgery. His suspicions were confirmed when during a court recess the solicitor on the other side approached the attorney with an offer to pay 1,000 pounds between solicitor and client, if the opposition was withdrawn. The barrister declined to give any opinion on this offer, beyond stating that he was convinced that the will would not stand. The case proceeded, and the will was set aside.

Then came a startling result. The client, Sullivan, subsequently failed to prove himself any relation to the deceased peddler. He never touched a farthing of the estate, and its entire assets reverted to the crown.

A more reasonable attitude was displayed by the participants in an affair which was told me by an investigator and heir-finder. He said that he was once in the probate court, when his attention was attracted to a proceeding in the estate of a deceased Roman Catholic priest. My informant, a Catholic, was shocked to hear the estate being claimed by a young woman who asserted that she was the illegitimate daughter of the deceased. Her attorney stated to the court that the priest was a native of Syria who had immigrated to this country, and who apparently had no other relatives, as far as they had been able to discover. He said that the claimant was a daughter of the priest and his housekeeper, and had been received as such into the only family which he maintained.

The investigator determined not to allow a pastor of Holy Mother Church to be besmirched without some protest. He accordingly stood up and said, "If the Court please, I wish to enter my name in the records of this proceeding as the representative of George Massow, also known as George Massof, presently a native of Syria, who is a nephew of the deceased and who intends to file a petition for distribution of this estate to him."

His appearance was duly noted in the record, and the matter continued. When they left the courtroom, the attorney for the alleged daughter came up to him and proposed that some settlement be made between the claimants. He said, "My client tells me that her father frequently spoke of his nephew George Massow, but we had supposed that he was dead."

Finally a written agreement was filed in the estate, dividing it equally between the young woman—who probably was not related to the deceased—and George Massow, also known as George Massof, who did not even exist. The woman's attorney paid the latter's share over to the investigator as his assignee, and nothing more was heard of the affair.

I once defended a man in an action on a promissory note for $2,500. My client had had numerous dealings with the plaintiff over many years, and he furnished me with a receipt, wholly written and signed by the latter, which bore a date approximately two years later than that of the promissory note.

The plaintiff was a heavy drinker and had every appearance of being such. On the trial I showed him the receipt, which he examined with amazement. He acknowledged the writing and signature, but said that he had no recollection of having written it or ever having received the payment evidenced by it.

The defendant then took the stand and testified that he had paid the sum and received the receipt on the date stated on it, but that the plaintiff had been somewhat intoxicated at the time and may not have remembered it. The court gave judgment in his favor.

When we walked out into the corridor, the plaintiff came up and apologized profusely. "But, Joe," he said, "why in hell didn't you come to me when I filed that suit, and tell me you had paid me?"

"To tell the truth, Billy," replied the other, "I mislaid the damned receipt and couldn't find it until a few days ago. You know how bad tempered you are when you're drinking, and I didn't want to get in an argument with you."

When we got outside the building, he chuckled. "He gave me that receipt on another deal back in 1910," he confided, "and I just changed the one in the date to a two and brought it up ten years. I figured his brains were so addled with booze that he wouldn't remember the other deal."

A somewhat similar story is told of a man who filed suit for money alleged to be owing to him by a firm whose premises had been completely destroyed by fire a few days before the action was instituted. He testified to the debt and its nonpayment.

On cross-examination he was handed a piece of paper and asked if he recognized it. He surveyed the document, handed it back to the counsel, and proceeded to leave the stand.

"What's all this? What's all this?" asked the bewildered judge.

"Only the gentleman's receipt in full for the amount claimed," replied the attorney.

The plaintiff, half out of the witness box, turned to the judge with the air of a man who has been cruelly misled. "I take my solemn oath, Judge," he said earnestly, "I would never have brought the action, only I was led to believe that the receipt was burned."

All witnesses should be questioned as closely as possible before they are placed on the stand. Those who are particularly difficult should be interviewed frequently, allowed to repeat their stories, and questioned within the probable scope of cross-examination.

It must be remembered that—except under unusual circumstances—you will not be permitted to ask your own witnesses leading questions in court. Therefore, where the separate elements of an event are material, the witness should be required to fix them in his memory, so that he can recite them without prompting or suggestion.

I once represented an extremely stupid man who had been defrauded as a result of certain misrepresentations made to him. He could recite these, if given sufficient time and allowed to ramble at great length through immaterial matters. I subtracted from his long account five statements which were important, and I wrote them down on a sheet of paper. Then, for two months prior to the trial, I had him come to my office each day, at which time I would ask him just one question. "What did the defendant tell you about the property you were buying?"

If he omitted any of the items, I had him go into another room, reread the statement, and return, upon which I would repeat the question. Then, to insure that everything went as rehearsed, we agreed upon a device to be used on the trial. After asking him the above question, I would place my hand over the lower part of my face. As he recited each part of the answer I would close one finger into the palm, and the answer should not be considered completed while any finger on that hand remained visible.

He did well enough on the stand, but forgot one of the five items. While I sat with my thumb against my cheek, he struggled to recollect it, now and again regarding the remaining digit with a puzzled frown. Finally it came to him, and he triumphantly finished the list while I lowered my hand with a sigh of relief.

This procedure can hardly be overdone. It is dangerous to leave any part of it to the witness himself. Tom O'Connor once learned this to his discomfiture. He was defending a murder case in Nevada, representing one Sunburnt, who had crowned an illicit amour by killing the woman's husband. The plea was self-defense. In developing it, O'Connor instructed the defendant that it was necessary that he bring himself within the definition of a person of ordinary prudence in estimating the necessity he had been under to fire the fatal shot.

He pointed out that, to avail himself of the defense, he must show that the deceased had acted in such a way that a person of ordinary prudence would consider that his own life was in danger, and that less than this would not excuse the killing. The defendant was warned against any acknowledgment that he had acted under the stress of panic or unreasonable fear. He was cautioned to answer any question relating to his state of mind during the alleged assault by affirming that he had been cool and collected at all times.

Apparently the phrase "cool and collected" was not impressed sufficiently upon the defendant, who was at best of slow comprehension. On the trial he told his story with reasonable clarity, and then the attorney called for his state of mind during the affray.

The witness leaned forward and answered with manifest sincerity and a strong Middle-European accent, "Mr. O'Connor, I vas absolutely cold-blooded!"

It is highly advisable to interview witnesses, even though they are known to be adverse. Sometimes they have a distorted view of the controversy, from having heard only one side of it, and may be won away by presenting the other. Even if they continue inimical, an interview can be of use. If a witness refuses to discuss his testimony with you, this may be brought out on cross-examination, to show his bias to the jury. There is no reason why a fair witness should not tell his story to both sides.

Of course, there is some danger in this procedure. In criminal cases, especially, you may find yourself accused of "tampering with witnesses." Do not be dismayed by this. It is not only your privilege but your duty to investigate all available evidence. You need only tell this to the jury on the argument. They will probably feel that if they were in the defendant's position they would want a lawyer who missed no chances.

On occasion a witness of this kind may accuse you from the stand of having attempted to influence him improperly. If his testimony is strong enough, you can take the stand and deny it. You can also argue to the jury that the defense lawyer is always in danger of such charges if he is conscientious in consulting the safety of his client. You might even tell them that you have known of district attorneys—not this one, of course—instructing witnesses to make such accusations.

If possible, a written statement should be procured from such witnesses as may later prove recalcitrant, but this cannot protect you entirely. Confronted with such statement on cross-examination, the witness will usually come up with some prepared explanation, and this may prove more harmful than his original testimony.

In a case in San Francisco a woman was indicted for conspiracy to commit abortions. She was alleged to be working with one Doctor May, who had served a term in the federal penitentiary for performing plastic surgery on the notorious gangster John Dillinger.

The prosecution produced a taxi driver who identified the defendant as the woman who had called him to drive the complaining witness to a hospital after an unsuccessful attempt to abort her.

On cross-examination of this man, the defense counsel presented a statement signed by him, repudiating the identification. The witness admitted signing it, but then explained. He said that an acquaintance of his, who professed to come from the defendant, had pointed out to him that he was dealing with gangsters; that May was a dangerous man to antagonize; that a taxi driver is frequently required to drive passengers to remote and lonely places; and that unless he withdrew the identification, his life was in danger. This helped convict the defendant.

There are ways of guarding against such backfires. Archer Zamloch was once placed in a similar position, but had the caution to prepare countermeasures in advance. He sent an investigator to interview an important state witness in a murder case. The agent returned with a statement, signed by the witness, which established a plea of self-defense. On the trial he gave quite contrary evidence. When he was confronted with his signed statement, he alleged that it had been extorted from him by force. He said that the person who procured it had compelled him to enter an automobile at the point of a gun, and had there made him sign the document.

Zamloch then called the investigator, who denied any such coercion and stated the conversation between him and the witness. However, the matter was not left to a mere conflict of credibility between the two men. During the interview in the automobile, a wire-recording dictagraph had been operating under the cowl. This was now produced in court and played off to the jury. Its authenticity was comfirmed by the unmistakable accents of the two witnesses.

The verdict was acquittal. The fact that he was a prosecution witness, of course, saved the impeached witness from an indictment for perjury.

CHAPTER 11

Archaic Laws

IT HAS always been a source of wonder to me that people should go to such pains and expense to prevent others from engaging in any kind of sexual play which they don't happen to care for themselves. Probably their concern arises from a too-literal belief in the story of Sodom and Gomorrah. The residents in one part of a state may apprehend a rain of fire and brimstone upon themselves if those in another part yield to temptation or experiment in sexual taboos.

Certainly the fear is very much with us. And the unfortunate who ends up in the legal bag for engaging in some sexual dido not approved by society can expect little sympathy from court, newspapers or public.

One of the most celebrated sex cases was that which involved Oscar Wilde. He was having an enormous success with such plays as *The Importance of Being Earnest,* when his crisis came.

Wilde was a pronounced homosexual—that is to say, he had more feminine components in his composition than the average male. He became involved in a "love affair" with Lord Alfred Douglas, youngest son of the Marquis of Queensberry. The Marquis took the strongest measures to "save" his son, whose own sexual anomalies were such that he did not desire to be saved.

Queensberry finally called at Wilde's club and handed the porter a card addressed "To Oscar Wilde, posing as a Sodomite."

With the utmost folly, Wilde filed a complaint against him, charging him with criminal libel. Before doing so, he had consulted his attorney, Sir Edward Russell, who warned him of the danger of bringing such a proceeding if there were any possibility of the defendant establishing the justification of the statement by its truth. Wilde swore that there was not the slightest basis for the libel.

When the case went to court, Russell was permitted to act as special prosecutor. It was supposed that the Marquis would support his plea of truth upon certain passages in Wilde's works. The most important of these was his novel *The Picture of Dorian Gray* and the contents of a letter he had written sometime before to Lord Alfred Douglas. Wilde had no thought that there could be anything further than this, and had so advised his attorney.

Upon the trial Lord Russell took the bull by the horns, and in his opening statement read the incriminating letter aloud to the jury. He suggested that it was really nothing more than a sort of prose sonnet, and that it had indeed been translated into a French poem. The words, he said, might sound extravagant to those engaged in writing commercial correspondence, but that no invidious construction should be placed upon it.

The letter was as follows:

> MY OWN BOY—Your sonnet is quite lovely, but it is a marvel that those red roseleaf lips of yours should have been made no less for the music of song than for the madness of kisses. Your slim gilt soul walks between passion and poetry. I know Hyacinthus, whom Apollo loved so madly, was you in Greek days. Why are you alone in London, and when do you go to Salisbury? Do go there to cool your hands in the grey twilight of Gothic things, and come here whenever you like. It is a lovely place— it only lacks you; but go to Salisbury first. Always with undying love. Yours, OSCAR.

Russell must have been a very naive man not to recognize the implications in that letter. Confronted with it, the most ordinary advocate in the Hall of Justice would have laughed and sent Wilde away with the advice to forget it.

Having read it, however, he stated that Mr. Wilde would satisfy the jury that there was nothing to be ashamed of in it, and he looked up for assurance from it. He might have been warned by the dissatisfied countenances of the jury.

The foreman asked ominously, "What is the date of that letter?"

The attorney answered that it was undated, and he passed on to surer ground.

The defendant was represented by Sir Edward Carson. With Wilde on the stand, he entered upon the very course the complainant had anticipated. His cross-examination began with an inquiry as to certain passages contained in Wilde's books and plays. In this the witty author was quite at ease. He kept judge, jury and spectators in gales of laughter with clever bon mots. His mercurial temperament contrasted sharply with Carson's somber demeanor.

The latter called his attention to one of his more suspect compositions. "Is it good for the young?" he asked.

"Anything is good that stimulates thought, in whatever age."

The lawyer next turned to *The Picture of Dorian Gray,* and said that a decadent construction could be put upon it.

"Only by brutes and illiterates," retorted the witness.

"But an illiterate person reading *Dorian Gray* might consider it such a novel?"

"The views of illiterates are unaccountable."

Carson put further questions as to the views of ordinary individuals upon *Dorian Gray.*

"I have no knowledge of the views of ordinary individuals," Wilde replied.

"You did not prevent the ordinary individual from buying your book?"

"I have never discouraged him."

The examination shifted to the views expressed by characters in the book, and referred to one who had adored another man "madly." Did Wilde ever entertain such adoration?

"I have never given adoration to anybody except myself."

There was loud laughter at this, but Carson treated it with cold scorn. "Suppose a man who was not an artist had written this letter, would you say it was a proper letter?" he pursued.

"A man who was not an artist could not have written that letter."

The laughter which greeted the sustained wit of his dialogue was now mixed with a low murmur of approval. The audience liked Oscar Wilde.

"You are of the opinion that there is no such thing as an immoral book?" Carson asked him.

"Yes."

"May I take it that you think *The Priest and the Acolyte* was not immoral?"

"It was worse—it was badly written. I do not believe that any book or work of art ever had any effect on morality whatever."

"Listen, sir. Here is one of the 'Phrases and Philosophies for the Use of the Young': 'Wickedness is a myth invented by good people to account for the curious attractiveness of others.' You think that is true?"

"I rarely think anything I write is true."

" 'Religions die when they are proved to be true.' Is that true?"

"Yes, I hold that. It is a suggestion toward a philosophy of the absorption of religions by science, but surely it is too big a question for you to go into now."

"Do you think that was a safe axiom to put forward for the philosophy of the young?"

"Most stimulating."

" 'If one tells the truth, one is sure, sooner or later, to be found out'?"

"This is a pleasing paradox, but I do not set very high store on it as an axiom."

Carson took another of Wilde's extravagant letters to Douglas. "Is that an ordinary letter?" he asked.

"Everything I write is extraordinary. I do not *pose* as being ordinary."

Wilde had asked another young man, employed in a publisher's office, to an expensive dinner at a hotel.

"Was that for the purpose of having an intellectual treat?" asked the advocate.

"Well, for him, yes," answered the witness.

Once more the jury laughed, but it was almost the last kindly laugh that the case aroused in any of the audience. Carson had been playing at cat and mouse with the complainant, and the literary inquiry was designed only to lay a foundation for a grimmer inquisition.

For months detectives employed by Queensberry had been investigating Wilde's activities. The chance remark of a prostitute that male whores were getting the money of Oscar Wilde and his friends set them upon the track which led to his ruin. They discovered a cache of letters addressed to young men. The aid of these was easily purchased, and Queensberry had gone into court armed with statements of witnesses, prepared to prove—both by direct admissions and circumstantial evidence—the truth of the alleged libel.

Something in the atmosphere alarmed Wilde, and his composure began to desert him.

Carson mentioned the name of a young servant at Oxford almost casually. "Did you ever kiss him?" he asked with sudden emphasis.

Wilde made a gesture of disgust. "He was particularly plain," he said. "He was unfortunately very ugly. I pitied him for it."

It was of course a ruinous answer, and he struggled in vain to explain it. Other names and circumstances now poured in on him, and he realized too late the trap he had entered.

Next morning he failed to appear in court, and his attorneys withdrew the charges. Queensberry's lawyers immediately sent to the public prosecutor the statements of the witnesses.

The perverse instinct which has prompted me to engage in so many crusades detrimental to my financial interests has also led me to write letters to editors, protesting the preservation of laws the chief function of which is to facilitate the blackmailing of homosexuals.

A very important and objective book, *The Kinsey Report,* has disclosed the percentage of homosexuality to be much larger than was formerly supposed. The investigators who compiled the volume estimate that five-sixths of all people have homosexual traits to a greater or lesser degree.

The same work demonstrates that a "sexual perversion" is something that you haven't happened to try yourself, and that such expressions as "the infamous crime against nature" are nonsense, nature taking no interest in the matter.

It is under the last designation that anal copulation is condemned by our codes. It is probable that dogs, apes, and other dumb creatures who practice this, must know of nature's abhorrence of the act. It is therefore curious that no effort has been made by law to punish such activities on the part of animals other than human. Neither am I sure that some moral imperative will instruct us of its wickedness. I remember in the days of my boyhood innocence, being surprised to learn that intercourse with a sheep is unlawful. I could not reconcile that inhibition with the owner's right to kill the animal. It seemed to me that, if given the choice, the latter would choose to survive in shame.

Of course there are vested interests involved here also. Numerous blackmailers and extortionists would be thrown into the army of the unemployed by the repeal of these statutes. In addition, they enable certain police officers and prosecutors to augment their own scanty salaries.

The taboos connected with this anomaly are such that homosexual persons may even be murdered with impunity. Some years ago John Taafe defended a man who had shot to death one of his son's associates. His defense was that the victim was homosexual and that the father had desired to rescue his son—who was probably homosexual himself—from destruction. The plea was successful, and the defendant acquitted.

Shortly afterward, a young religious leader of a local congregation was beaten to death by a sailor whom he had persuaded to come to his hotel room. The killer was arrested in Texas and returned to San Francisco, but the officials of the victim's church persuaded the district attorney not to institute a prosecution, to avoid a scandal. Their request was complied with, and the killer walked out unscathed.

A short while ago five youths from "good families" were cruising the streets of San Francisco in an automobile, looking for "queers to beat up." They encountered a young high-school teacher, who was waiting for a streetcar, knocked him unconscious, and left him lying on the tracks where he was struck and killed by a streetcar. In reporting the trial of his assailants, the newspapers reiterated with monotonous regularity that "There was no evidence that the victim was, in fact, a homosexual." And the district attorney stressed this in his arguments to the jury. The defendants were convicted of second-degree murder. I then wrote to the two newspapers and the district attorney, inquiring whether, if the deceased had "in fact" been a homosexual, his murder would have been justified. But the query went unanswered.

Some doubts on this subject appear to have arisen in England. A couple of years ago Parliament appointed the Wolfenden Committee to study the subject. It recommended the abolition of all laws punishing homosexual acts between consenting adults. Unhappily, however, the Victorian tradition had more influence than a scientific inquiry, and the recommendation was disregarded.

It therefore came as something of a pleasant shock to me when in May 1962, the American Law Institute, in approving a model penal code which has been under preparation for ten years, adopted the recommendation of Judge Learned Hand that the criminal law should not punish any kind of sexual relations, normal or abnormal, between consenting adults in private. Those now alive may see the day when the state legislature will accept this view and abolish these archaic laws, but I doubt it.

Just as crimes involving sex bring down the fury of society, so do crimes involving the use or sales of narcotics. But here something more important has a hand: Money.

Narcotics addiction, with its concomitant traffic and resulting criminal prosecutions, illustrates how a profitable symbiosis can be maintained between lawyers who defend addicts and peddlers and the liars, hypocrites and frauds who promulgate and enforce the laws against them.

Please do not understand that I use these latter terms in any hostile spirit. Undoubtedly there are softer synonyms, but I do not care to spend the time discovering them. Also, the people to whom they are applicable are sufficiently hardened not to be annoyed by them. In addition, they are sustained by the apathy, ignorance, and misinformation of the general public, and particularly that portion of it whose vocal vigor is inversely proportional to its knowledge of the subject.

Centuries ago man learned to use the juices of the poppy, the fibers of the hemp family, and other such means of temporary escape from the stresses of reality. The necessity to evade life which the user of narcotics feels appears not to differ essentially from that which drives others to alcohol, religious ecstasy or even suicide.

Just as some physical organisms perish in an environment in which almost identical ones flourish, so the moral structure of one man may not survive pressures which affect his fellows little or not at all, and he seeks escape in some available mechanism.

That addiction to narcotics is a personal and social evil goes without saying. The remedy which the sick man uses to relieve his misery increases it, and he becomes a burden to both himself and to society. It therefore is society's duty to eradicate it. To this, all agree. Division of thought occurs when it comes to the method to be employed.

There are two conflicting schools in the United States. One is composed of doctors, scientists, and people with social consciences. The other is a vested interest. It consists, essentially, of the officials charged with enforcing the narcotic laws.

It would seem that the first of these forces, by virtue of its moral stature, its prestige and disinterestedness, would easily prevail over the few persons who compose the second. To believe so is to misunderstand the political pressure which, in this country, can be mustered by an entrenched bureaucracy which believes its power or tenure in danger.

For several years medical and social organizations have been pressing a campaign to treat narcotic addicts as sick people and addiction as a medical problem. In February 1959, for example, a conference on the subject held by the Ethical Culture Society and the Community Council of Greater New York heard Dr. Herbert Berger, a former president of the New York City Medical Society, demand a change in the laws so as to allow physicians to treat addicts as patients and end prosecution for the mere use of drugs. "The only approach to the narcotic addict," he said, "is to treat him as a weak, sick person. He seeks, through chemical means, to make his peace with 'society.' "

The consensus of those at the conference was that doctors should have the legal right to treat addicts, even to give them narcotics, and many speakers urged that the American Medical Association and local affiliates take the lead in advocating this.

Shortly prior to this, the public health committee of the New York State Bar Association proposed an amendment to the Public Health Law, making it possible to distribute drugs to the state's estimated 17,000 addicts, saying, "We do not believe any solution of the addict's problem is practicable without some form of legal distribution of narcotic drugs."

This last sentence furnishes the solution of the problem. Cheap or free distribution of narcotics to addicts is a requisite step in their elimination. In the first place, it would end the traffic in them almost literally overnight. There would be no incentive for illegal sale or for recruiting new customers. The gang murders between rival sales forces would cease, and other crimes would be sharply diminished.

At present the ordinary addict is almost necessarily condemned to a life of crime. The danger run by the vendor makes illegal narcotics extremely expensive. It costs about $50 a day to satisfy the habit. Such an amount can not be procured by ordinary work. Male addicts become petty thieves, pickpockets, holdup men and burglars; almost all the women take to prostitution.

In a recent criminal prosecution in Brooklyn Felony Court,

two young women, aged twenty-seven and twenty-eight, were ar-
raigned on a charge of stealing $35,000 over a period of two
years by forging money orders. Both were narcotic addicts, and
stated that their addiction cost them $100 a day.

The Federal Bureau of Narcotics states that the victims of
narcotics addiction paid $300,000,000 a year to the infamous
Maffia for heroin alone, and that their activities to procure this
sum accounts for 30 percent of crime in the United States each
year. The easiest way for an addict to procure narcotics is to
become a peddler of them. It is estimated that 85 percent of those
who sell drugs also use them.

I have talked with many narcotics addicts and peddlers who
have confirmed these facts. One old man, who had spent half of
his life in prison, said bitterly, "If they had dispensaries where an
addict could buy cheaply, I could have lived a useful life, even
with the habit. I could have worked all day, gone to the dispensary
and taken a shot at night, gone home and gone to bed, and gone
to work the next morning so that nobody would notice it."

However, if the furnishing of narcotics to addicts in government dispensaries would put the peddlers out of a job, it would
do the same to the officers making their living arresting them.

These have more influence than either the unfortunate addicts
or the humanitarian groups which seek to correct the situation.
They do not approach the problem in any scientific way. Their
top man at that time, Federal Commissioner of Narcotics Harry
J. Anslinger, met the suggested remedy with a demogogic appeal
to passion and prejudice: "If we are to have a dispensary for
narcotics addicts on the first floor," he said, "let's have a saloon
for drunkards on the second, and a brothel for sex perverts on
the third."

It would hardly be expected that he would say, instead: "If you
kill off the narcotics traffic, what is to become of me and my staff
of enforcement officers?"

In the symposium discussed above, Dr. Berger characterized
Anslinger as "a despot, interested only in maintaining the *status
quo.*"

It is said that there are 50,000 narcotic addicts in the United

States. In England, where the government has adopted the method advocated by the medical groups here—that is to say, by the maintenance of dispensaries where addicts can procure cheap drugs—there are only 300 addicts in the entire country.

The same method prevails in the Soviet Union. In a conference which I had with A. B. Chevloff, Deputy Director of the Institute of Public Health, he stated that narcotic addiction is considered a psychoneurotic medical problem and is treated in dispensaries where free drugs are provided as required. In addition, he said that addicts are given warm baths, change of residence or type of work, and involved in social activities. They may spend their nights in sanitariums, under the supervision of doctors, and may obtain sedatives in them so as to insure normal sleep. He claimed that he could count the narcotic addicts in Moscow on his fingers.

The chief general deputy prosecutor also informed me that narcotics addiction posed no problem in the Russian Federated Republic, which contains 60 percent of the Soviet population. He stated that in the eastern republics, where narcotics have been used for centuries, there is some difficulty in eradicating them. The use of drugs is not a criminal offense, though the private production or distribution of them is.

The experience of both Great Britain and the Soviet Union demonstrates the correctness of the narcotics control method advocated by the medical profession and the humane organizations above described. Of course, a lawyer who advocates this advanced approach is throwing away a valuable source of income. Tons of heroin are imported into and distributed throughout the United States. Elaborate networks of police officials, spies and informers, make their livings stalking the numerous vendors. While the take is usually limited to small-fry pushers, occasionally a big distributor is caught in the net, and a lawyer can come up with a splendid fee. Even the small fry are good for potboilers, and their cases are usually not difficult to handle, since all expect to be convicted and few are disappointed in that respect.

Even where no vested interest is involved, religious or moral superstition may provide a field from which profitable harvests may be reaped. Outstanding among these are the laws which involve criminal abortion. The Spanish author Ibáñez entitled one of his books *Los muertos mandan,* meaning "The Dead Command." It has to do with the restrictions which ancient customs impose upon the living. Prominent among these tyrannies is that which involves unwanted pregnancy. For centuries the shamans and hypocrites have united to force women to bear babies which they don't want.

Not long ago, militaristic nations made no pretense about the matter. They wanted cannon fodder. It is estimated that over a million abortions were performed in Germany in 1930, the laws forbidding it being largely ignored. When Hitler launched his program of conquest, these laws were strengthened, and inducing an abortion was made a capital offense. Similarly in Japan, abortion was illegal because the militarists wanted an army. After their defeat in the Second World War it was legalized.

Mass murder having declined in popularity since that cataclysm, this reason for outlawing abortion has been largely hushed and moral and religious clichés are substituted for it.

"Life is sacred!" is the protest, not only of priests, but of some doctors and others with pretensions to scientific outlooks. Of course, it is sacred only when in the womb. Once released, it may be slaughtered with the blessings of both groups.

The scientists invent the instruments of destruction, and the ecclesiastics consecrate them. Christian missionaries wail at induced terminations of Japanese and Korean pregnancies. Christian airmen, with the approval of these spiritual guides, blast living children with atom or napalm bombs.

As might be expected, the United States of America, with its inheritance of Puritanism, abides by its religious and moral taboos in this matter. The State of California, which professes to be one of its most advanced members, expresses this spirit in its criminal code. In that State inducing an abortion is a felony, unless it is necessary to preserve the life of the expectant mother. Moreover, it is a felony to give information on, or to furnish contraceptive materials. Physicians and druggists are exempted from this last provision.

In 1958, the Planned Parenthood Federation of America and the New York Academy of Medicine held a conference at which numerous persons furnished information and suggestions. The discussion was chiefly concerned with therapeutic abortion, few venturing to suggest that it should be legalized on other than medical grounds.

The chairman opened the conference by stating, among other things: "The Law does not recognize that a woman suffering from serious heart disease, or who, in early pregnancy, contracted German measles, should have an abortion: although the first may make serious demands upon her, and in the second one you may expect in 20 percent of the cases the child to be born blind, mentally retarded, or otherwise affected."

Physicians from the Scandinavian countries, where the laws have relaxed in recent years, informed the audience that in Norway abortion is legal, if the pregnancy "endangers the health" of the woman; and that in Sweden a socioeconomic cause was added in 1946. Under this amendment the operation is now legal, if under the conditions of life of the woman and other circumstances her physical or mental strength would be seriously reduced by the birth and care of a child.

Almost all those opposed to extending permissible causes for therapeutic abortion based their position upon pretended scientific grounds. This was true of some doctors who practiced in Roman Catholic Hospitals where even therapeutic operations are banned. The general pretext was "traumatic effect" upon the woman involved. No woman was called upon to discuss the traumatic effect on a sixteen-year-old high-school girl of being forced to bear an illegitimate child.

The reactionaries based much of their position upon an opinion of United States Circuit Judge Thurman Arnold that an abortion for the purpose of avoiding social disgrace, poverty or illegitimacy, is "offensive to our moral concepts."

Little concession was made to the fact that the situation is practical and not a theoretical one, although the consensus of the conference was that about one million illegal abortions are performed annually in the United States.

This estimate was supported by that of Dr. Samuel A. Cosgrove, chairman and professor of obstetrics and gynecology at Seton Hall College of Medicine and Dentistry, in Jersey City, New Jersey, in an address to the Society for the Scientific Study of Sex given in New York on November 8, 1958. He lamented efforts to extend legitimate abortions beyond merely medical reasons.

The New York Times quoted him: "This objective is demonstrably sparked by the psychiatrists and—God help us—by nonmedical social workers." The article continued: "In reply to an indirect question about his religious background, Dr. Cosgrove identified himself as a Protestant, although he teaches at a Roman Catholic school."

Other groups, including government agencies, confirm the above estimate. Additionally, they claim that of this 1,000,000 illegal abortions, only about 800,000 are performed by medical doctors. The remaining 200,000 unfortunate women submit their lives and health to the efforts of nurses, midwives, chiropractors, veterinarians, or whoever else is bold and callous enough to assume the task.

These 200,000 women are victims of economic disparity. A speaker at the Planned Parenthood conference above mentioned stated that qualified abortionists practicing in New York were charging fees of $1,000 to $1,500 for the operation, and that the present laws foster crime by bringing the underworld into what should be a medical problem.

Another participant presented statistics of a poll taken among unmarried women, showing that 88 to 95 percent of conceptions among them had been terminated by illegal abortions. In a similar poll of women who had been married, 10 percent admitted that they had had abortions by the time they were twenty years of age, and 22 percent by the time they were forty-five.

Numerous studies have established the growing promiscuity of quite young people in this country, with its necessary concomitant of unmarried pregnancies. A similar study in England, involving a poll of 6,251 British women, showed that 25 percent of the unmarried women in the United Kingdom had had sexual relations, and that among married women 40 percent had had premarital intercourse. Most girls had had their first sexual experience between the ages of eighteen and twenty.

There are three other countries in the world in which the American record for abortions is equal or exceeded. These are the Soviet Union, China and Japan. However, in all three abortion is legal. The Japanese dismiss moral objections with the cynical observation that a country which has endured modern warfare can scarcely be compunctious about removing a few grams of protoplasm from the uterus. In the Soviet Union the only limitation is that the abortion must be performed in a hospital and by a medical doctor. The cost is graded to the economic status of the woman, but in no event does it exceed 50 rubles ($56). In addition, the matter is treated as a medical case, and the woman is entitled to her wages during the period required for the operation and her recovery from its effects.

Of course, in advocating the same procedure in this country a lawyer is again cutting off a source of income. Doctors who perform abortions with some discretion and with a proper regard to the nature of their clientele are rarely involved in criminal prosecutions. However, their fees are high, and many women can not afford to pay them. They therefore fall into the hands of chiropractors, midwives, veterinarians, and others having only a limited knowledge of the technique. The danger which the patient runs is heightened by the strain under which the operator works. He must always consider the possibility that his client is a police agent and that he may be sent to the penitentiary by a hypocritical judge enforcing an unrealistic law. Many of them perform their work with their courage strengthened and performance confused by alcohol.

These frequently bungle the operations. They may then be informed upon by their patients. In some instances their incompetency may result in the death of the unfortunate woman and they may be indicted for second-degree murder. Not infrequently an attempt may be made to dispose of the victim's body, sometimes with as little skill as was displayed in the original operation. Photos of a young woman's naked cadaver dumped into a ravine can enhance both the probability of conviction and the size of the fee which may be demanded.

In a case tried in San Mateo County, California, the district attorney's advantage in this respect was heightened by the fortuitous circumstance that when the police photos were taken, a lizard was perched upon the corpse. On appeal, this fact was held not to have prejudiced the defendant.

CHAPTER **12**

The Press and Justice

IN 1890, Émile Zola explained how he was able to read the newspapers. He said that each morning he ate a toad whole and alive; with such a diet he was able to swallow the lies of the French newspapers without nausea.

Leon Trotsky wrote on the same subject:

> One may say that the newspapers tell the truth only as the exception . . . Zola wrote of the French financial press that it could be divided into two groups: the venal and the so-called "incorruptible" that sells itself only in exceptional cases and at a very high price. Something of the sort may be said of the mendacity of newspapers in general. The yellow press lies as a matter of course, without hesitating or looking back. Newspapers like the *Times* or *le Temps* speak the truth on all unimportant and inconsequential occasions, so that they can deceive the public with all the requisite authority when necessary.

Mendacity, corruption and cynicism are the primary qualities of newspapers. They are controlled by advertisers. They have great power. Pity the wretch on trial for his life or liberty, if one of them decides to launch a campaign for his conviction. Judges fall into line. Possibly there are some brave and honest enough to protect a defendant from a judicial lynching, but who will attempt to undo the prejudice created by inflammatory editorials and slanted news items? I have never met one who would.

Shortly after I was admitted to practice, I discovered how a newspaper handles a susceptible judge. A dog bit a small boy. It is the practice, in such instances, to impound the animal for rabies. If it shows symptoms of the disease, it's assumed that the person is infected. He's given serum. There's a wild superstition that if the animal is put to death before the symptoms appear, it can no longer develop rabies, and neither can its victim.

The parents of the boy—believing this nonsense—agreed with the owner of the dog that if he would kill it, they would waive any damages for the child's injury. The owner, eager to rid himself of a dangerous claim so cheaply, agreed to have the dog gassed.

An afternoon paper heard of the affair and sent a reporter to interview both families. He found that the animal's owner also had a boy who loved his dog. Next day there was a "human interest" story with photos of the child mourning the coming death of his pet. One animal lover phoned the paper, eager to accept custody of the doomed dog. But the superstitious parents of the injured boy, convinced that if the dog lived past the seven-day period of rabies incubation he would endanger their child's safety, refused and insisted on its death.

The owner was ready to oblige, despite the paper's sentimental readers. But the city editor had a good story. He called me and explained that, as a matter of continuing reader interest, he wanted to prevent the execution. A Superior Court Judge, he said, had agreed to issue an injunction to prevent the killing, if a petition requesting it were presented by even an outside person.

I prepared a complaint on behalf of a reporter on the paper. This interest was so intangible that I did not dare have the document verified. It prayed for an injunction to stop the impending tragedy. The proceedings were transacted with all possible drama. The reporter and I waited until it was too late for the rival newspaper to run anything on the matter. We then hurried to the city hall, where the friendly magistrate awaited us in his chambers. He signed a temporary restraining order and an order turning the custody of the dog over to my reporter. We whirled off to the city pound, where another newsman was waiting with a camera. The poundman had been fixed to delay the fatal blow until our arrival. The doors were opened to the four-footed culprit, and after due flashing of photo bulbs, we sped forth to hide the corpus, i.e. the dog, for future purposes.

Next day we appeared in the cooperative magistrate's court on a motion to make the injunction permanent. The parents of the injured boy and the owner of the animal appeared with an attorney. He pointed out to the judge that the dog was the personal property of his client, who had a right to do with it as he pleased, and that I and my client were only officious intermeddlers without a vestige of right in the matter. He also produced authorities to show that the proceedings for an injunction were void, because the complaint was not verified as required by the code in such matters.

I would have been embarrassed to answer these contentions, but the court did not require me to do so. He merely stated that he had given the matter much thought and felt that the dog should not be killed for what was probably some unintentional mischief on his part. He signed a decree forbidding the defendants to kill the animal and granting its permanent care to my reporter friend.

Theoretically, the defendants could appeal and reverse this judgment. But this would have cost them about $150, and they could not afford it. We walked out of court with the dog which the reporter then gave to a rancher in a nearby county. Some days later it bit another child, and the rancher shot it.

The circumstances of that case were trifling, but viewed against its perspective, you can imagine how a lawyer feels when he glimpses the headlines which inform him that some newspaper has decided to raise a hue and cry against a client of his on trial for his life or liberty.

Shortly after the dog incident I was on that side of a newspaper lynching bee. I was employed to represent John Tipton, one of the defendants in a celebrated California murder trial, generally known as the "Windmill Murder" case. The supposed crime had taken place in Kings County, the seat of which is Hanford, a drab, hot little town in the central valley of the state.

Jennie Laura Brown and her husband had been farmers in Kings County for a great many years. Childless, they had adopted three children, Lee Camp, his sister Laura, and Bob McCamish. All three grew up at the Brown farm. But Laura Camp had quarreled with Mrs. Brown and left the place several years before the events leading to the trial. She had married humbly and was living in Hanford, but was not on speaking terms with the remaining members of the Brown household.

Brown had suffered a paralytic stroke some years before and was confined to his bed. Mrs. Brown, with the aid of the two husky foster sons, her uncle John Tipton, and the ranch foreman Fred Mills, carried on with such success that she was the envy of neighbors. She was a hard-bitten little woman with few friends.

One Sunday morning about ten o'clock Lee Camp and Tipton were removing a windmill fan from the roof of a tankhouse within a stone's throw of the county road and in plain view of persons passing upon it. Tipton went to get additional rope, and while he was absent Camp slipped upon the mossy shingles of the roof and plunged to the ground. His head struck upon a portion of the windmill machinery which was lying there. When Tipton returned, he found him bleeding and unconscious. The injured man was rushed to the farmhouse and thence to the county hospital, where he died some hours later.

Camp's sister Laura started telling friends in Hanford that her brother had been murdered. A San Francisco newspaper heard of it and sent a reporter. Within a few days the paper began to headline the incident, recounting all the vague gossip, rumors, innuendoes and whisperings.

Laura Camp was interviewed by the district attorney. She told of attempts against her own life during her stay at the ranch. One yarn took a particularly bizarre form. She said she'd been fed capsules full of phonograph needles. The Grand Jury decided to investigate. Each new item furnished fresh headlines. Several of the San Francisco papers were by now beating the drums, which in turn excited new Grand Jury action.

It employed Oscar Heinrichs, an eminent criminologist, whose reputation for ability and honesty was widespread, to investigate. After a survey, he reported that Lee Camp had in fact fallen from the roof of the tankhouse. He'd received the fatal injuries by striking his head upon the machinery lying on the ground.

He had found, he explained, two scrape marks in the slippery moss, extending from the comb to the edge of the roof. Moreover moss was still upon the heels of the dead man's boots. In falling, his body had torn loose an electric wire high up on the side of the tankhouse; the nail which held it had been pulled out. It was rusty for part of its length, but still shiny where it had been embedded in the wood before being torn loose. Part of the insulation on the wire had been scuffed off and remained as a stain on the victim's trousers. Near the machinery upon the ground was a bench nailed to the side of the building. The under wall and the underside of this bench were drenched with blood which had evidently spurted from the cranial arteries of the injured man. There was no blood above the bench. Obviously he had received the fatal injury upon the ground.

But the crusading newspaper was lusting for a kill. It gave so much space to the Camp case and made such direct and venomous charges, that the Grand Jury was caught in its fervor. It insulted Heinrichs by asking him if he had been bribed by the prospective defendants. It also questioned Tipton, Mills and McCamish. All three gave the same versions of the incident. It developed that Camp's life was heavily insured in favor of Mrs. Brown, although there was no evidence that she knew of this. Camp, it seemed, just couldn't say no to insurance salesmen.

There was no question but that there would be an indictment. As Tipton, Mills and McCamish had testified so strongly to the same effect, it was not expedient to omit any of them from the charge. The Grand Jury returned an indictment, charging murder against Mrs. Brown, Tipton, Mills and McCamish—in other words, against everyone on the ranch except the paralyzed Brown. I never did find out why they omitted him.

Then the fun really began. The metropolitan scandal sheet, having commenced the prosecution, undertook to finish it. It hired a lawyer of known demogogic talents and slight scruples to act as special prosecutor. The district attorney complaisantly surrendered his duties to this worthy for the duration of the trial. The paper's investigator ranged far and wide, stirring up further suspicions and prejudices. Its headlines became more lurid. Its rewrite men strained for flamboyant new phrases to excite prejudice. The farm near Hanford became "The Ranch of Regrets"; a photo of the defendants entering the courtroom under heavy guard was solemnly entitled, "The Leaves of the Judgment Book Unfold." This ruthless newspaper erected the stake and piled up the fagots. The defendants' good neighbors danced happily around them.

Two weeks were consumed in selecting a jury. We finally got twelve honest farmerfolk, none of whom had ever had or expressed the slightest opinion as to the guilt or innocence of the defendants. The special prosecutor, worthy of his employer, was a thorough and unprincipled scoundrel. While the newspaper whipped up the mob outside its mouthpiece inflamed them within. And as it turned out, the judge was already with them.

I had carefully gone over the testimony before the Grand Jury. Three-fourths of it was inadmissible, being mostly hearsay. Matters designed to prove motive were not connected with any defendant. Indeed there was no proof that a murder had been committed. I'd spent weeks researching the cases. I had incontrovertible authorities on every point involved assembled upon the counsel table. Yet, the first time I rose to make an objection the judge informed me that I would be permitted only to state the objection. I was not to argue it, and I would not be permitted to read from any of the decisions upon which I relied.

Not one single objection which the defendants made was sustained. No discussion beyond the bare statement of the point was allowed. A hostile mob growled and glowered from outside the rail. The special prosecutor, supported and sustained by the court, raved and roared within it.

Meanwhile, the newspaper continued to so inflame the rustic inhabitants of the sweet little hamlet that I found it risky to walk outside during the recess periods, with surly bumpkins, obviously calculating whether they could take me in a fist fight.

The trial lasted two months. The temperature averaged 113°. By the end of the case the prosecution had not even established the corpus delicti of murder—that is to say, it had not shown that Camp had met his death by unlawful means. There was not a word to offset the plain proof of accident. Motions for directed verdicts on that ground were as futile as the idle wind. We proceeded to argument to the jury. The regular district attorney led off with a disarmingly reasonably plea. Each of the defendants had his own attorney. All made convincing arguments. The local gazette described mine as "easily the outstanding oratorical achievement of the pleadings." I pointed out, among other things, the improbability that a conspiracy to murder would carry out its purpose in plain sight of the open road on a Sunday morning, and the added improbability that the conspirators, having delivered less than a fatal stroke, would rush their victim to a hospital where he might recover consciousness and denounce them.

Then the special prosecutor rose to address the jury. In hours of invective and insult to both the defendants and their lawyers, he shouted and roared around the tribune. Scornfully assuming that the slaying had been proven, he depended his conclusions on a negative argument. He magnified trifling contradictions among the statements made by the defendants when they testified before the Grand Jury. Actually, these only demonstrated that they were not telling a prepared story. He invented a motive more exciting than that of any financial gain which Jennie Brown might derive from Lee Camp's death. He asserted that an illicit sexual relationship had existed between them and that it was about to end. This, he contended, was demonstrated by two pieces of evidence: one, that Mrs. Brown had been seen to kiss her foster son goodnight; the other, that he had paid some attention to a neighborhood girl. This, he thundered, had aroused the defendant's fears that the dead man was about to desert "her bed of passion and her couch of delight." If there should be an acquittal, the decent people of Kings County should arm themselves and prepare to defend their homes, he cried.

The defense counsel were on their feet from the start of this. We tried to stop it with objections and assignments of misconduct. Not one was allowed. Finally the judge, fearing that we were lessening the force of the argument by such interruptions, forbade us to make any more. He informed us that we should not again interfere with the special prosecutor's speech, and at its end we would have such exceptions as we might be entitled to. He stated that he would also instruct the jury to ignore such portions of the argument as might, in fact, be objectionable. The other defense counsel succumbed to this admonition. I refused to do so and kept up the objections.

Within the next hour or so I objected to practically every sentence uttered by the prosecution. I even argued two of them after being ordered to take my seat, and was twice adjudged in contempt of court, and fined $500.

When the special prosecutor finished his tirade, he was without coat, necktie or dignity, sweating like a bull, from the sheer physical demands of his performance.

Thereupon the entire crowd of spectators, filling every seat and swelling the aisles, broke into applause, stamping, clapping, shouting and whistling for several minutes. The judge looked blandly on, making no effort to quiet the hullabaloo. It continued until the newspaper investigator, who had been seated at the prosecution table throughout the trial, leaped upon it like a football cheer leader and quelled the clamor with outstretched arms.

The jury was instructed and retired sometime in the afternoon. The announcement that it had reached a verdict came precisely at midnight. Meanwhile a great crowd, mostly of men, had assembled around the courthouse. It was a common rumor that, if the defendants were acquitted they would be "strung up." I went into court with a loaded revolver in my hip pocket, ready to use it if a lynching attempt were made.

But the jury was not courting trouble. It found three of the defendants guilty of second-degree murder and acquitted McCamish. Of course, it was first-degree murder or nothing. The verdict was a concession to the mob.

A few days later Jennie Brown's attorney, Harry Brown, was killed in an auto accident. She employed new counsel to conduct the appeal for all defendants. The Supreme Court reversed the convictions, particularly on the ground that no crime was shown to have been committed. It excoriated the special prosecutor for his conduct on the trial. It also ordered the indictment dismissed upon a motion which I had made early in the proceedings.

The three defendants were reindicted, but the court transferred the trial to another county. They were acquitted on a directed verdict.

Shortly after the conclusion of this case, a woman was arrested in one of the mountain counties on a charge of having poisoned her husband. Scarcely had she been accused, when this same newspaper dubbed her "The Borgia of the Sierras." This fixed things up for her. Sometime after, the same technique was used on a youth also accused of murder. As he had considerable hair on his body, he was titled "The Ape Man." Later, one of my associates struggled in vain to overcome the prejudice resulting to a murder defendant from the charitable description, "The Gorilla Murderer." He was considered fair game for this merely because he was a man of great physical strength. The jury convicted him, but the Appellate Court reversed the judgment, holding the evidence insufficient as a matter of law.

But people will go on believing newspapers. Still, just as a matter of record, I want to say that nobody should accept a newsstory as having the least value in establishing the guilt of a person accused of crime. In the first place, a crime is a story; an accident is not. Papers are printed to be sold, not to disseminate truth. The public can be whipped up to buying more and more of them by suggestions and innuendoes which increase its suspicions. Everybody becomes an amateur sleuth. In this way the circulation of detective and mystery stories has been greatly increased in recent years.

Police reporters consider cynicism synonymous with professional ability. As a matter of trade practice, they scoff at any innocent interpretation of human conduct. They start off with the assumption that every accused person is guilty. They shrug off the suggestion that their distorted accounts may have sent an innocent man to the gallows or prison.

Once in a while all this is admitted in a death-bed repentance. Fremont Older, editor of the San Francisco *Bulletin,* spent several years trying to put Abraham Ruef, the city's political boss, in prison. Finally he succeeded, but after reflecting on the methods which had been used for that purpose, he spent several more years trying to get him out. In a public speech he told the story of his crusade and its result. Then he said:

> And then it dawned upon me for the first time that my life, too, had been filled with evil; that I had done many cruel things; that I had at no time been fully fair to him, or to the others who were caught with him; that I had been striving, as he had, for success; that I had been hurting others in order to make money out of a successful newspaper; that I had been printing stories that made others suffer that I might profit; pandering to many low instincts in man in order to sell newspapers; that I had told many half truths and let many lies go undenied.

Years ago I was once naive enough to visit a judge in chambers at the start of a celebrated murder trial and to demand that he curtail the activities of a newspaper so as to protect the rights of the defendant. I would never think of doing such a thing now. It would be like inviting a little child who is afraid of ghosts to go into a dark wood and drag out a wolf. It wouldn't matter that there was neither ghost nor wolf there, the terror would be as dreadful as if there were.

The trial which most involved me with newspaper sensationalism was that, in 1932, of Frank Egan, the public defender of the city and county of San Francisco. Only one other public official had been tried for murder in the state of California. The Egan case had enough bizarre developments to make the most fantastic TV whodunit sound plausible. In addition to the stature of the defendant, it had violence and mystery, a young and flamboyant lawyer—I was thirty-four years old and given to unpredictable procedures—with a cagey investigator and even a beautiful sweetheart to assist him.

Frank Egan, while a patrolman in the San Francisco police department, had attended night law school, gotten himself admitted to the bar, and when the office of public defender was created in the state, ran for that office in his native city and was elected.

I first came to know him when he called at my office to inquire about the progress of an action involving a friend of his whom I was representing. He was so satisfied with the results of this litigation that he started referring cases to me, and occasionally dropped into my office.

He was a strange sort of man, six feet tall, rangy and vigorous. He affected at times a fierceness of manner, with loud and indignant denunciation of judges, assistant district attorneys, or others who had incurred his displeasure, and often fell into the device of referring to himself in the third person. Meanwhile, a certain hesitation in speech, a softening of his light blue eyes, and diffidence in the presence of those whom he respected, betrayed an underlying insecurity. Ultimately there was something childlike and pathetic in the trust and reliance which he came to repose in me.

Few cases in the world have attracted as much publicity as that of the *People of the State of California vs. Frank Egan*. It began with the discovery, one dark night, of the dead body of a woman named Jessie Hughes sprawled in the roadway of a San Francisco street, the apparent victim of a hit-run driver. A few days later the papers carried a story that Chief of Detectives Charles Dullea had sought to question Public Defender Frank Egan in connection with the woman's death, and that Egan had refused to be questioned.

A day or two later came the startling news that Egan had disappeared, having apparently been kidnapped. Dullea informed the newspapers that the missing official had phoned him the preceding evening, whispering nervously and excitedly, "Charlie, this is Frank Egan; two men are holding me down here near the ferry building. . . ." At this juncture the voice faded away and the call was disconnected.

Soon Dullea stated—and the papers broadcast—the suspicion that the death of Jessie Hughes was somehow connected with the disappearance of the public defender; in addition, the police officer revealed that he had put out a bulletin for the apprehension of two ex-convicts, Albert Tinnin and Verne Doran, whose paroles Egan had recently procured, and who had similarly disappeared. Egan's wife was interviewed; the police took prints of his automobile tires, and otherwise heightened the suspicion that he was involved in Jessie Hughes' death. All of these matters were done quite openly, and the newspaper accounts were lurid with suspicion and innuendo.

After three or four days of this, Lorraine Egan came to my home one evening and confided to me that her husband was in hiding and that he wished to talk to me. She gave me the address where he could be found.

I went there and found Egan on the verge of a nervous collapse. I quieted him down sufficiently to discuss the situation. It seemed to me that the longer he was absent, the greater would be the excitement engendered by his disappearance and the more suspicion would fasten upon him in connection with Jessie Hughes' death. It had been revealed that her life was insured in his name in the sum of $50,000, with double indemnity in case of accidental death.

I felt that it would be extremely dangerous to allow him to be questioned in his present demoralized condition, and that we had to solve the problem of how to return him to public observation without the embarrassment of interviews with either the police or the press.

I communicated with a doctor friend, who arranged to have Egan placed in a private sanitarium to which I immediately took him. The physician there put him under sedation. I informed Dullea and the newspapers that Egan had returned, was in my charge, and that his physical and mental conditions were such that I had been required to put him in a hospital.

I agreed that they would be permitted to see him the next morning in my presence, but that no questions were to be put to him, nor was he to be disturbed by any discussion of the matters which had raised such a storm. Naturally, if Egan were involved in any crime, I wasn't going to permit him to furnish the means of his own destruction.

Next morning I arranged for the police and reporters to see the missing man. While they adhered to their agreement, they besieged me with inquiries as to where he had been, the manner in which he had come under my charge, and what facts he had revealed to me regarding his disappearance and his possible connection with the death of Mrs. Hughes. To all of these I maintained a firm front, relying upon the confidential relationship existing between attorney and client, promising them that as soon as Egan was well he would give a complete explanation.

Next I moved Egan out of the sanitarium and back to his office. Suspicions and accusations against him had mounted, and so did the insistence that he furnish a statement of his activities and his whereabouts during the period of his disappearance.

Finally the papers published a list of questions which they asserted the authorities were interested in having answered. These, in effect, accused Egan of some complicity in the death of Jessie Hughes, and called upon him to answer or refute a number of suspicious circumstances connected with it. I at once took the position that the police were harassing Egan, were charging him by innuendo with involvement in a crime, and that we were not going to lend ourselves to any circus as Dullea had stirred up by dignifying the questions which he had proposed. I also concocted a device to shift the onus for this reticence onto my shoulders.

I permitted him to make a general statement to the reporters in my presence, but as soon as they asked anything dangerous I would snap in with a direction to Egan not to answer the question. Upon this he would turn to me with the greatest air of innocence in the world and inquire, "Why, Vince, I have no objection to answering that question; these boys are all friends of mine. I'm willing to answer anything they ask me." But he would shrug and follow my instruction. This would lead to protests by the reporters, and Egan would again express his willingness to answer anything they said. I would close the act with the ultimatum: "If I'm going to represent you, Frank, you're going to do as I tell you. I'm not going to fall for Mr. Dullea's little game of character assassination by innuendo. If he has any accusations to make against you, let him make them, and then we'll answer them. Meanwhile, we're not lending ourselves to any inquisition based on his malice and innuendos."

When the newspaper men persisted, I would become truculent and quarrelsome; Egan would subside into a surly compliance; and the interview would end rather unhappily.

The device had the desired effect. Presently the newspapers began criticizing my attitude and by-passing Egan's. He confided to me that lawyers of our acquaintance had called upon him, suggesting that I was damaging his case and that he would do well to get rid of me. His attitude during the numerous efforts to interview him had made it obvious that he had nothing to conceal, and my insistence upon his silence was both pointless and damaging.

Warrants for the arrest of Tinnin and Doran had been issued for violation of their paroles. I set about to contact acquaintances and friends of theirs so as to have them surrender voluntarily. In the first place I thought that this would be valuable as an indication of innocence; also, I wanted them represented by counsel from the moment of their arrest so that they could not be subject to any brutality or coercion which might evoke a confession. Unknown to us, Tinnin had been apprehended. Instead of booking him at the city prison, Dullea had held him in a hotel room, where with other police officers, he had worked on him both to procure a confession and to discover the whereabouts of Verne Doran. The chief device employed was to keep the prisoner from going to sleep, and when he started to doze off, to question him sharply in the hope of evoking some answer while he was half conscious. Tinnin was a Spartan, and three days of this treatment failed to provoke a single incriminating word. Finally Dullea had him booked at the city prison, and the newspapers headlined his arrest.

While I wanted to keep some control over both Tinnin and

Doran, at the same time I did not want to involve Egan too closely with them. Accordingly, I employed Nathan Coghlan to represent Tinnin and to make immediate contact with him in jail. He informed me that Tinnin was a rock, had said nothing, and would say nothing.

I then set out to locate Doran. I felt that he could not much longer evade arrest, and I wanted him represented at the very moment he came into the custody of the police. In addition, I felt that this voluntary surrender would be an argument in favor of innocence. I located friends of his who knew his whereabouts. I employed Walter McGovern, a well-known trial lawyer, to protect him, and brought Doran to McGovern's house one night. Next morning he surrendered him into custody.

Now we thought we had the situation pretty well in hand. Apparently all that the prosecution had was some bizarre conduct on Egan's part, the fact that the woman's life was insured in his favor, and a dogged detective who seemed determined to convert these into a capital charge against a popular, elected official.

We did not know that all this time Dullea was in possession of facts which were not revealed until after the trial was over, and which led him then to inform me: "When I learned that Jessie Hughes had been killed, I knew that Frank Egan had killed her, and I only had to find out how he had done it."

Some days passed without any further developments. Egan stayed as close to me as possible. I owned a small summer cottage at Emerald Lake near Redwood City, about thirty miles from San Francisco. I had built an outdoor boxing ring on the property. This and the lake made the place a mecca for all my athletically inclined friends, and during the summer we spent practically every weekend there. I took Egan along, for he had confessed that he felt lost when I was not around.

It was a Sunday afternoon. The customary group of young men and women were assembled at the Emerald Lake cottage. There had been much boxing and swimming, and now we were playing bridge and listening to the radio. Frank Egan sat close beside me, watching my play.

Suddenly the music on the radio stopped to permit an announcement which froze us in our seats: "Verne Doran has confessed to the murder of Jessie Hughes. He has implicated Albert Tinnin in the crime and says that they were employed by Frank Egan to kill the woman, so that he could collect her insurance."

I jumped up and caught Egan by the arm. "Come on, let's get out of here," I commanded. I knew that it wouldn't take long for the police to find where I was, and they would surmise that the public defender was with me. It was a good guess. Within ten minutes of our departure they were at the cottage. There wasn't any thought of Egan's running away, but we wanted time to find out exactly what had happened, and we wanted to arrange his arrest without giving the police the opportunity to employ the same tactics they had used on Albert Tinnin. Egan was at the cracking stage, and I wanted him to regain his balance. I drove him to San Francisco and stowed him away where he would be safe for the time being. There was nothing improper in this: he had not been indicted; no charge had been filed against him; and he was under no obligation to turn himself in.

This is where the girl enters and the TV "love angle" begins. I want to make a digression to explain that girl and my subsequent involvement with her. At this time I was a confirmed bachelor, or thought I was. I was also personable and athletic. I had risen spectacularly from poverty to wealth and from obscurity to at least a parochial fame. I was a San Francisco personality. I enjoyed my physical prowess and would do nothing to diminish it. I neither drank nor smoked. As to more personal vices, having thrown away the monkish morality with the daffy theology of the Roman Catholic Church, I embraced a pagan hedonism. I loved the girls and there was no shortage of them. However, there was one thing I was completely sure of, and that was that none of them could ever inveigle me into matrimony.

One evening a friend, one of a party which was going dancing at a local hotel, phoned me. His car had broken down, and he asked me to pick up his date en route to the affair. He gave me her name—Vivian Moore—and her address. I called for her quite casually, but when she opened the door I almost literally lost my voice. She was beautiful. She had a face and figure to turn any man's head. During the ride to the hotel, that's just what she did to me; I couldn't keep my eyes off her, and she was frankly delighted to meet me. She said that she had heard of me and wanted to meet me for years. I didn't know it at the moment, but by the time we got to the hotel I was roped and tied. I would have rejected any suggestion to that effect with scorn; I was thirty-three years old and she was nineteen.

We had a wonderful summer; the days were longer and sunnier than they had ever been before; the nights were warm and full of stars and moonlight; the skies had brighter hues; the birds had learned new songs. I didn't admit it, even to myself, but I was in love. Vivian had nerve too. We took up horseback riding, and on the fourth or fifth ride her beast ran away with her. She turned him up a hill and kicked him along until he stopped, exhausted. Then she calmly rode him back again. She terrified me by plunging into the icy water off Monterey and starting off toward Japan. When she made it back to shore, I was so torn between fury at her recklessness and relief at her return that I didn't know whether to slap her or kiss her. Now I had to enlist her courage in a delicate incident in the Egan case.

Having deposited Egan in a safe place, I decided to take a day or so to find out how the land lay and then surrender him. This easy plan was thwarted by an unexpected development. When I arrived at my own home, I found an automobile containing four men parked directly opposite it. As they bundled out of their vehicle there was no mistaking their trade—plain-clothes cops.

The leader flashed his badge and announced, "We have orders to take you down to headquarters."

"What's this about?" I demanded.

"Dullea wants to talk to you," answered the detective.

"Have you a warrant for my arrest?" I asked.

"No we haven't," he conceded.

"Then you're not taking me to headquarters or any place else," I asserted defiantly.

The officer looked somewhat nonplussed. "Do you mind if we go in and call the chief on your phone?" he asked.

"Not at all. Come on in."

The detective dialed the police chief's office and was presently explaining to him that I refused to accompany them. I could hear the official sputtering at the other end of the line, and finally I said, "Here, let me talk to him."

"What's this all about?" I asked the chief.

Chief William Quinn, usually an easygoing sort of man, sounded as though he were on the verge of hysteria. "What's it all about?" he shouted. "Listen, Hallinan, this town's in an uproar; you get Frank Egan in here right now or I'm going to charge you with complicity in the murder of Jessie Hughes."

I answered him with exaggerated iciness. "Frank Egan will come in and surrender, if there is any complaint or indictment filed against him," I informed him. "If you or your men interfere with my movements, I'll sue you for false arrest. You'd better simmer down and realize that you're an officer of the law, and stop letting your office be run by the newspapers."

I handed the phone back to the detective. After some minutes of conversation, most of which, at our end of the line, consisted of "Yeah" 's and "Unh-hunh" 's, he hung up. He turned to me. "The chief says that you don't have to come down to headquarters unless you want to. But we're going to stay right here with you, and we're not supposed to let you out of our sight until Egan comes in and surrenders."

"Make yourselves at home," I assented cheerfully. "I'll cook us up a pot of coffee."

I stepped into the kitchen, went right out through the back door, over the next-door fence, out the alleyway and to the home of a friend whose automobile I borrowed.

I was now in a quandary. I wanted Egan to go in and surrender before he could be arrested, so as to use that fact as an argument of innocence later. I surmised that every prowl car would be alerted to look out for me, and as I was fairly well known to a great many policemen, it was likely that I would be picked up before I could make contact with him.

I had to enlist someone else to advise him, and first choice fell to my adventurous girl friend. I phoned her and asked her to meet me at a secluded place on the outskirts of the city, as I had a somewhat difficult job that I wanted her to do for me. I drove to the appointed place and waited longer than I had expected. She finally arrived, flushed with excitement.

As I had expected, as soon as my absence was discovered an all-points bulletin had been put out to pick me up. What I had not expected was that the police would know of my sentimental involvement with Vivian, and acting upon a long established principle, stake out her residence as the likeliest place to apprehend me. Scarcely had I concluded my phone conversation with her, when her doorbell had rung. She'd answered it, and two burly plain-clothes men had stepped by her, the leader barely flashing his badge and announcing, "We're looking for Vincent Hallinan."

"Well, he's not here," she said.

"We'll just take a look," replied the officer.

This was Mike Desmond, a ponderous old veteran of the department, famous for his pungent comments and awkward errors. He disliked Arthur Jonas, one of the assistant district attorneys. Surveying him through the glass window of the courtroom door one day, he announced in his broad Irish brogue: "Arthur Jonas! By Christ, he's well named, he's the original throw up on the sands!" He was once sent to apprehend a woman swindler who was a passenger on a ship which docked at San Francisco, and by mistake he was directed to the cabin of a prominent European noblewoman. She endeavored to establish her identity, but Mike would have none of it. "Look," she protested, endeavoring to show him her passport, "I am the Countess So-and-So." "Sure, ma'am," agreed Mike amiably. "And I'm the pope." And he hauled her off to the hoosegow, creating an international incident which required an apology from the State Department.

Now he sat down with mock amiability, announcing, "Well, we're just waiting here until he comes."

Vivian had protested. "But he isn't coming here; I don't know him that well. I may not see him for weeks."

"Oh yes you will," Desmond returned, with bland assurance. "You're his girl, and he'll be getting in touch with you."

She sat for awhile, wondering how to meet this emergency. Then she stood up and started to walk from the room. Desmond barred her path. "You're not leaving this room, young lady," he informed her.

"I hope I'll be permitted to use the bathroom," she replied icily.

The detective stepped aside with some embarrassment, and she entered the bathroom. She opened the window, stepped upon a stool, climbed out into the porch below, descended the apartment-house stairway, tipped over a flowerpot—which enabled her to climb over the low fence—and hurried into Golden Gate Park. Ten or fifteen minutes later she heard the sirens wailing around her, and hid in the shrubbery until they had disappeared. Then she hailed a cab and drove to the spot where I was waiting.

I was upset at the position I had put her in, but she was elated and insisted on carrying out the errand. She took a cab, left it a couple of blocks from where the public defender was holed up, went to the address I had given her and delivered the message. By this time headlines were out that I too had disappeared. Some sort of pandemonium was averted when Egan strolled into an outlying police station and calmly surrendered.

In procuring his indictment, the prosecution had moved in such manner as to insure him the smallest chance of defending himself. Doran had been taken before the Grand Jury, where he gave the barest outline of the circumstances of the crime and of Egan's and Tinnin's asserted connection with it. The jurors were requested by Isadore Golden, the deputy district attorney, not to ask him any questions. This was to hamper the defendants in subsequent cross-examination and also to deprive them of the opportunity to contradict his statements. Dullea filled in enough to avoid a dismissal on the ground that the accomplice's testimony was uncorroborated. This made the skimpiest sort of record upon which to work.

Since then the law has been liberalized to require the prosecution to furnish the defendant in a criminal case with copies of the statements of prospective witnesses, and he is furnished other means of discovery which prevent the "blackjack" proceedings that were available to the prosecution in the Egan case.

However, I had in my employ an investigator named William Shaughnessy, who proved a veritable Sherlock Holmes in discovering just what the prosecution had. Thanks to his diligence, we entered the trial better prepared than the district attorney had supposed we would be.

Unhappily, the newspapers had built up such prejudice and hostility against the defendants that it was impossible to procure them a fair trial. In addition, they had a judge who was determined to hang them. This was Frank Dunne, a withered old tyrant. He had presided at a series of trials involving the bribery of public officials of the city and county of San Francisco back in 1906, and had conducted himself then about as unfairly as he did now in the Egan case.

Coghlan and I fought him every inch of the way, but the evidence was tough and the prejudice created by the long newspaper campaign put a win out of the question. The jury was out for seventy-two hours, but returned a verdict of guilty as to both defendants. However, we were able to raise enough doubt so that they fixed the penalty at life imprisonment instead of death.

Then came the real shocker. Detective Captain Charles Dullea gave an interview to the newspapers, revealing some matters which had not emerged at the trial. One of the people whose names had figured in the case from time to time was a Dr. Nathan Housmann. He was a close friend of Frank Egan's.

Dullea now revealed that for some time Housmann had been suspected by the police of having acted as a surgeon to the underworld, particularly in the removal of bullets from some of its denizens who had been wounded by the police. A police officer had been killed and his assailant, though wounded, had made his escape. Believing that this man would seek the assistance of Dr. Housmann, the police had installed a dictograph in the physician's office, and for a considerable period had listened to everything that had transpired there.

Dullea now asserted that on two separate occasions the officers stationed at the listening device had heard Frank Egan and the doctor discuss at length the proposed murder of Jessie Hughes and how the same could be made to appear accidental so as to procure double-indemnity insurance.

Dullea said that he had gone to Mrs. Hughes' home and warned her that Egan was plotting to murder her, but that she had dismissed the warning with a laugh.

Questioned as to why he had not used this evidence upon the trial, he said that both he and the district attorney's office were certain they had a perfect hanging case without it, and they had not wished to reveal the fact that they had been engaged in such espionage as he now revealed.

If the newspapers had been aggressively hostile to us before this disclosure, they now became ferocious. The savage penalty of life imprisonment imposed upon the defendants was denounced as unconscionably lenient. As it put the defendants beyond further vengeance, they concentrated on me, meanwhile blasting Dullea for not producing the evidence which they were sure would have resulted in the execution of the two defendants.

There were editorials demanding that the Bar Association move to punish me for my conduct during the trial. The device I had employed to shield Egan from newspaper inquiry and from questioning by the officials was assailed as an unethical stratagem to thwart justice.

During the trial Dunne had found me guilty of contempt of court and sentenced me to twenty-four hours in jail, and had ultimately and during the closing argument of the prosecution expelled me from the courtroom and appointed another lawyer to represent Egan. Throughout the proceedings the newspaper descriptions of my conduct had gradually deteriorated. First I had been "resourceful and combative"; then "crafty and truculent." Now I was "unscrupulous and insolent."

All this had an influence upon the general public. Only the experienced criminal lawyers approved my conduct of the case. Walter McGovern told me that on one occasion during the early part of the inquiry he had sat at the same luncheon table with a number of Superior Court judges and prominent lawyers of the city. During the meal there had been a great deal of discussion of the Egan case. He said that the consensus was that I was injuring Egan by my truculence and by forbidding him to discuss the case with the newspapers and other officials. They felt that Egan's obvious willingness to talk was a strong indication that he had nothing to conceal. McGovern said that he had to sit there silent, smothering within himself the desire to burst out: "If all you goddamn fools knew what Hallinan knows about the case, you'd know that he's doing exactly the right thing."

The impression which the situation made upon the general public, and the picture which had been constructed of me, can be best illustrated by the fact that one day a woman called at my office and offered me $5,000 to have her husband murdered.

Business fell off, and I had plenty of time on my hands. I started spending more and more of it with Vivian. Then she gave me a shock. She and her mother were going to Los Angeles to spend a couple of weeks with an aunt. Actually, I feared I was a little more involved than I wanted to be. When we waved good-bye, I felt a certain sense of freedom. In a few days I got a letter from Vivian. She was having a wonderful time; there were all kinds of parties and dances; she was meeting many new and interesting friends. I was depressed.

When she had been absent about a week, Bill Shaughnessy came into my office and sat down. "Listen, Vin," he said with a laugh, "cut out acting like a grizzly bear who has lost her cubs, or everybody in this office is going to walk out on you. For Christ's sake, phone down and have that girl come back home."

I looked at him with astonishment, but a light had dawned. My ugly mood flew out the window; I knew exactly what I was going to do.

A few days later the lady returned. The round trip was made on one of the coast steamers which then carried passengers between San Francisco and Los Angeles, and which has since been discontinued. I was waiting on the dock when the ship berthed. I could scarcely contain myself when I saw my sweetheart at the rail. I hurried up the gangplank to meet her, interfering with the exit of the other passengers. As we stood hugging and kissing I blurted out, "Will you marry me?" An old fellow whose progress we had impeded smiled indulgently and said: "Sure, she'll marry you. Now please let us get off this ship."

Next day we drove to Reno and were married. That evening I said to her, "I am supremely happy, and do you know, I never thought I would marry you or anyone else." To which she replied, "The first night I met you I knew we'd get married." When I recovered from this one, I went on, "I really got nervous when I found you were having such a good time in Los Angeles—" "Oh," she interrupted, "I didn't have a good time at all; I was miserable."

"But you said in your letter—" I began. "Oh, Vin." She laughed. "I love you, but you are really a terrible fool, and you don't know a single thing about women."

We settled down to domesticity, and gradually business picked up. However, I didn't make a decent fee until a case broke which required just about those qualities which the newspapers had accused me of possessing.

In November, 1933, Brooke Hart, twenty-two-year-old son of a wealthy San Jose family, was kidnapped. Anticipating a ransom demand, the police tapped his parents' telephone so as to enable them to trace immediately any calls received upon it. Finally the expected contact was made. The caller's location was established at once, and the police sped to it and seized John M. Holmes as he was leaving the telephone booth. According to the newspaper accounts which followed, the arrested man confessed, not only to the kidnapping, but to the murder of the boy. He named as his accomplice Thomas H. Thurmond, who was quickly taken into custody. The story published was an atrocious one. The two men were said to have bound their victim's limbs with wire, affixed a weight, and thrown him from the San Mateo Bridge. When he had somehow managed to gain a pier and cling to it, they dispatched him with pistol shots.

Public opinion was naturally inflamed. The Santa Clara County newspaper and radio went to outrageous lengths to whip it up further. A lynching atmosphere was created which became critical when the ghastly remnants of the boy's body were recovered from the spot indicated by his slayers.

Holmes' father, a quiet and respectable man who conducted a tailoring business in San Jose, employed me to protect his son's rights. He paid me a considerable fee. I arranged to meet him the following morning at the Santa Clara county jail where we would have a conference with the arrested man. I then communicated with the governor's office to demand state protection for the accused men.

That evening the San Jose radio broadcast two disconcerting notices. One was that the crafty and insolent lawyer who had all but thwarted justice in the Egan case had been employed to extricate Holmes and Thurmond from their just deserts. The other was that James Rolph Jr., Governor of California, had replied to that lawyer's demand that he furnish protection to the defendants with the flat statement that if they were lynched he would pardon the lynchers.

To be quite truthful, I was rather elated to be in the case. There was an exhilaration in coming to grips with fate in a desperate cause. Also, we needed that fee.

Shortly after dinner the background radio music was interrupted to allow a news flash. A mob was storming the Santa Clara county jail, intent on lynching the murderers of Brooke Hart. I grabbed the phone and called a local newspaper. It confirmed the radio report. It had an open line to San Jose and furnished a running account of the grisly incident until the two men were dangling from the trees of Saint James Park, across the street from the county jail.

A couple of days later I returned the money received from Holmes' father, and shortly afterward filed an action on behalf of his wife and two minor children for damages for his unlawful death. I joined as defendants Governor Rolph and the Santa Clara County radio and newspaper. I included a large number of John Does who were either participants in the lynching or cops who had stood around and watched it, without attempting to rescue the victims. I had press photos of several of the latter with automatics strapped on, looking singularly detached while murder was being committed before their eyes. As Rolph was a resident of San Francisco, I was able to file the action in that county. However, he died shortly afterward and the defendants had the case removed to Santa Clara County where it died too.

The Egan case also died. Egan and Tinnin each served twenty-five years in prison before they were released on parole. I had made numerous efforts to procure paroles for them, but was thwarted by the continued hostility of one of the San Francisco newspapers and the fear which it engendered in the parole board.

Finally the managing editor who had kept the hate alive passed away. Judge Dunne and Prosecutor Golden had long preceded him. Egan, now seventy-three years old, finally emerged to move like a shadowy ghost among the scenes of his former triumphs. In a couple of years he was dead too. Of all who had been so diligent in his prosecution, only Charles Dullea survived.

I have often been asked: "Was Egan really guilty?" To which I can only reply in one way. I never bothered to ask him.

Part III

My Most Important Case and Politics

CHAPTER 13

The Case Which Changed
My Life

IN 1949, James Martin MacInnis, although only thirty-eight years old, had an established reputation as a trial lawyer. He had a long record of victories in both civil and criminal actions. Brilliant and resourceful, he was frequently employed by other lawyers to try difficult cases. Thus he had gained experience beyond his years. He had encountered almost every situation in which a trial attorney can find himself.

It was therefore surprising when, in the course of the trial in which he was then engaged in the United States District Court, with an overflow crowd in attendance and reporters from all over the country recording almost every word uttered, he stepped to the rostrum and addressed the presiding judge. "Your Honor, in all my experience I have never seen anything like this morning . . . In the course of what was transpiring I told my clients, 'This isn't really happening; you are just dreaming. Forget about it!' . . . To say that I am astonished is a weak word!"

The statement did not cause the surprise one might expect. For it expressed the sentiments of most of those who heard it. Also, their capacity for dramatic novelty had been about exhausted by preceding events.

I had been the central figure in these events. At a command from the judge, two bailiffs had stepped behind the chair in which I was seated. They had seized me by the arms. They had pulled me from it. The order they were obeying had climaxed a half-hour denunciation of me from the bench. It included a sentence of imprisonment in the Federal Penitentiary and a decree striking my name from the list of lawyers licensed to practice in United States courts.

I had moved for a stay of execution of these decrees. A specially appointed deputy to the Attorney General of the United States had vigorously objected to any such stay. He had urged the immediate carrying out of the sentence. He had referred to me as a "mad dog."

The chief deputy in charge of the fraud division of the Attorney General's office had joined in his associate's objection and had stated that he would not refer to me as "counsel," since to do so was to "prostitute" that title, and said that I was making "a bawdy house of the Temple of Justice."

The chief deputy of the United States Attorney of the district in which the trial was being held had added his voice to that of his two confreres, had insisted upon the immediate execution of the decree, and had given his opinion that representation by me was detrimental to my client.

What crime had I committed which drew upon me this storm of insult and injury?

None.

What had I done or said which was improper, unethical, contrary to correct legal procedure, or even discourteous?

Nothing.

I had been asked by some friends to undertake yet another criminal case. It involved the celebrated labor leader Harry Bridges, who, with two other officers of his union, Bob Robertson and Henry Schmidt, had been indicted by the United States Government on a charge of conspiracy to procure citizenship by fraud. I had met Bridges briefly about a year before, but had had no further acquaintance with him. I had a general idea of his history, but did not learn the details until I had become involved in his case and had read the records of his previous hearings in order to prepare for the coming one.

He was a native of Australia who had emigrated to the United States in the 1920's, finally gravitating to the San Francisco waterfront as a stevedore.

He had found conditions there atrocious. The work, which was hard and dangerous, was sporadic and uncertain. To procure it, the men were required to "shape up" daily—that is, to assemble on the docks so that working crews could be selected from those available. This selection was done on the basis of "kickbacks" to the labor boss in charge. The stevedores were ground between these corrupt leaders and the powerful Waterfront Employers' Association. The latter facilitated the extortions of the bosses, in return for keeping wages low and hours long.

This system was deeply entrenched. It had been in operation for many years. It is still employed on the docks of New York City. A movie, *On The Waterfront,* with Marlon Brando, defined the problem. I state this so that you will understand the difficulty of the task which Bridges confronted in undertaking to destroy it.

He was adroit, courageous and uncorruptible, and he had a social conscience. When his activities became threatening, he was visited by a well-known retired pugilist, who presented him with two alternatives. One was a loaded pistol; the other $20,000 and a return ticket to Australia. Bridges turned on his heel and walked away.

Finally, in 1934, enough insurgency had been generated to risk a strike. It extended to all the ports on the Pacific, and was a long and bitter one. Police and soldiers were used against the strikers, many of whom were killed. The excessive violence of the employers and the authorities working with them produced an unforeseen effect. It swung public sympathy to the workers. A general strike was called by other unions, and this brought victory to the longshoremen.

A subsequent strike in 1938 consolidated their gains and led to the formation of the strong and militant International Longshoremen's and Warehousemen's Union, with Bridges as its president.

During the strike and continuously thereafter the Waterfront Employers' Association made strenuous efforts to get rid of the plaguy Australian. When he could be neither frightened nor bought, a campaign of slander was opened, with the purpose of exciting public opinion against him and facilitating the employment of Government agencies to do the dirty work. He was stated to be a British agent sent here to destroy the American maritime industry.

By 1938, the British bogey was pretty well washed up as a haunt. It had, however, been replaced by an even scarier one. The Soviet Union, still groaning from the pangs of a terrible birth, was even more foreign than Great Britain. Its hostility to capitalism was identified with its contempt of religion. In the instant crisis, it was a natural.

The British-agent charge was abandoned. It was now alleged that Bridges was a Communist, devoted to the forcible overthrow of the United States Government. In this he was stated to be serving the Russian-led world revolutionary movement.

The waterfront employers, who considered their interests synonymous with those of the nation, did not propose to allow moral abstractions or legal niceties to interfere with their protection. They invoked the aid of the United States Immigration Department to accomplish their objective.

At this point I interrupt to suggest a startling thesis which may shock you. Simply stated, it is: *In dealing with many agents of the U. S. Government you must assume, until the contrary is completely established, that these representatives might commit felonies, suborn perjury, conceal evidence, bribe witnesses, intimidate jurors, convey information to judges, and otherwise engage in practices which would be the cause for disbarment or imprisonment for a private attorney.*

For the ultimate of such venality, corruption, force and fraud, one can turn to the Department of Immigration. Let there be a strike of agricultural workers in California or Texas, you will find its agents scouring the lettucefields to seize and deport recalcitrant immigrants pointed out by planters. Let an alien sea-man assert some right by law or contract, and his employer can count on the minions of this agency to quiet his complaints.

The victims of these activities are not only foreigners; they are poor and obscure foreigners. You will not hear their cries for justice, save in the anti-Americanism of embittered wetbacks south of the Border, or in the hatred of mariners marooned on alien shores.

The Immigration Department agents turned to ridding the waterfront employers of Bridges. Tenacity is a virtue rarely recognized as such. But we must at least concede this virtue to Immigration. For it permitted neither rain nor snow, dark of night, defeat, disappointment, disclosure of its corruption and fraud, decisions of the U.S. Supreme Court, scorn and contempt of those who viewed its works, to stay the swift completion of its appointed task. It persisted day and night, by fair means or foul, to accomplish the destruction of Harry Bridges. *And it kept this up for over twenty years.*

By the time I entered this panorama the department had already completed several hearings. The first had been held before a regular immigrant department examiner. The proof was not forthcoming. There was no evidence which would support an order for deportation. The hearing had ended without an adverse finding.

Then the department really got to work. Bridges said that agents tapped his telephone and dictagraphed his sleeping quarters, dogging his every step; they subsidized enemies; they threatened friends; they intimidated the weak; they bribed the venal. In this fashion they accumulated a quantity of gossip, rumor, perjury, venom and other legal garbage, which they sorted out, arranged, classified and labeled.

Then they filed a petition for deportation. But here luck intervened to undo their frantic efforts. President Franklin Roosevelt had appointed James Landis, former Dean of Harvard Law School, to conduct the inquiry.

In the meantime the wily Bridges had not been sleeping. His union maintained a small staff for the special purpose of anticipating just such evidence as was now presented. For years it had collected and filed every scrap of information it could gather concerning potential hostile witnesses. This list included enemies of the union or its officers, professional stool pigeons and informers, renegade Communists, strikebreakers, Red squad cops, and others. Its files were full of transcripts of testimony before congressional and state committees, facsimiles of court records, copies of speeches, books and pamphlets, photostats, microfilm, newspaper clippings, affidavits, personal histories and memoranda of conversations, all ingeniously indexed. It required only a few minutes to produce the dossier of any particular individual. Such foresight was amply repaid in the trial before Landis.

The Immigration Department poured out a swarm of skid-row bums, drunkards, professional strikebreakers and Red-baiters. These witnesses swore that Bridges had said he was a Communist, or had been, or intended to be; that he had expressed kindly feelings for one or more known Communists; that he had failed to express hostility to others; that he was opposed to war or imperialism or colonialism or the use of troops in strikes.

In every instance the defense produced from its astonishing files some statement of the witness, usually sworn to, which impeached his testimony. In addition, he was shown to have been in contact with forces openly out to get the bothersome labor leader, or was being paid for his testimony, or had a private grudge to satisfy.

Landis heard the evidence with a sour look, and promptly found it unbelievable. He decided that there was no credible testimony that Bridges was, or had been, a Communist, or that he had "affiliated" with Communists within the legal meaning of that term.

The Immigration Department shook off this reverse. With a stubbornness worthy of a more appealing cause, it began anew, joined by the State Department and the Federal Bureau of Investigation.

The wire tapping and dictagraphing were redoubled. They rented apartments in the neighborhood of the victim's home, and from these kept watch and ward. They photographed his visitors, calendared his entries and exits, trailed him afoot or by automobile, looked, spied, delved, questioned, asked, cross-examined, glared, threatened and menaced.

Finally they collected a basketful of "proof," about equal to that which had upset Landis' digestion, and filed another petition for deportation. This time the Department of State picked its own umpire, who probably had to swallow hard, but found that Bridges was indeed a Communist.

The State Department's board of appeals promptly reversed him. Dean Acheson, an attorney for the House of Morgan, performing his tour of duty in Washington as Secretary of State, as promptly reversed the board. He ordered the battered labor leader deported.

The union appealed, first to the United States District Court, and then to the Circuit Court of Appeals. It lost out in both. Then the U.S. Supreme Court granted a hearing. Justice Frank Murphy wrote its decision, annulling the order of deportation. His opinion was a blistering document. It narrated the years of persecution which Bridges had endured and damned the conspiracy which had nurtured it. It said in part: "The record in this case will stand forever as a monument to man's intolerance of man ... Seldom, if ever, in the history of this nation, has there been such a concentrated and relentless crusade to deport an individual because he dared to exercise the freedom that belongs to him as a human being and that is guaranteed to him by the Constitution."

But the Immigration Department wasn't through yet. Bridges filed a petition for citizenship. Two officers of his union, Bob Robertson and Henry Schmidt, were invited to sign the customary formal affidavits attesting his good character, an honor accorded them as a reward for the years of effort they had expended in his cause. They were to pay well for it.

The petition for citizenship came on for hearing in the Superior Court in San Francisco. An official of the Immigration Department attended it. He informed the court that the department had no objection to offer, although it was not satisfied that the applicant was not, or had not been, a member of the Communist Party.

The judge turned to the witness. "Mr. Bridges," he said, "are you now, or have you ever been, a member of the Communist Party?"

"I am not and I have not been," was the answer.

The applicant had given this same testimony on each of the three preceding investigations.

An order granting him citizenship was entered. The Immigration Department shed its coat, rolled up its sleeves, and was off once more. It exploited treason, rewarded treachery, intimidated loyalty, fostered discontent, heated resentment and capitalized on domestic and foreign strife. Best of all, it bided its time until every circumstance appeared to have fallen into the pattern assuring success.

The great Red hunt was in full fury. Everyone from senators to comic-strip characters was assailing the Communists. A New York daily justified narcotics addiction in Asia as a preventative to Communism. Gangsters grumbled about police spoiling their little pranks when they should be concerned with the master menace. Russian émigrés, nuts, con men, and frauds, emerged with wondrous tales of conspiracy and were lionized, stuffed with chicken à la king at luncheon meetings, and ushered into congressional boards of inquiry.

Then the U.S. Government indicted the Communist leaders. They stood their ground, shouting defiance, while the estimated 75,000 Communists in the United States—one to every 2,000 in the population—all patently accused of the heinous plot to overthrow the country, fought back. Old men who advocated public ownership of the means and instruments of production and were now political criminals, raised bail and circulated petitions. Drab workingwomen picketed courts and circulated petitions. They damned imperialism, condemned the atom bomb and Cold War, fought for Negro equality, and demanded peaceful relations with Communist countries. The Government took their schools off tax-exempt rolls, plagued them with excessive income-tax assessments, seized their funds, and padlocked their offices and news-papers.

The charge was tenuous. Technically, it accused them of having engaged in a conspiracy to teach and advocate the desirability of overthrowing the Government of the United States by force and violence when the opportune moment should present itself.

The public, by now, wasn't interested in philosophical refine-ments. Its critical sense dulled by the wave of propaganda, the public was assured that the victims were automatically guilty of treason and espionage. Further, they were plotting to turn the country over to Russia. This was trite stuff; but it worked. McCarthy, Martin Dies, and smaller vermin, spread the miasma of credulity, panic and hysteria over the intellectually unwashed like a plague.

In such happy circumstance the Immigration Department pro-cured a criminal indictment against Harry Bridges in its fourth try.

This charge in *United States vs. Harry Renton Bridges* involved some complicated legalisms. It was based upon the contention that he had committed perjury during the hearing on his applica-tion for citizenship when he had stated that he was not, and never had been, a member of the Communist Party. However, this had occurred more than five years before, and a charge of perjury was barred by the three-year Statute of Limitations. As the lay-man puts it, it was "outlawed."

The Immigration Department found a way around this ob-stacle. There was a section of the United States Criminal Code which punished frauds against the Government, and a six-year limitation statute applied to it. The Government, therefore, charged that, in obtaining his citizenship, Bridges had defrauded it out of that intangible commodity. It alleged that Bob Robertson and Henry Schmidt had conspired with him to perpetrate this fraud, and it made them codefendants in the indictment.

Too, the department had a new friend. Thomas C. Clark was Attorney General. Although a newcomer in the ranks, he was not to be outdone in zeal by his cocaptains. In frankness, he outdid them. There was a strike of the ILWU in Hawaii. Clark boldly announced that he hoped the indictment would break it. Subsequent to the Bridges trial, he was promoted to the Supreme Court of the United States by President Truman, and is now its most reactionary member.

As I have stated, I did not know any of these facts concerning the Bridges case until after I had entered it. Up to that time, my ideas concerning politics and economics had been pretty fuzzy. I was not taken in by that anti-Bolshevik campaign. Thirty years before, I had thought that the Russian Revolution was the greatest step humanity had taken forward since the French did in their tyrants, and I had heard nothing credible to change my opinion. I did not believe that the Soviets ever intended to attack the United States, and I was aware why it was pretended that they did. I believed that capitalism, as an economic and political system, was outmoded and would be replaced by some form of socialism. I did not like to see the Communists, or anyone else, pushed around. But I was personally well off. It was no skin off my nose. I did, however, sign some petitions, contribute some funds, and express indignation at the witch hunt when anyone asked me about it.

In a hazy way I still believed the ancient lessons in constitutional law thumped into every student: the Government's power is divided into three bodies—executive, legislative and judicial—and the latter stands as a bulwark between the Government and the people. It would seem that a reasonable amount of cynicism should have thrown doubt on this. After all, the three departments were part of the same government. Would it be strange that the right hand should release what the left hand bound? Would it be eccentric to believe that a corrupt politician—suddenly elevated to the bench—might not really change?

When Bridges came to me I listened, admittedly with wry amusement in part, to his story. I had only a vague outline of the background I have just narrated. But I knew the law was not easily warped and twisted to satisfy the whims of any economic class.

I had read with amazement of the alleged antics of the attorneys for the principal officers of the Communist Party who had been before Judge Harold R. Medina in the U.S. District Court in New York. The newspapers contrasted the fairness and patience of the magistrate with the rudeness of the lawyers. They pictured the judge, sticking to the issues with firmness and courtesy, faced with what was apparently a deliberate effort to disrupt the proceedings and get a mistrial by fair means or foul.

He had come through his experience lionized, finding the defendants guilty, and sentencing them to the maximum terms allowed by law. That he had quite naturally found their attorneys guilty of contempt of court and sentenced them to maximum terms, only brought new praise from bar associations and the press.

The Bridges case was presented to me only two months before the date set for the trial in November 1949. There was not much time for preparation, let alone formalities. I was first approached to learn whether I would handle the case. Having expressed willingness, an appointment was made for the defendants to come to my home.

They were an arresting and interesting trio. Bridges and Schmidt were about the same age, that is to say in their late forties, but there the resemblance ended. Bridges was tall and wiry, with sharp features and an aquiline nose. Indeed, his aquilinity did not end there. He had the bold glance and fierce courage of an eagle. Some part of him was always in motion. He was possessed of a restless energy which kept his hands, his shoulders, or the features of his face, involved in some activity. His speech was of the same character. He came quickly to the point of discussion, and any questions which he asked were sharp and incisive.

Schmidt was a Dutchman in the traditional pattern. His complexion was pink and white, and his thinning hair was blond. In temperament, he was almost phlegmatic. When he spoke, which was seldom, he did so quietly and deliberately, but what he said disclosed an active, vigorous mind. For the most part, though, he sat quietly smoking his pipe and allowing the conversation to be monopolized by his more voluble companions.

Robertson was a big, strongly built man. He looked much more the working-class type than either of the other two. He had been a prize fighter in his youth, and his nose bore some marks of that trade. He was high strung, and to him everything was black and white.

The contrast between the three men can perhaps be best illustrated by their conduct, when long after this they learned that the Supreme Court had reversed their convictions and thrown out the case against them. This good news arrived while the three were engaged in conference with other officers of their union. Bridges sat silent, and a tear rolled down his cheek; Robertson fainted; Henry Schmidt took another puff on his pipe.

At this first session these defendants shared a gloomy view of their prospects. From this I assumed that they were guilty and knew of evidence which would convict them. I had tried some fairly desperate criminal cases and supposed that this would be one of that description.

I was much surprised by the first statement they made concerning it. Acting as spokesman for the three, Bridges informed me that we would begin with the understanding that they had complete confidence in me and would withhold nothing from me; that I could start out with absolute assurance that the testimony he had given in the Superior Court was true and that neither he nor either of his codefendants had ever been members of the Communist Party.

This announcement was as pleasing as it was surprising. I had won many actions in which I had to dispute indisputable facts and refute irrefutable evidence. Taking apart a manufactured case was child's play. Yet I puzzled over the inconsistency between the defendants' declarations and their pessimistic outlook. I asked them to explain.

"First," said Bridges, "you must understand that this is a political case. Ever since '34, the Government has been working with the waterfront employers to get rid of me."

He outlined the history of the proceedings. "After the Supreme Court reversed the deportation order," he continued, "the United States Senate passed a bill ordering me deported, 'notwithstanding any act or decision.' It was the first act of attainder ever passed in this country. The Attorney General advised them that it was unconstitutional, and it was never sent to the House of Representatives. When they will go that far, you can see how anxious they are to put me out of circulation.

"The anti-Communist hysteria they've stirred up is just what they need to do it. They've been whipping it up for years, and they're using the courts to destroy the Communist Party. Right now, anyone who can be shown to have associated with Communists, or to have worked with them, won't have a ghost of a chance.

"During the '34 and '38 strikes we got a lot of help from the Party. Most of their people were old-time labor leaders, and they knew organization and strike tactics. We were taking help from whoever would give it to us, and we used their printing presses and lawyers. They helped us get bail and represented the strikers who were arrested. We sat down with them a thousand times, and we took their advice when we thought it was useful.

"I've admitted all this in the other proceedings.

"The New York case opens the door wide for them. Anyone who had ever had anything to do with Communists will be considered just as bad as they are. Every judge in the country will copy Medina. They want their pictures on the magazine covers too.

"They'll hand-pick juries and frame evidence.

"Also, don't forget what happened to the New York lawyers. I know some of those men, and they're damn good lawyers.

"We're not crying, and we're fighting every inch of the way, but we know what we're up against.

"They'll show that we played around with the Communists; they'll get a couple of stool pigeons to say they signed us up in the Party, or that we told them we were members, or what-have-you—and we'll land in the bucket."

"Mr. Bridges," I said earnestly, "don't let anyone tell you that. I only know about the New York case from what I read in the papers, but it seems to me to have been badly handled. In the first place, there were too many lawyers. The trial of a case is as much an art as a science. By that, I mean that all sorts of things must be done or left undone, for which you can give no reason. You just feel that it's the right thing at the time.

"When you have several lawyers, acting independently, you lose that element.

"I think, too, that the New York lawyers let themselves get too much involved, personally. They acted as though they were on trial themselves. They lost their tempers and let the judge put them in a false position.

"However, I don't know enough about that case to pass a worthwhile opinion on it; but I will tell you this. I have been practicing in this city for many years and have had many cases in the Federal Court. I know all the judges out there, and they are decent men. Frank Hennessey, the United States Attorney, is completely honest. I think that if he knew a government witness had committed perjury, he would expose it himself.

"The juries are selected from the great register of voters. They are ordinary people, like ourselves.

"Despite the newspapers, you are well thought of in San Francisco. Nobody has ever questioned your integrity.

"We'll pick a jury very carefully; we won't start off with any bias against the judge. If he starts off with one against us, we'll win him over. I don't believe that the United States Government will produce false witnesses against you. If it does, it will be very remarkable if we don't expose them."

The defendants regarded me doubtfully.

"In each of the Immigration hearings," Bridges informed me, "they put on ten or twelve of the worst perjurers you ever heard. My lawyers exposed them all right—but the Government went right ahead, and they found a decision against me on one of them."

"This time," I assured him, "you are in a court and before a jury. The hearing officer in an immigration proceeding is part of the department which is trying to get you. That department can't use the Federal Courts in the same way they can use their own employees. The very fact that there have been so many previous attempts will warn the judge that there is some improper motive behind them.

"San Francisco has always been a strong labor city. Things like that have an influence on both the court and the jury. If they try to use false witnesses, we should be able to show them up. The exposure of even one such witness is usually enough to finish off the prosecution's case. The jury feels that it is being imposed on and looks with suspicion on all the evidence.

"If the judge isn't fair, we'll take care of that all. I've seen juries lean over backward to acquit because they thought the judge was helping the prosecution.

"No. I can't see any reason for pessimism in your case. Of course, any. case can be ruined by bad handling, but you can be sure this one won't be."

These sagacious observations having passed without further dispute, I proceeded to more practical things.

"From what you tell me," I said, "the prosecution will not be able to produce any authentic application for membership in the Communist Party which has been signed by any one of you, nor any membership card bearing your signature, nor any canceled check in payment of dues. Is that correct?"

"Nor any document of that nature whatever," asserted Robertson.

"What kind of witnesses did they produce at the Immigration hearings?" I asked.

"Bums," replied Bridges, "derelicts, drunkards—the kind the Waterfront Association can pick up for a dime a dozen in any Embarcadero saloon."

I smiled deprecatingly. "Believe me," I assured them, "if the Government tries to make a case before a jury on that kind of evidence, we will have a field day. Let me read the transcripts in the Immigration hearings. They might change my opinion, but I doubt it."

Next day, I received the reporters' transcripts of the two Immigration proceedings. The testimony in both had been much alike. There was a great deal of it to the effect that the strikers had accepted help from the Communist Party in the 1934 and

1938 strikes—which Bridges freely admitted. A few witnesses had stated that he had made admissions to them over the years, either directly to the effect that he was a member of the Party, or that which could be taken as inferring membership.

These witnesses were shown to have "scabbed" on the strikes, been expelled from the Union, or have been on the payroll of organizations dedicated to the crusade against Bridges. Every one of them had been impeached in some manner, usually by previous contradictory statements in writing. The trial would be a breeze.

There was one disturbing element. The case had been assigned to the Department of United States District Judge George B. Harris, and I had some personal difficulty with him. Although I had no information that he did, I feared that Harris might entertain some animosity from this event. I sent for the defendants and acquainted them with the facts, suggesting that we might ask for another judge. Some months before, Harris had been trial judge in a proceeding in Hawaii in which the ILWU was a party, and had given a decision in its favor. From this and other circumstances, they believed that he would be as fair as any other available judge, and perhaps a bit fairer.

By this time I had completed reading the transcripts of the prior proceedings. At the end of our discussion I said to them, "Generally, lawyers try to paint cases blacker than they really consider them. Then if things go wrong, they can point out that they had expected it. On the other hand, if they go well, they can claim some extra glory. I don't believe in raising false hopes, nor in scaring people. If a case looks bad, I say so; if it looks good, I say so. Usually they turn out about the way I predict. There's a lot of work still to be done on this one, but I think I have a fair grasp of it now. I don't think the Government will put on the kind of testimony the Immigration Department did. If they do, we'll demolish it in short order. We're going to get a fair trial and get a quick acquittal!"

CHAPTER 14

The Bridges Trial

THE Bridges Trial started in November 1949. MacInnis and I had laid out a program which we supposed would avoid the circumstances which had so prejudiced the Communist defendants in New York. As I have said, we had accepted the newspaper accounts of their trial. We had taken for granted that the defense lawyers had been guilty of the misconduct with which they had been charged. We were not acquainted with any of them, and had no knowledge of their abilities or experience. Thus, we did them the injustice of believing that they had conducted themselves as the newspapers had described.

There was to be nothing like this in the Bridges case. We would assure that the defendants received all their legal rights; we would be vigorous and persistent; but we would carefully avoid anything which could be construed as discourtesy to the judge or opposing counsel.

The Government had appointed two Washington, D. C., lawyers to conduct the prosecution. When we entered the court we went up to these two, introduced ourselves, welcomed them to San Francisco, offered our cooperation in anything which would facilitate the trial of the case and even contribute to their comfort and entertainment while they were in the city. They responded affably, and we seemed to have started out on the course we had determined upon. When Judge George Harris took the bench and bestowed a friendly smile and greeting upon the participants, we repaid his cordiality with interest. By the time the jurors were selected we had apparently established a camaraderie in which we imagined the case would float to a happy conclusion.

This illusion was speedily undone. The prosecution made a short opening statement, and I rose to give the jury an outline of our defense.

It is my practice in criminal cases, wherever the circumstances permit, to make an extensive opening statement on behalf of the defendant immediately after the prosecution has concluded its own. I consider this to be of vital importance. If the prosecution is permitted to conclude its evidence before any word from the defendant is heard, the jury will probably arrive at a judgment which must then be torn down and another constructed in its place. If the defense has already cast doubt on the prosecution's case, the jury will probably reserve judgment until it has a chance to hear from the other side.

In the present instance it was absolutely necessary to get before the jury the history of the continued persecution of Bridges, the interests behind it, the corrupt and dishonest means employed to destroy him, and the fact that the present prosecution was but a continuation of the old campaign.

Otherwise we probably would have a trial in which several witnesses would swear that the defendants were members of the Communist Party and they would swear that they were not.

Accordingly, I had prepared an opening statement which it would take several chapters to narrate. Believe me, it was a dramatic and revealing narrative, and I felt that its successful conclusion would establish an atmosphere for the trial which would reveal its real purpose and put anything the prosecution could produce under immediate suspicion.

I commenced as disarmingly as possible. I informed both court and jury that the purpose of the statement was to give a general outline of what the defense would be, so that they could determine the purpose of such cross-examination as we might employ and the direction which our evidence was to take. I said that such time as was consumed in it would, therefore, ultimately save a great deal more. I stated that of course the facts I was about to narrate were not evidence, and were to be understood by the jury only as a general outline of the nature of the defense.

I was careful to make courteous reference to the prosecution attorneys and flattering observations on the legal ability and judicial demeanor of the trial judge. The chief prosecution attorney, a man named Donoghue, had been specially appointed to conduct this case. He was fiftyish in appearance, with a ruddy face and one eyeball deflected somewhat from its normal orbit. He had probably been an officer in the Army, wearing the shoes affected by that profession. The hair on the sides of his skull was clipped extremely close, to eliminate its gray.

As my statement progressed he sat complacently absorbing the courtesies which I now and then directed toward him. Not so the judge. I had run along for about an hour when I noticed that he was regarding me with a look of apprehension.

Presently he suggested, in a mild enough manner, "Mr. Hallinan, I don't want to interrupt you, but it seems to me that you are going somewhat afield in this matter. I really do not see what the history of the turmoil on the waterfront has to do with the charge of perjury against Mr. Bridges."

I hastened to assure him of the propriety, legality and materiality of the matters I was propounding. I advised him that we proposed to show that such witnesses as the prosecution would produce were actuated by motives stemming from the situation on the waterfront which I had been describing. I stated that we knew the names of several of the prospective witnesses, and that we wished to warn the court and jury in advance of their biases, prejudices, interests and connections. I repeated that the time consumed in my opening statement would result in a great saving of time and trouble later, since court, counsel and jury would know the purpose of the questions which would be thereafter addressed to these witnesses.

His Honor sat back, apparently at a loss. Then one of the

prosecution's staff, Robert McMillan, began to object to my procedure. McMillan was a grizzled old-timer who had spent many years in the United States Attorney's office. He affected a folksy, homespun way. Up to this time he and I had always been on terms of affability.

Harris frequently attempted to curtail my address. I plodded on, yielding—or appearing to yield—where necessity required. I felt that it was absolutely necessary to get in that opening statement, and I was not going to be prevented from it except by some irresistible force. I succeeded to the extent that by the end of the first day I had painted a picture which could never be eliminated from the minds of those who heard it, and which of necessity had to color their final opinions concerning the case of the *United States vs. Harry Bridges.*

Meanwhile, McMillan's objections increased, and finally Donoghue joined in. The judge's comments became more acrid and pointed. However—and this is most important—he never made any flat ruling that the matters I was enlarging upon were improper, nor did he require me to exclude any specific subject from them. At most, he would say, "It seems that my rulings do not have any great effect upon you, Mr. Hallinan. You seem to ignore them."

Legally, I could not consider these as rulings at all. The statement I was making was entirely proper, and I was entitled to make it. If I had desisted from doing so upon comments such as those above, then—if things went wrong—I would have no basis for an appeal on that ground. The Appellate Court would have held that the trial judge had not made any ruling, and that under the circumstances I was entitled to continue with my statement; that if I chose to stop upon mere comments by the magistrate, then I had no ground for complaint.

Harris was fairly new to the bench. A more experienced judge might simply have said: "That is all, Mr. Hallinan. Sit down. Mr. Prosecutor, put on your first witness." Which would have finished the incident.

By the evening of that first day Harris was interrupting more and more frequently, in a way which would have disconcerted a less experienced campaigner, and the prosecution's lawyers were also interrupting with objections at every available opportunity.

What was worse, Bridges himself appeared very unhappy. When I got home, I found out why. The courtroom was crowded with newspaper reporters from all over the country. During the afternoon recess two of them, who were on friendly terms with my defendant, approached him and his wife, one of them inquiring anxiously: "Harry, what the hell's the matter with Hallinan? This judge is a good fellow, and he'll give you a fair trial, but Hallinan's rubbing him the wrong way. You'd better get him to lay off antagonizing Harris, or you're going to lose your case right at the start."

The defendants called a council of war and acquainted me with this advice.

"That isn't so, Harry," I warned him. "Those fellows didn't get the picture, and apparently you haven't yet. It's quite plain what Harris is up to. He has seen Medina's picture on the cover of *Time* and he is going to out-Medina him.

"This is his golden chance to be a great national figure. You're more important than the Communists in New York, and I'm a more shining mark than any of their attorneys. He set out to get a conviction on you in the calmest and most legal fashion imaginable; incidental to this was the necessity of squashing me. He hasn't been able to do either of these things yet, and he sees his plans going astray, so he's blowing his top.

"If I take program from him in the way your friends indicate, you'll have a nice, clean, short trial. Eight or ten stool pigeons will swear that you were a member of the Communist Party with them; you'll swear you weren't; and the jury won't be out half an hour."

After a lot of arguing back and forth, I left him half convinced, but it was obvious that I had to win over more than the jury. The clients, the newspaper reporters and the spectators, believed that I was butchering the case.

Next morning when I recommended my opening statement, the atmosphere became charged with electricity. I had scarcely uttered six sentences when McMillan was on his feet.

248] *A LION IN COURT*

"Your Honor," he demanded, "these statements that Mr. Hallinan has just uttered are in direct defiance of the rulings that you made yesterday. I submit that he is in contempt of court, and I suggest that this court take some steps to vindicate its own dignity. Mr. Hallinan and I have been friends for many years, but I am more concerned with the dignity of the United States Court than I am with that friendship, and I say now that he should be punished for contempt of court."

I was astonished at the statement.

"Mr. McMillan," I said, "aside from the friendship which you mentioned, I am astounded that any lawyer should stand up in court and demand that his opponent be cited for contempt of court. The statements I have been making are perfectly proper and material; and it is certainly a lamentable spectacle that you should endeavor to incite the court and to arouse any ill feelings, on his part, against me."

"I do not think Mr. McMillan's remarks are ill-timed at all," said the judge, "and unless you watch out, Mr. Hallinan, you are going to find out that I may have to take exactly the remedy that he has suggested."

"Your Honor," I remonstrated, "I have the highest respect for both you and the court, and under no circumstances would I attempt to circumvent your ruling. However, I am compelled to assign the statement that you have just made as misconduct on your part and to ask you instruct the jury to ignore it."

"I will do no such thing," he all but shouted, "and I warn you that a great deal of the matters you have been talking about have no place in this trial. I am not going to say anything further, and I will leave it to you to conduct yourself in accordance with the wishes which I have expressed."

Here was another avoidance of a direct ruling. I went right ahead with my discourse.

"We will show you," I continued, "that the United States Immigration Department, in its efforts to destroy Harry Bridges, installed dictaphones and other listening devices in his hotel room—"

Donoghue was on his feet, screaming. When he paused McMillan took up the refrain.

Harris glared and growled, "I warn you now, Mr. Hallinan, not to mention that subject again in your statement. The charge you have just made is improper, and you know it is improper. You are displaying a constant contempt for this court, and I am not going to permit it."

"I am again compelled to assign the court's statement as misconduct," I said. "I ask that you instruct the jury to ignore it. It is entirely improper for the court to so characterize my statement and to threaten counsel in the presence of the jury."

That was the pattern for the remainder of this particular matter. Every paragraph brought forth a protest from the prosecution table and an assignment that I was guilty of contempt. Every objection was sustained, upon which I shifted to other grounds and went blithely on.

By noontime the atmosphere was really electric. Nobody was speaking to me. The defendants, their families and friends dined together, but I was not asked to join them.

When court reconvened, the Government put on its first witness. He was an innocuous enough individual, an Immigration Inspector named Gardner. He established a few technical matters, and was surrendered to me for cross-examination.

My first question caused the roof to fall in. I asked him, "Mr. Gardner, did you ever have anything to do with installing a dictaphone in a room occupied by Harry Bridges in a hotel in Portland, Oregon?"

Harris hit the ceiling. He ruled that the question was improper and in direct defiance of the rules he had laid down during the opening statement. I demurred gently that I was entitled to show the witness' hostility. He answered that the witness had said nothing except what could be proven by public records. I demurred that the witness nevertheless subjected himself to the ordinary cross-examination; that I was entitled to show his bias. Abruptly, Harris called a recess and stepped from the bench into his chambers. An hour or more elapsed before he returned.

He then read off a statement of two pages or more, reciting my alleged misdeeds and misconduct. He finished by announcing: "I find you, Vincent Hallinan, in contempt of this court, and I sentence you to a term of six months in the Federal Penitentiary, and I further order that your name be stricken from the list of attorneys licensed to practice in this court." He motioned to the bailiff. "Take him into custody," he ordered.

Pandemonium broke loose in the courtroom. Two deputies, one on each side, seized me by the arms. I was not the least disconcerted; indeed, the extravagance of the proceeding made it amusing.

With the two officers clutching my elbows, I stood up and addressed the court with exaggerated *sang-froid*. "I desire at this time to address a motion to the court," I said.

"What do you want to say?" the judge snapped back.

"I can state it more in conformity with the dignity of a court," I replied, "if these gentlemen will release my arms."

"You'll get used to them," replied Harris. "You will find them very cooperative."

"I have not the slightest doubt of that," I answered affably. "Meanwhile, I assure Your Honor that I have not the least intention of endeavoring to escape."

"Let him go," Harris ordered.

I walked to the lectern as unperturbedly as though I were engaged in the most ordinary discussion. "The motion I wish to make is this," I stated. "The case on which we are engaged is a complex one; I have spent the time available to me in learning its details and am better prepared to defend Mr. Bridges than any other lawyer whom he could procure in time to continue with the trial. I therefore request a stay of execution upon the judgment which you have just pronounced until the termination of this case, so as to enable me to continue to represent the defendant."

This casual approach disconcerted Harris. He of course wished to avoid a possible mistrial, and knew that it would be impossible for Bridges to procure counsel to proceed with the case, as it then stood. He called Bridges to the witness stand and questioned him as to whether or not, if I were summarily removed from the case, he could procure another attorney to continue with it.

Bridges rejected the suggestion. "I have chosen Mr. Hallinan to defend me," he said, "and if he isn't allowed to do it and things go wrong, I'll never think I had a fair deal."

Harris turned to the prosecution bench, hoping to secure some suggestion from it which would enable him to effect a dignified retreat. "Mr. McMillan," he said unctuously, "of course we are dealing here with a fellow attorney; as you say, you and Mr. Hallinan have always been on friendly terms, and I would like your opinion as to the motion he has just made. That is, whether he should be permitted to continue in the case at this time, or whether my original order should be carried out."

McMillan dumped him. "In my opinion he should be removed from the case right now, and the sentence of the court carried out," he stated dogmatically. "I dislike to take this position, but I feel that my duty to this court compels me to do so."

Harris turned to Donoghue. "Well, Mr. Donoghue," he said, "will you give us your opinion on the matter? You have had a great deal of experience in Washington and other places, and the court would appreciate your views on the matter."

Donoghue moved to the lectern, squeezing the muscles of his head and face together until his neck turned red, and went all out. "Your Honor," he charged, in vigorous denunciation, "this man has been raging through this court like a mad dog ever since the inception of this case. I do not believe that Mr. Bridges will be harmed in the least by his expulsion from the case; in fact, I believe that he will be much better served by any other lawyer who can come in here and try it."

As a last resort Harris turned to the other Washington prosecutor. The latter was a tall, bony fellow, with a hooked nose upon which his spectacles customarily rested while his head was thrown back to prevent them from sliding off his proboscis. I am not sure that I ever really did know his name; he hailed from Tennessee and was known by the defense table, throughout the case, as "Sowbelly."

"Yo' Honah," he intoned, his head thrown back and the

spectacles bobbing in their place, "Ah hav nevah seen a spectacle lak this man has created in this coht. He is makin' a bawdyhouse uv the Temple uv Justice."

The prosecution trio had picked up the wrong cue. The judge was looking for an escape hatch, and they had failed to open it for him. He sat in thought for some moments, and then announced: "I want to take a recess at this time, to give this matter some thought. I'll make my ruling on the matter later."

He left the bench and entered his chambers. After half or three-quarters of an hour he emerged, quite bland and composed. "Gentlemen," he announced, "I have decided to grant Mr. Hallinan's request and permit him to remain in the case. This is done upon the understanding that he will hereafter conduct himself in a correct and courteous fashion. I do not wish to do Mr. Bridges an injustice, and I hope that everything will now go smoothly and that we will be spared any further recriminations or difficulties."

Under such happy auspices as I have described, the case proceeded. By this time the defendants, their wives and retainers, were pretty sure they had made a grave mistake in employing me to handle the case. To be sure, their attitude was more one of sorrow than of anger, but I was not accustomed to defending my conduct to my clients, and I didn't propose to let the newspaper reporters prescribe my tactics in a court.

It was an astounding trial. Personal enemies, Communist renegades, professional perjurers and similar riffraff, paraded in and out of the witness stand. Most of them were complete strangers to the defendants. The door to the hallway would open, a new witness would amble across the front of the courtroom toward the chair, and we would ask the defendants: "Who's this?" Almost invariably the answer was: "Never saw him in my life before."

None of them was difficult to deal with. Two or three had been enemies of Bridges for many years, and had put their sentiments regarding him on print in labor and other publications. These now served to destroy, or at least seriously damage, their testimony. Others narrated insignificant facts, usually as compatible with innocence as with guilt. Many, it developed on cross-examination, were subject to deportation or had some member of their families in that unhappy situation. They told of meetings between the defendants and Communist Party leaders during strike periods. In the opening statement I had warned the jury that the defendants, as leaders of the embattled Longshoremen's Workers Union, had accepted the help of Communists, Democrats, Republicans, and anyone who would lend a hand during the bitter strikes on the San Francisco waterfront, so these witnesses did us little if any harm.

MacInnis and I alternated on the cross-examination, and felt that we were effectually nullifying the Government's testimony.

Then, on the 21st day of the trial, came its most important break. The stand was taken by a short, middle-aged, jaunty Negro, who looked the audience over with the easy familiarity of the practiced witness. This was Manning Johnson, and we had considerable information about him.

As I have stated, during the many years the Government had been trying to get Bridges the wily Australian had been constructing his defenses. In addition to their ordinary functions, all the members of his staff had special tasks to perform—collecting, indexing and filing every scrap of information which presented itself, touching any past informer or anyone who might reasonably be expected to become one.

When the anti-Communist witch hunt got under way, there was added to this collection whatever could be garnered concerning the group of "professional witnesses" which the Government was using against the Communist Party leaders.

There was a stable of these worthies. In my opening statement I had warned the jury of them under the description "the Government's cageful of trained cobras"—a designation which has stuck with them ever since.

For several years Manning Johnson had been one of this unholy crew. When he announced his name from the witness stand, a messenger (whom we retained in court for the purpose) hastened to the Union building to discover what there was in the files concerning him, and he found plenty. Johnson had appeared often before the House un-American Activities Committee, and had dragged an obscene trail across the United States: here testifying against an embattled labor leader; there against a liberal school teacher. We had transcripts of all his testimony. He claimed to have been a member of the Communist Party for many years and to have gotten religion.

Now he denounced his old associates with a revivalist fervor. Asked by Donoghue under what circumstances he had left the Party, he declaimed, "I left because you cannot serve God and *'Beezlebub'*!"

I grabbed the opportunity to interrupt his narrative. "Just a minute," I demanded. "Could we have the name of the last person this witness mentioned? I would like to have this 'Beezlebub' identified before we proceed further."

The judge smiled benignly. "Maybe Mr. Donoghue would help us identify him," he suggested.

Donoghue rose to his feet, smiling, a bit embarrassed. "Your Honor," he began, "it is well known that Beëzlebub [pronouncing it correctly] is the Prince of Darkness."

"Well, now we're talking about two different people," I protested. "The witness is talking about Beezlebub and Mr. Donoghue, about somebody else again."

Having thus thrown a dash of the ridiculous into the witness' appearance, we sat back to hear, with considerable astonishment, a bizarre invention which was supposed to identify Harry Bridges as one of the leading members of the Communist Party of the United States.

Johnson testified that in 1936, as a member of the Communist Party, he attended its national convention, and that he was present when on June 28, the last day of that convention, the chairman announced to the audience that Bridges had been elected to the Party's national committee. He testified that during the announcement he could clearly discern Bridges standing in the wings of the stage from which it was being made.

MacInnis gave the witness a considerable twisting until the evening recess. We wanted him held for further cross-examination until we could consult the defense records for whatever might be available concerning him. Donoghue protested vigorously against compelling the witness to return, but could give no reason why he should not. Harris overruled his objection.

The objection became understandable when we had finished our researches in the magic files. We found plenty to impeach the witness' credibility, but we found something much more important.

Bridges had a phenomenal memory. Here we were, in 1949, and he started exploring the crannies of his recollection back thirteen years, in an effort to figure out just where he had been at the time the witness said he had seen him at the Communist Party's national convention in 1936.

"I'm pretty sure," he said, "that there was a Coast convention in San Pedro that summer, and that I reported on it to several of the locals; and it must have been just about the time Johnson says he saw me in New York."

Armed with this lead, some of the staff members began consulting union publications of that period. Several hours had elapsed when one of them strolled in, almost casually. "Here it is," she said. She presented an issue of a Stockton, California, daily newspaper of June 29, 1936, and indicated an item describing the appearance on the preceding evening of Harry Bridges at a special meeting of the Stockton ILWU local. The account gave a general outline of the speech which he had delivered on that occasion.

A telephone call to the Stockton union cinched the item. Its minutes showed that on the evening in question Bridges had spoken at length before the meeting, explaining the proceedings and programs of the Coast conference.

Now if we could pin Manning Johnson down to the exact time at which he claimed to have seen Bridges in New York, we could demonstrate to the jury that it was physically impossible that he could have done so. Next morning MacInnis adroitly committed Johnson to the exact hour at which the alleged incident had taken place.

He showed him a copy of the Communist Party's New York publication *The Worker*, which stated that the national com-

mittee had been elected on June 28, the last day of the convention. Johnson agreed that this was so. He was then induced to
fix almost the exact moment at which Bridges' election had been
announced. He said that it was almost precisely at 4:30 P.M.,
because he remembered that very shortly afterward the meeting
adjourned.

That did it. The minutes of the Stockton local showed that
Bridges had begun his talk at 8 P.M., and that preceding it he
had had dinner with some of the union officials. It was physically
impossible that he could have been in New York anywhere
around 4:30 P.M. and in Stockton, California, at 8 P.M. Jet
flight had not yet been invented, and the fastest planes took ten
hours to make the trip.

Having set this up, we bided our time. We supposed that some
other witness might be gently led into the same trap, and we
would wait to spring it when it would be too late for retreat.

The very next witness justified our patience. He was another
professional stool pigeon, Paul Crouch, who had testified as a
witness in dozens of cases for the Government, but he sat upon
the witness stand twisting and untwisting his fingers, his little
gimlet eyes darting above the enclosure of the courtroom, and a
look of apprehension upon his face.

Sure enough, he testified that he had once visited the Soviet
Union and had been made an honorable general in the Red
Army. Donoghue, apparently accepting this absurdity as true,
bowled right along with the witness until he finally led him into
the convention hall of the Communist Party in June 1936, and a
confirmation of Manning Johnson's testimony that he had seen
Harry Bridges there, and that he had heard the announcement
of his election to the Party's national committee. On cross-examination he confirmed, almost to the minute, Manning Johnson's estimate of the time this had occurred.

He knew, of course, what Johnson had testified to. I put my
questions in such a fashion that he assumed I was trying to get
him to contradict the latter's testimony, and took every opportunity to bolster his companion's story.

By the time the examination was finished he had committed

himself, unequivocally, to the statement that the appearance of Bridges in the wings of the convention hall and the announcement of his election to the national committee had occurred at 4:30 P.M. on June 28, 1936, give or take not more than ten or fifteen minutes either way.

Meanwhile we had prepared photostatic copies of the Stockton union's minutes and of the other available documents. Next morning we brought them, together with the originals, to court. I had determined upon a maneuver to interrupt the flow of the prosecution's case and to throw doubt upon it at its very apex.

I waited until the court had opened and the jury was in the box. Then I stepped up to the lectern with my bundle of material, laid it upon the clerk's desk, and announced: "Your Honor, I am constrained to interrupt the present testimony and to present to the court a matter of the utmost urgency. I have here conclusive evidence that the preceding witnesses, Manning Johnson and Paul Crouch, have both committed abject perjury. I have here absolute proof that at the time they say they saw Harry Bridges in New York at 4:30 P.M. on June 28, 1936, he was in Stockton, California; that he made a talk there before the ILWU local union at 8 P.M.; that he had preceded that by having dinner with some of the officers of the union; and that the occasion was recorded in the Stockton paper of the following day.

"It is my duty, as an officer of this court, upon learning such facts, to immediately lay them before the court. I am not allowed, even if I wish to do so, to retain this matter for defense or rebuttal and to allow the trial to proceed without informing the court of what has transpired.

"I now request leave to place on the stand evidence which will demonstrate that, as I have said, the witnesses Johnson and Crouch have committed perjury, and thereafter to move the court to take such steps in relation to it as will vindicate the dignity of the court and punish this contempt upon it."

The prosecution and the judge were caught flat-footed. The jury, of course, heard the entire statement. Nobody undertook to argue my contention of what I owed to the court, under the circumstances. Finally Donoghue arose and suggested, somewhat mildly, that the matter be heard outside the presence of the jury. To this the judge assented, and the jurors were led from the courtroom. The damage had been done, and the court had little choice but to pursue the path which I had suggested. I didn't give the prosecution lawyers time to think out whether or not the procedure was proper. I called Bridges to the stand the instant the door closed on the last of the jurors. He denied that he had been in New York in June, 1936, and asserted that he had, particularly, been in Stockton at the time I have stated.

We followed with the Stockton Union officials, introduced the pertinent documents, and in general used up the remainder of the day on that side issue. Next morning we got an unexpected assist. A gentleman came to my office, informed me that he had read the newspaper account of the preceding day's activities and could support the point we were making. He said that on June 28, 1936, his sister had been married at Stockton, and that following the ceremony the wedding party had gone to a local café; that a group of men at one of the tables had made remarks concerning the formal attire of the wedding guests, upon which one of them came to the wedding table and apologized for the misconduct of his companions; that he had assured the victims of their remarks that there would be no more of them.

This man was Harry Bridges, and so introduced himself, and the man offered not only to appear in the court and testify himself, but to bring with him several of the persons who had been present in the café on the night in question.

He had with him a copy of the Stockton paper of June 28, containing photos of the newly wedded couple, and said that this was what enabled him to be definite as to the time and place of his meeting with the union leader.

Of course we embraced the offer eagerly, and placed this gentleman and several of those who had been with him in the Stockton café on the stand to substantiate Bridges' alibi. We further produced the records of all of the major airlines operating between New York and San Francisco, and established that it was absolutely impossible that Bridges could have been in New York at any time during the afternoon of June 28, 1936, and in

Stockton that same night. At the conclusion of the showing I demanded that the court refer the matter to the grand jury and that the two witnesses, Johnson and Crouch, be placed in custody awaiting its action.

Naturally, we did not expect that this motion would be granted. Harris felt he had to do something, however, and did instruct the United States Attorney that he should refer the matter to his office to determine what proceedings should be taken. Of course we also knew that this was a mere gesture for the sake of the spectators and newspapers and that nothing would come of it. However, we had delivered a stunning blow to the prosecution and a general air of skepticism began to pervade the court and even to color the newspaper accounts of its subsequent proceedings.

In any proceeding except a political trial in the United States District Court, the prosecution's case would have been destroyed. If any remnant of it had remained, the next witness would have given it the *coup de grâce*.

He was a smooth, cocky fellow who gave his name as Lawrence Sedon Ross. As he did so I glanced toward the door and saw our faithful messenger departing to learn what information concerning him might be found in the magic files of the union.

The witness had just the proper background for a champion of good, honest Americanism against a foreign ideology. He said that he was born in Kentucky, the son of a small planter, and was a graduate of the University of Kentucky. He testified that he had been a member of the Communist Party for many years. He explained his entry into it on idealistic grounds, and his eventful disillusionment on a similar basis. He said that during part of the time that he was a member he had been editor of its publication the *Western Worker*. He claimed to have been a delegate to the national convention of the Communist Party in 1936 and to have heard Harry Bridges nominated and elected a member of its national committee. To this extent, he supported Manning Johnson and Paul Crouch.

However, he said that he had not seen Bridges in person at

the convention. This, of course, was to permit the argument that Bridges had been elected to the national committee at the 1936 convention all right, but that Johnson and Crouch might have been mistaken in their identification of the person they claimed to have seen there. Ross was not to be trapped in the pit into which Johnson and Crouch had fallen.

At noon we hastened to the union headquarters and examined the material which had been collected on this witness. Among this were the copies of the *Western Worker* for June, 1936, a period during which Ross had been its editor. Included also were transcripts of certain proceedings of the House un-American Activities Committee. These hinted at a possible discrepancy in the witness' testimony, which MacInnis was to exploit with devastating effect upon the prosecution's entire case.

A considerable time was spent upon articles appearing under Ross' by-line, as well as sworn testimony which he had given before investigating committees. All of these flatly contradicted the testimony he had given on the witness stand, in this case, as to the alleged illegal purposes of the Communist Party. Here he had sworn that that organization advocated the overthrow of the Government by force and violence, and in his preceding appearances he had sworn directly the opposite.

His cross-examination was resumed, and the newspaper articles were called to his attention. The accounts in the *Western Worker* of the 1936 Communist convention confirmed their testimony that the central committee had been elected on the afternoon of Sunday, June 28. He refused to confirm the fact. He said that the newspaper was loosely edited and could not be relied upon to establish the chronology of events at the 1936 convention. This, of course, was to give Johnson and Crouch another out. Possibly they had been mistaken as to the exact time at which they had seen Bridges present in New York.

Ross was a wily and experienced witness, evading fairly well the traps which the cross-examination set for him. He excused his past perjuries with the universal device: "At that time, I was a Communist."

MacInnis then switched to a subject which was to destroy the witness. In the transcript of his testimony before the un-American Activities Committee was a letter which he had written in July 1941, to its secretary. In this he had denounced the "slanders" which the committee had published concerning him.

Included in this letter was the following statement:

> Another such fanciful and fantastic touch put in to make the report more disagreeable, I assume, is that my real name is Rosenfeld and that I was born in the Bronx . . . however, I am not much perturbed at this barter since I recall reading some anti-Roosevelt campaign publicity in the 1936 election, in which the accusation was made that Roosevelt's real name was Rosenfeld.

MacInnis now began a cautious survey of this item. For greater clarity I will quote the transcript, verbatim, where it may be useful to do so.

Q. [By Mr. MacInnis] Now, Mr. Ross, where did you say you were born?

A. Bell, B-e-l-l.

Q. Bell County, Kentucky. And what date?

A. June 24, 1903.

Q. And your name has always been Lawrence Ross?

A. Yes.

Q. [By Mr. MacInnis] What was your father's name?

A. My what?

Q. Your father's name.

A. Sedon—S-e-d-o-n.

Q. Sedon what?

A. Ross.

Q. Where does he live?

A. He isn't living now, sir.

Q. Where did he live?

A. In Bell County.

Q. What was his occupation?

Mr. McMillan: Oh, may it please your Honor—

Mr. MacInnis: I have a purpose in this.

Mr. McMillan: Haven't we gone far enough in cross-examination?

Mr. MacInnis: I am not sure who this man is.

The Court: I think, not only with respect to this witness, but many of the witnesses who have been produced in this case, have been subjected to probably the most searching cross-examination of any case in which I have ever participated.

Mr. McMillan: Yes.

The Court: And I think that having gone this far, we might just as well go to the extent of finding out who his father was and his occupation. I will overrule the objection.

Mr. McMillan: May it please Your Honor, the other day, very respectfully I asked Your Honor to lay some limitation upon the extent of this cross-examination, and really, as I said then with becoming diffidence on my own judgment and out of all respect, it has really begun to get interminable, and I really don't want to personally sit here until the frost is on the pumpkin and the fodder is in the shock.

This was the first effort on the part of the prosecution to curtail the examination of Ross on this matter. They followed with a barrage in support of that purpose. The court having overruled these objections, the cross-examination continued:

A. He was a small planter, farmer, for awhile—most of the time.

Q. [By Mr. MacInnis] When you joined the Communist Party in 1927 in New York, didn't you state that your father worked in a clothing factory?

A. I don't recall that, no, sir.

Q. Do you recall whether you did or did not?

A. He didn't.

Q. Was your father a member of the ILGWU—the International Ladies' Garment Workers Union?

[Ross laughed incredulously.]

A. No, sir.

Q. You are positive of that?

A. Oh yes.

Q. What was the date of your first marriage, Mr. Ross?

Mr. Donoghue: I think, if Your Honor please, that there are some personal privacies in a man's life to which he is entitled to guard even as a witness.

The objections of the prosecution becoming more vociferous, the court finally adjourned the session to his chambers, where the Government lawyers instituted a new tack; that is to say, they set out to force MacInnis to disclose what information he had concerning the witness.

Thus the transcript discloses the following:

> *Mr. Donoghue:* I think, if Your Honor please, Mr. MacInnis should make an offer of proof. What does he expect to prove by questioning this witness with respect to the circumstances? I assume that is in his mind. . . . I think he should make an offer of proof.
>
> *Mr. MacInnis:* I don't see why I should tell these gentlemen.
>
> *Mr. Donoghue:* Well, if Your Honor please, I want to say for the record that I am an officer of this court and I am sure that Your Honor has, with respect to every lawyer who is an officer of the court, a confidence in his integrity.
>
> *Mr. McMillan:* Counsel has just stated he sees no reason for making an offer of proof and advising counsel for the Government of the nature of this proposed proof. Yet Your Honor will recall that he started to put the question in the presence of the jury, and the next step that was taken, he stated, was such a matter that he wanted to take it up with Your Honor. Now to me it is a most extraordinary situation, one of the most I ever saw, that counsel in a courtroom starts to ask a question before a jury, and upon objection being made, states to the Court that it is such a matter that he first wants to take it up with you, and you as a Court, and then steps in here and says he doesn't care to reveal the matter to counsel for the Government; when he was ready to put the question to the witness on the stand in the presence of the jury.

Finally, after an interminable wrangle, Harris ruled that MacInnis need not disclose what he had in mind in cross-examining the witness.

This ruling could scarcely be called generous. It would be utterly contrary to the very purposes of cross-examination to compel a disclosure of its purpose to the opposite side.

When the session was reopened in the courtroom, Donoghue

shifted to another device to discover how far our information went. He stated:

> In order that we may not be put in a position where we may have to ask for delay, and that we may be ready with another witness when the cross-examination of this witness is concluded, I wonder if Your Honor might inquire of counsel about how much longer they expect to have this witness on cross-examination?

MacInnis thereupon disclosed that he was expecting some information from the East Coast, touching the witness on the stand, and that he might be compelled to request the court to continue the cross-examination until the following Monday morning—this being Friday afternoon.

The examination continued:

> *Q.* Now, Mr. Ross, you told the Court and jury under oath on your direct examination that you were born in Bell County, Kentucky, did you?
> *A.* Yes, sir.
> *Q.* In what town in the county were you born?
> *A.* Not far from Middlesboro.
> *Q.* Not far from Middlesboro?
> *A.* Yes.
> *Q.* And you say that you went to the University of Kentucky?
> *A.* Two years.
> *Q.* And those years were what?
> *A.* Twenty-two and twenty-three, *I believe.*

MacInnis, who was still young and had clinging about him some of the filaments of his collegiate career, paused in unbelief at the phrase "I believe." That anyone should be uncertain concerning his golden college years was something beyond his comprehension. He pressed the inquiry further:

> *Q.* Where is the University of Kentucky?
> *A.* Lexington.
> *Q.* And under what name did you go to that school?
> *A.* The same name, sir.
> *Q.* Lawrence Sedon Ross. And you are quite sure you went to that school?

A. Yes, sir.

Q. Can you remember anybody in your class at that school?

A. I'm afraid not.

That did it. It was sufficiently incredible that the witness should not know the years during which he attended college, but that he should have forgotten the name of every other student in his class was really beyond belief. MacInnis knew he had him. He went on:

Q. Can you remember one person who was a college classmate of yours at that school?

A. No, sir; I took special courses and—

Q. Yes. You didn't go there at all, did you?

A. Yes, sir.

Q. Did you? Where did you go to high school, Mr. Ross?

A. Middlesboro.

Q. You are positive and you affirm now that you went to the University of Kentucky in the years that you have mentioned, under the name of Lawrence Sedon Ross?

A. Yes, sir.

MacInnis now requested that the cross-examination be continued until Monday morning and that the witness be held pending the arrival of the information which he expected from the East Coast.

At once a storm of objections broke out from both the prosecution table and the witness. Again Donoghue demanded that MacInnis be required to state exactly what he expected to prove on the material which he hoped to get. Ross broke in with an impassioned request to be freed, so that he could return forthwith. There was a special edition of his newspaper coming out. This was an obscure sheet published in Memphis, Tennessee, called the *Cotton Trade Journal.* The witness described its predicament:

It is an annual forecast edition, which we are way behind on. It would be terribly inconvenient to stay over until Monday, almost would demand a suspension of the publication. But it would amount to a monetary loss for the paper if that edition

didn't come out on time. . . . I spoke to my employer in Memphis
on the telephone Wednesday night. I told him then I had been
on the stand for that day and probably would be off the next day.
That was yesterday. He said, "Take care of yourself. We need
you here very badly. I am having to send out wires in order to get
some material in that only you can get. I doubt if I can get it.
And please start back as soon as you can, we need you here very
badly."

Harris inquired if he could go to Memphis, complete the
edition, and then return to the court for further cross-examination.

> *The Witness:* Well, that would be very difficult, for this reason,
> that beginning with this month, January, we have a series of
> special convention numbers. This month we have an annual fore-
> cast edition which is a rather bulky edition, which we get out
> every January. That is the edition I am referring to now. Then
> early in February we start a series of special convention numbers
> dealing with various segments of the trade, the cotton trade and
> industry. And from now until, I should say, June or May thirtieth,
> I think is the last one, these are published periodically. They re-
> quire my presence there.

Again, there was an adjournment to chambers, and again
Donoghue endeavored to discover how far our information went.

By this time MacInnis had in his possession a telegram from
the president of the University of Kentucky stating that no one
named Lawrence Sedon Ross had ever attended there.

He had a telegram from the principal of Middlesboro High
School to the same effect, and containing the additional information that, in response to a telephone call, he had sent a wire
conveying the same information to Bruce Barber, of the United
States Immigration Department, at the very courtroom where we
were trying the case.

In other words, we now knew that the prosecution attorneys
had definite information that their witness was lying. It took no
great acumen to understand that they were trying to ferret out
how much we knew and that they intended to slip their witness

out of the court's jurisdiction so as to prevent further examination of him.

Donoghue suggested that possibly a stipulation could be entered into as to what we had in mind. The court furthered this suggestion. MacInnis declined to comply with it and pressed for the requested continuance. The transcript continues:

> *Mr. Donoghue:* He isn't entitled to it, and ought not to interrupt the normal, ordinary processes of a trial for that purpose. If he has some definite objective, some valid reason for believing that if he were allowed time, he would impeach this witness, and would designate the point and tell us whether the point was, we wouldn't be in a position to say to Your Honor not to keep him here.

Finally and reluctantly, MacInnis showed his telegrams to Judge Harris. We had wished to avoid this, feeling sure that Harris would inform the prosecution of their contents.

There was no reason whatever for the long and involved wrangling about the continuance until Monday morning. Under ordinary circumstances, such requests are granted without prolonged discussion. The assurance, by the lawyer, that he has matters of importance to develop at the later date ordinarily suffices to procure such continuance.

The weekend was crowded with effort and excitement. On Monday morning we entered the courtroom armed to the teeth. We knew all about Lawrence Sedon Ross. However, when MacInnis rose to continue his cross-examination of that worthy, Donoghue interrupted him with unctuous formality. He first asked the judge to excuse the absence of Robert McMillan, who had become ill—the latter probably could not stomach the developments which he knew would ensue. After a lugubrious exchange with the bench on this subject, he continued:

> And now, if Your Honor please, since the adjournment of court on Friday, I have conferred with the witness Lawrence Ross—

Here MacInnis interrupted, demanding the right to continue the cross-examination of the witness without the interposition of any statement by the prosecution attorney. The *entente cordiale* between that worthy and Harris insured that the former would be heard. Permitted to proceed, he went on:

> *Mr. Donoghue:* Yes, Your Honor. As I was saying to Your Honor, since the adjournment of court on Friday last, I have conferred with the witness Lawrence Ross, quite contrary to my usual practice, with respect to a witness who is still under examination. My reason for so doing is to be found in the series of questions asked of the witness by cross-examining counsel, questions obviously purposed to show either that the witness Lawrence Ross is not the same Lawrence Ross who for some period of time was the editor of the *Western Worker* and a prominent active member of the Communist Party in San Francisco, or that be he the same Lawrence Ross, he was at some time during his lifetime known by some name other than that of Lawrence Ross. I feel it is my duty to call to the attention of this Court and jury the information which I have received since we last adjourned. However, rather than making the information available to the Court and jury by a statement of my own, I ask Your Honor at this time to permit the witness to make a statement now by way of correction and in explanation of certain testimony heretofore given by him—not with respect to any statement he has made in support of the allegations contained in the indictment, but only testimony he has given with respect to his name, his origin and his education. I think by every rule of law, if Your Honor pleases, a witness still on the stand is entitled to the right to make any explanation or change in his testimony which he feels proper, and on that basis I ask Your Honor that he be awarded, or afforded, that opportunity at this time.

Of course, permitting the witness to make such explanation would allow him to present it in terms most advantageous to himself, but the Court permitted him to do so.

Afforded this grace, the witness then informed us:

> Both on direct and cross-examination I made several misstatements. Those misstatements refer to my origin, my education, my name, my father's occupation and name. First of all, I was not born in Kentucky. I was born in Western Poland and came

to this country, I believe it was 1910, at the age of seven, in company with my mother, her sister, my brother. My father already was here at that time. I am a citizen. I think the technical term for it is a derivative citizen, based upon my father's naturalization papers, which I have asked Mr. Barber to check. I did not recall on Saturday, and do not of my own memory recall now, the date of that naturalization. I am informed, however, that it was sometime in 1915 and that both my father and I then became derivative citizens. I have never had any certificate of derivative citizenship, although I understand my brother has had for some years. . . . My education next. I never attended school in Kentucky. I attended grammar school in New York, high school in the Bronx, New York. . . . As a matter of fact, I didn't change my name at all. I Americanized it. The name originally was Rosenstein. I Americanized it to Ross at the time I was approximately sixteen, possibly seventeen years old, and since that time have not been known under any other name. So that for thirty years of my forty-six years of life—perhaps twenty-nine—I was known to everyone as Lawrence Ross. The reason for the change, of course, was an attempt at Americanization. That also was the reason for my adoption of Kentucky as my native state. . . . Now, as to my father. His name was, and still is, Rosenstein. He was perhaps—may be still, although I don't know—he is probably up in years—a member of the International Ladies' Garment Workers' Union. [He closed with the following sanctimonious exordium] The problem I was faced with, Your Honor and the Court, was a serious one in my life, perhaps the most serious I have ever faced. I had two alternatives, as I say it, as I wrestled with myself in the wee small hours of the morning: Shall I still keep these facts from the Government and from the Court, brazen it out, stick to my lies in an effort to save my marriage and my standing in the community, or shall I purge myself once and for all, altogether, and make a clean breast of it? And this I have elected to do. It was to me a great decision, a very difficult decision. I believe, I am sure, I have made the correct decision. I asked for help in this decision, help of a higher judge than sits in this court, and I was struck by one proverb I read: "Commit thy works unto the Lord and he shall establish thy thoughts." I have done my best to do that. This is the statement.

MacInnis developed these admissions on further cross-examination. Having established that the witness came to this country from Poland in the year 1910, the cross-examination proceeded:

> *Q.* And what was your first name at that time?
> *A.* I don't know. It has been Lawrence, certainly ever since I arrived here, I know. Arrived in this country, and that was at the age of seven. Now I assume that Lawrence is an Americanization of another name, but I don't know what that was.
> *Q.* You don't remember what name you were given in those years of your life?
> *A.* I know when I went to public school, first started public school, it was under the name of Lawrence. I am sure of that.
> *Q.* Well, you were seven when you left Poland and came to the United States?
> *A.* I would think so, if 1910 is correct, and I believe it is.
> *Q.* And were you able to talk at that time?
> *A.* I suppose so.
> *Q.* Well, what was the name given you in Poland? It wasn't Lawrence, was it?
> *A.* I wouldn't think so. It was Lawrence soon after my arrival here, I am positive.
> *Q.* Well, what was it up to the time you were seven years of age and came across the ocean?
> *A.* I believe I have it. It started with an L. I believe it was L-i-p-m-a-n, possibly L-i-p-m-a-n-n, I think. The name of Lawrence was given to me upon my arrival. Under the name I attended public school and have used it ever since.

To help expose this deception, MacInnis then inquired:

> *Q.* The report of the Dies Committee existed in printed form in the archives of our Government since July 31, 1941, carrying the accusations against you that I have read?
> *A.* I assume so.

Again Donoghue attempted to head off this inquiry. He demanded:

> If Your Honor please, is this examination still going to be examination unlimited?

Mr. MacInnis: Your Honor, times have changed since Friday last.

Mr. Donoghue: If so, in this way they have changed, if Your Honor pleases: Instead of requiring an extended cross-examination by the defense to develop certain matters, we made the disclosure forthwith this morning. Now, certainly in the light of that fact and in the light of the type of questions that have been asked here all day long, I again ask Your Honor to impose a limitation on this cross-examination.

The argument involving this request covers seventeen pages of the trial transcript.

Soon after that Donoghue produced a telegram from the University of Kentucky which—he was prepared to state—would show that the information had not been received by them until late Friday afternoon.

Of course, we were not going to accept his unsworn statement, and in addition here was another opportunity to let the jury know exactly what we thought about the prosecution counsel. I therefore initiated another discussion:

Pardon me, Your Honor. Are we to be bound by what this man says here now? Why should he be allowed to make a statement of that kind? Let him take the stand so we can cross-examine him to show their real interest in this case. We have accused him of being part of this conspiracy, accused him of it in open court, and he gets up here and vouches for another fellow who is just his tool, gets up here and reads a telegram and wants us to take his word for it.

The Court: Mr. Donoghue, reserve your showing, then—

Mr. Donoghue: This, if Your Honor pleases, is with respect to an objection to a question asked of this witness by Mr. MacInnis, in which he states that Mr. Barber made a phone call about noon on Friday to the University of Kentucky registrar.

Mr. Hallinan: We know he did, Your Honor, and let Mr. Barber take the stand and testify he didn't. We will show them whether he did or not. . . .

MacInnis called to the court's attention a question and answer which Ross had given after the disclosure of his identity and pursuant to the inquiry as to what statements he had made to the prosecution lawyers:

> Mr. Witness, so far as you know, if you had not made this so-called voluntary disclosure, these men were prepared to let you go ahead and stick to your story?"
> *Witness:* Yes.
> *Mr. Donoghue:* If Your Honor please, of course Your Honor knows as well as I do that in all these cases where the allegation in an indictment has something to do with Communism or the Communist Party, that the methods of defense are always the same: "Don't try the defendants, try the witnesses," and these men—and I feel I can state this freely now in the absence of the jury—these men have sunk so low that they have called me this morning a liar. I did not reply at that time, if Your Honor pleases, because my reply might not have been with the same measure of dignity with which I now address myself to Your Honor. It is a very difficult position in which I find myself, not as Mr. Donoghue, a member of the bar, but as a special representative of the Attorney General of the United States, in which capacity it would not be seemly to engage in a brawl with brawlers.

However, in enlarging on this theme he made the following devastating admission:

> *Of course, if Your Honor pleases, we are not fools, and it was apparent to me when Lawrence Ross on the stand on Friday afternoon was unable to identify a single student in the University of Kentucky, that perhaps he might never have gone there, and for that reason at my direction on Friday afternoon the telegrams heretofore identified were sent. . . .Of course, I knew that the Dies Committee or an investigator of the Dies Committee had sent a telegram and put it in evidence that Lawrence Ross was known by another name.*

This gave me exactly the opportunity I had been looking for. The fact that we were in a courtroom imposed considerable limitation upon the language which I would be required to use to express my complete opinion of Donoghue, but I did the best I could. The transcript recites:

Mr. Hallinan: Might I speak briefly on that, Your Honor? Now, we have the remarkable situation of this counsel, this special prosecutor, getting up here and admitting that he knew while the witness was on the stand and the questions were being addressed to him that he had committed some deception concerning his name and his identity; and that after the adjournment of this court, he suggested to Mr. Barber that he wire these people. What did he do when he suspected that the witness was deceiving the Court and the jury? He fought as vigorously as he could to get him out of that witness chair, out of the court and out of the state. He made a determined and vigorous effort, bolstered by the witness himself, to prevent the Court, the jury and counsel from determining whether or not there was any falsehood or any deception in the witness' testimony. And this man vigorously, actively, almost fiercely, importuned the Court as to the injustice and the wrong that was being done the fellow because he couldn't get out his special edition of the paper, and his children couldn't get back to school, when he stupidly—because I don't think he does it honestly—admits that he knew from the witness' demeanor and answers that he was telling lies on the witness stand.

The witness who followed Ross proved the means by which we could expose further trickery on the part of the prosecution. His name was Louis Michener. His testimony was unimportant, but a circumstance involving his appearance proved otherwise.

Government agents had worked diligently for years, not only to build up a case against Bridges, but to produce confirmation, or rather what could be called confirmation, of their witnesses. For example, when a witness would testify to some meeting that he had attended in San Francisco, a hotel record or some similar matter would be introduced to show that he had actually been in San Francisco at that time. They seemed to think that these "confirmed" the witness' testimony.

There is a hill in Ireland which has a large depression on its summit. Nearby is a heap of debris roughly corresponding in bulk with the cleft on the hill. This spot is called "The Devil's Bite." The natives affirm that St. Colum was chasing the devil out of Ireland, and the latter—in order to hinder the saint's pursuit—bit a chunk out of the hill and spat it back in his pursuer's path.

The skeptic is asked how he can have any doubt about the truth of the story, since there is the bite and there is the bit.

This was somewhat the same reasoning as moved the prosecution to suppose that such indications established the veracity of the witness' testimony. However, they went along with the device until they were almost drowned in records in the cases of Johnson and Crouch.

Now, for Michener, they abandoned the procedure. On cross-examination he testified that at one meeting in which Bridges had been present he had stayed at a certain hotel in downtown San Francisco. As he was specific both as to the time and the persons who accompanied him and stayed at the same hotel with him, we checked that item. During a recess MacInnis and I went to the hotel and were permitted by the manager to examine its records for the time involved. There was no card showing that Michener had stayed there at any time near the date which he had assigned. We asked the manager if there were any other records which might disclose that, and gave her the name we were seeking. She replied that there was nothing else that would show it and that the records she had given us were complete. We subpoenaed her to bring the records to court and she duly appeared.

Thereupon Donoghue, obviously embarrassed, got up, holding in his hand one of the hotel's registration cards. It showed that Michener had in fact registered there at the time he had stated.

Being questioned, the manager stated that the Government agents had come to her hotel some weeks before, had gone through the files, and extracted the card showing Michener's registration. She was asked why she had not told us this when we appeared and questioned her about it. She said that the Government agents had instructed her not to tell us that the card was in existence.

Obviously it was the prosecution's intention to keep the card secret, to produce it if it served their purposes, and to repress it if it did not.

Such was the atmosphere in which the case of the *United States vs. Harry Bridges* was tried. We smashed witness after

witness. We exposed item after item of fraud, corruption, suborna-
tion of perjury, and complete dishonesty on the part of the
prosecution agents. Under ordinary circumstances there could be
no question of the outcome. The case would be a breeze.

Unhappily, there were elements that we could not overcome.
One was the anti-Communist hysteria which was being whipped
up to its highest point at the time, and which necessarily infected
everything connected with the case.

Next, there was an intimidated jury, and it was kept so deliberately. A Federal jury is ordinarily in that condition *ab initio*.
Here the prosecution maintained a garrison atmosphere, with the
courtroom swarming with Federal agents. The prosecution
lawyers were not only permitted but encouraged to insult and
berate both the defendants and their counsel.

On the last day of the trial the Government stationed an FBI
agent outside the home of each juror, releasing to the papers a
statement that it was done for the protection of the jurors.

Toward the end of the case the two reporters who had so
criticized my conduct during the opening part of the case came
up to Bridges, his wife and mine, who were chatting together
during a recess.

"Harry," said one of them, "we have something we want to
get off our chests. We owe Vince Hallinan an apology, and we
haven't guts enough to go up and say it to him. This judge is a
son of a bitch! He was out to get you from the very start of the
case, and Vince was the only one who saw it."

One turned to my wife. "Will you tell your husband that?" she
asked. "We're ashamed we said what we did, and we should have
known better."

Somewhat later the United States Circuit Court of Appeals
directed an oblique but biting criticism toward Harris in his conduct of the Bridges case. The defendant, while on bail, had
delivered a talk to his union in which he criticized the American
government for intervening in the Korean Civil War. Upon this
ground, Donoghue moved to revoke his bail. Harris granted the
motion that threw the labor leader into prison. The Appellate

Court reversed the order and restored the defendant to bail. In its opinion it said, in part:

> There was a period in English history when high judges prostituted themselves to the role of mere instruments for carrying into effect the arbitrary will of the Crown.... In times of national danger the courts should, and have generally refrained ... from interfering with coercive measures of the executive ... but it is one thing to refrain from interference and quite another to become, themselves, the tools of military expedience.... It is the duty of the courts to set their faces like flint against the erosive subversion of the judicial process.

The case was on trial for five months—from November 14 until the following April 4. I used five and a half days in argument. The jury was out four and a half days and then returned a verdict finding the three defendants guilty.

Long afterward we found that the prosecution had pulled a trick on us which we had not discovered. A relative of Bridges had furnished the Government with an affidavit, not admissible in court under California law, which stated that Harry Bridges was in fact a member of the Communist Party, that she had seen the card which had been issued to him under a fictitious name.

However, on this trial Donoghue came forward with this document and asked to have it introduced "for the purposes of identification." We assumed that he hoped the papers would print it and thus bring it to the attention of the jury, and we were insistent that the court prevent any such disclosure. Harris then instructed the clerk to keep the document locked in his desk and not to allow any person to read it.

We wondered what use the prosecution intended to make of the affidavit. We supposed that some effort would be made to cross-examine Bridges concerning it, and thus bring to the jury's attention the fact that it existed. We were prepared to prevent this and to demand a mistrial if it were attempted.

The case closed without any such effort having been made, and the document was forgotten. That is to say, it was forgotten by us. We did not know what the real purpose was until, as I have said, years later, when some of the jurors informed us that—during their deliberations—this affidavit had been smuggled into the jury room, had been read by all of the jurors, and formed a large part of their reasons for finding the defendants guilty.

Harris beamed with delight when the verdict was returned. He complimented the jury upon its "intelligent understanding of the issues." He sentenced Bridges to five years in prison and Schmidt and Robertson to three years each. Then he sentenced me to six-months imprisonment for contempt and MacInnis to three months for the same offense.

The Supreme Court reversed the conviction of the three defendants and threw the case out upon the ground that the Statute of Limitations had expired at the time the indictments were returned.

CHAPTER **15**

I Run for President

QUITE awhile after the close of the Bridges case I arrived at a diagnosis of the political condition which had afflicted me. It is something epidemic among the American people, and it is called "Political Immaturity." The Government cured me of this affliction the hard way.

I was not the least concerned with the six-months sentence for contempt of court which Harris had imposed upon me. I knew my trade and I knew that I had not been in contempt. I took an appeal, serenely confident that the sentence would be reversed quickly. I was somewhat shocked when the Assistant United States Attorney assigned to handle my appeal delivered a vigorous argument, describing me in terms which would have been slanderous if applied to Caligula. My confidence was severely dampened when the Circuit Court of Appeals rendered a decision sustaining the sentence and delivering an opinion in about the same vein which Harris had employed in imposing it. I applied for a writ of review to the United States Supreme Court.

Meanwhile, I was outraged and indignant. I felt that the three defendants in the Bridges case, MacInnis and myself, had fallen victims to a Government program which was contrary to

278

every concept of Americanism as I understood it. That program was not only unjust, reactionary and repressive; it was completely unrealistic. It was designed to protect the existing economic order by fair means or foul, and it proposed to smash anyone who got in its way.

I proceeded to get squarely into that position. Bridges' union was anxious to acquaint American labor generally with what had happened in its case and to recruit forces to undo its consequences. I became its principal instrument for that purpose. A series of meetings were set up throughout the country, and with one or other of the defendants, I was called upon to address them. I spoke to labor groups amid the palm trees of Hawaii and the snowy stretches of Idaho. I was applauded in desert towns in New Mexico and in the metropolises of the East Coast. I spoke to English lawyers in the shadow of London's Big Ben, and was entering Canada to address a convention of miners when I was removed from the train by United States Government agents and served with a notice forbidding me to leave the continental limits of the country.

In the meantime, I was filling in a neglected part of my education. I read, I asked, and I listened. Gradually I came to believe that we are in one of those great periods of human progress in which the old economic and political order is dying out and about to be replaced by a new one. Just as the ancient slave economics had given way to feudalism, and they in turn to capitalism, so capitalism was now yielding to socialism throughout the world. This was a part of a steady progression in which the power of one man to exploit the labor of another was gradually being repressed. Slavery had been replaced by serfdom, and serfdom by hired labor. The machinery of production was in the hands of a few, and they used it to exploit the many.

Now that same many were moving to break the system and to take over the production of commodities for the benefit of all. That this was eminently progressive, humane and democratic, went without saying. Meanwhile it was equally apparent that the minority who controlled this power would not relinquish it without a struggle. Since these control the instruments of oppression—

namely the Government, with its police and armed forces—the contest was bound to be bitter and bloody.

I was on the side of the many. I was all for the colonial peoples in their efforts to shake loose from the shackles of imperialism; I thought that all the people of a country should own its natural resources and that they were foolish to leave them in the hands of a greedy minority.

In other words, I had become a complete socialist, and I did not propose to stand by and watch people who believed the same way I did get kicked around for trying to put our mutual principles into practice.

Even more important, the existing system threatened to drown the world in blood. The contest between the various capitalist nations for colonies from which to extract raw materials, and in which to sell their finished products, to establish trade routes and relations, and in general to exploit the labor and resources of backward nations, had now degenerated into a murderous struggle incomprehensible to any rational mind.

I had served a brief hitch in the United States Navy during World War I. I had no illusions that it was being fought to save democracy or for any of the other hypocritical reasons employed to justify it. I knew that it had started as a trade war between England and Germany, in which the stakes were African colonies and South American markets. This country financed England and its Allies, and finally had to get into the war to protect the investment.

Before the wounds of that war had healed, we were into World War II in which 10 percent of the population of the globe was killed, and this was scarcely over when we left 27,000 dead Americans in South Korea, to protect the investments of American corporations in that unhappy land. Meanwhile, at home, our Government was diligently smashing anyone who protested against this program, the Palmer raids of World War I, and the McCarthyism which followed World War II being only crests on the waves of repression.

I cried out with a loud and bitter voice against this attack on the dignity of man. A few heeded it; among them were the remnants of the Progressive Party, which had sustained a brave but vain battle to elect Henry Wallace President of the United States in 1948. Both his pride and confidence had been mortally damaged by the small vote which he received—about 1,500,000, to be exact. If he had stayed with the struggle and the Party and built on that 1,500,000 votes, he would have become a towering figure on the American political scene. The Progressive Party condemned the Korean War, and Wallace seized the opportunity to walk out on it.

This ended the Party as a political potential, but its rear guard decided to launch another campaign in 1952, hoping at least to acquire a platform from which to denounce the intervention in Korea. By this time most of its stalwarts had followed Henry Wallace, and it was necessary to find a candidate among its newcomers. So it was that the Progressive Party nominated me as its candidate for the Presidency of the United States in 1952.

The Democratic Party had an inordinate fear of the Progressive Party. In 1948 it had nullified the Wallace threat by campaigning upon practically the same platform which the Progressive Party had adopted, and which—up to that time—the Democratic Party had treated with scorn. Now it feared for the defection of its progressive elements once more. The Supreme Court was heavily packed with its appointees. My petition for a writ of review had been pending in this tribunal for almost two years. One week after I received the Progressive Party's nomination it denied the petition. Off to the Federal Penitenitary at McNeil Island, Washington, for the months of March through August, 1952, went the Presidential nominee of the Progressive Party for 1952.

The state bar moved to disbar me. However, they appointed a conservative—but very independent and honorable—lawyer, Webster V. Clark, as prosecutor. Clark could not see what the U.S. Circuit Court of Appeals and the Supreme Court had seen. He informed the state bar that he was unable to discern any contempt in my conduct of the Bridges case, and the proceedings were dismissed.

Despite the incarceration of its nominee, the Progressive Party was not going to be without Hallinans to trumpet its cause. Vivian and I had now been married some twenty years and had six sons. Neither of these things had noticeably diminished either her beauty or her courage. Taking with her the two oldest boys, Patrick, whom we called "Butch," and Terence, whom we called "Kayo," and without the slightest experience in the field, she launched into a political campaign. The Party's executives were astonished and delighted. She roved the country under their direction, speaking in great cities and country hamlets, on street-corner platforms and before factory gates. Butch, at seventeen, had the thrill of speaking to 15,000 people in New York's Madison Square Garden.

I got out of prison with less than a month left in which to campaign. I found the American Left torn by internal dissensions and unable to make up its mind which direction to take. I do not know whether any address could have united it, but I did not have the experience to even attempt it. Shabby expediency and disguised timidity betrayed the spirit which had founded the Progressive Party, and it perished in the election of 1952.

I returned to San Francisco like the defeated soldier to his ruined home. My law office was deserted; my associates had gone elsewhere; and there were no clients to care for. I thought that the newspapers had battered me around rather unfairly in the Egan case; it was nothing to what they did under the provocation of the Bridges case and my subsequent political activities. As Communism was being whipped up as the chief bogey, the most obvious ploy was to identify me with it. One publication suggested that it was my ambition to become a Communist commissar in a Soviet America, and the more exuberant patriots of Ross, California, daubed our gateposts with red paint.

All this bothered me not at all. I was even scornful when a former associate called upon me and warned me of more dangerous possibilities. He said that a friend of his who was a member of the FBI had warned him to steer clear of any association with me; that both his organization and the local United States Attorney's office had been ordered by their Washington superiors to "get" me. Shortly after, I was advised that some of my former associates were being questioned by Internal Revenue agents and FBI operators, concerning a transaction involving my office.

Some months before, a man named Paul Steffens had employed one of my partners to defend him on a narcotics charge in the United States District Court, and had given him a promissory note secured by a deed of trust on property which he owned in Palm Springs as payment for his services. Subsequently other counsel were substituted for this defendant, and the promissory note and deed of trust were transferred to them. I was astonished to learn, some weeks later, that these latter attorneys, their stenographer, a messenger who had recorded the deed of trust, and the notary who had notarized it, had been indicted by the United States Grand Jury for conspiracy to aid Steffens in defrauding the Government by a fictitious transfer of the property covered by the deed of trust. A week later my ex-partner, who had been the original beneficiary of the deed of trust, was added to the indictment. Sometime later, my stenographer was called to appear before that body. She told me that some questions had been addressed to her regarding the document, of which she knew nothing; that the jurors then began an inquiry as to my political affiliations, one of them asking her flatly if I were a Communist. The girl replied that she did not believe so, but that I was a fighter for civil liberties. Whereupon the Deputy United States Attorney and several of the jurors took her on with acrimony, inquiring into her own political beliefs and the identity of her personal friends and associates. In March 1953, they indicted me.

We went to trial. We were seven defendants, represented by four different sets of attorneys. The Deputy United States Attorney made a ringing opening statement in which he delineated a totally fictitious conspiracy involving the document in dispute. Then, pointing an accusing finger at me, he declaimed: "And we will show you that Vincent Hallinan was the mainspring and focal point of this conspiracy!"

As I had been in New York during all of the time that the "conspiracy" was in progress and had hotel bills and other receipts to prove it, I was somewhat puzzled as to just what proof would be evoked to establish that charge. None was forthcoming.

At the conclusion of the prosecution's case the judge gave a directed verdict, exonerating the investigator, the notary public, the stenographer and me. I was astonished that I was included in this clemency. I didn't think there was a Federal judge in the United States who would discharge me from any accusation. This one, Louis J. Goodman, operated outside his class; he had a sense of history. Later he was to rule for the defendant in an action brought by the Government to cancel Harry Bridges' citizenship. This he did upon the same kind of "evidence" that had been used to convict Bridges in the criminal case.

Following his ruling in my behalf, the other defendants besought me to absent myself from the courtroom, fearing that my presence might alienate the jury. I refused to do so. I told them: "I'm going to sit right through this trial, and when your defense lawyers are arguing, I want each one of them to turn and point his finger at me and say, 'There's the mainspring and focal point of this whole conspiracy, and he isn't even in the case any more. Then what about these little secondary springs and nonfocal points?' "

So I just sat there, and the Deputy United States Attorney got pale around the gills every time he looked at me, and the jury acquitted all the defendants.

Now, I said to myself, that's all to the good; they've shot their bolt and missed their mark, and they won't have the gall to try it again. This was to misunderstand the brashness of the U.S. Government's prosecution department's "on the make." Three months after my acquittal on the conspiracy charge, Vivian and I were indicted for income-tax evasion.

To be tried for income-tax evasion is tantamount to conviction. Only 3 or 4 percent of those tried are acquitted. The whole setup of the Federal Courts operates against the defendant. The judges, appointed for life and not responsive to the voters, are arbitrary and tyrannical, and almost invariably aid the prosecution. They will interrupt the cross-examination of a Government witness to take him off the hook, and rehabilitate him with comments designed to ingratiate him with the jury. They will sharply reject any criticism of the conduct of the United States Attorney, and become quite pouty if the defense lawyer lapses in courtesy toward a Government official.

For their part, the prosecution attorneys will engage in any trickery available, and the Internal Revenue agents will lie, and will conceal whatever might be useful to the defense. In our case most of the controversy related to deductions and payments which the Government claimed should not have been allowed. These had been openly claimed over a period of many years, and some of them involved disputes with the Internal Revenue Department. They entailed what is called in law "tax avoidance," which is legal. The prosecution now contended that these were in fact "tax evasions," which are illegal.

One such item will illustrate the point. Vivian, in addition to rearing six sons and running a home, had also gone into the apartment-house business. When the national economy started emerging from the depression of the 1930's, she began speculating in such properties, and ran a shoestring investment into a substantial fortune. Some of her properties were held by a corporation of which she was the sole stockholder. My father, who was in his early eighties, and my mother, in her early seventies, were naturally dependent upon me for their support.

My father was a proud old man, and we wanted to make it look as though he were earning his way; we made him secretary of the corporation. As such, he attended any meetings we had and signed the minutes as secretary. We paid him a salary of $700 a month, which we charged off against the corporation as an expense, and upon which he paid his own income tax.

For some time the Internal Revenue Department had been disputing this item, claiming that the salary paid was excessive and that the recipient did not render the corporation services sufficient to justify it. I took the position that it was none of their damn business what he was paid, and that he was as active as the secretaries of most corporations, except that he did not play golf. I was also prepared to defend the expenditure in the tax court, if the department should disallow it. At most it was a proper subject for a civil dispute. Whether or not such an item

constituted illegal "tax evasion" or legal "tax avoidance," was
a matter of intention. If a judge or jury found it to be the former,
the defendant was sunk; an Appellate Court would not interfere
with the finding.

Several such items were advanced against us in the trial, and
then the prosecution, "to show the standard of living of the
defendants," poured in a whole mass of expenditures in support
of persons and causes which were, even then, under fire by the
McCarthys of the period. To tell the truth, the list of recipients
looked like the Attorney General's subversive list. There were
large chunks for the defense of the Communist leaders in New
York and the Bridges case defendants in San Francisco. Our personal expenditures during the Progressive Party Presidential campaign of 1952 were marched in, as were our subscriptions to a
sheaf of "Left-Wing" publications.

We defended our position with vigor, but the prospects were
not promising. Toward the end of the trial Vivian laid out the
program we must follow when—not if—we should both be
convicted. She said quite calmly, but as firmly and impersonally
as if she were completing another real-estate transaction, "There's
no use fooling ourselves; we're both going to be convicted, and
we're both going to be sent to prison. Here's what we must do.
I'll go straight off to prison, and you take an appeal. You can
string that out for a couple of years, and by the time it's decided
against you I'll be out. Then you go on in. In this way, the kids
won't ever be left alone."

The jury was out for about twelve hours, at the end of which
they acquitted Vivian and convicted me. We hastened to a hall
where we were scheduled to address a rally of the Veterans of
the Abraham Lincoln Brigade, which we did without any more
concern than if we had just come from our home.

Next day the San Francisco *Chronicle,* reporting the verdict,
stated: "One of the jurors said that he still did not believe that
Hallinan was guilty, and that he had been convicted because
he had defended Harry Bridges and had been the Presidential
candidate of the Progressive Party."

Jim Purcell, who was representing me, made a motion for

probation. To my surprise, the probation officer vigorously recommended it. However, Edward Murphy, the Federal judge, turned it down. I had known him for many years. He was one of the lawyers who had testified against Thomas Mulvey when I was fighting the jury-planting racket in the San Francisco Superior Court. He was well-meaning, but weak. He told me afterwards that he would have granted probation, but that he was afraid that if he did so he would be impeached. I was convicted on November 15, 1953, and sentenced to eighteen months in prison.

In view of the controversial position I was occupying and the efforts that the Government had made to destroy me, the sentence was a moderate one. This put me in a quandary. It was the consensus of my friends and supporters that, if the Government could succeed in convicting me of anything, I'd be stuck away as long as the traffic would bear. We debated at length whether I should appeal. The consensus was that I better let well enough alone; if I reversed the conviction and came up for a new trial, the chances of drawing someone like Murphy were remote. There were plenty of Federal judges who would do just what my people had feared. In addition, I had received a valuable lesson from my previous experience. The Circuit Court of Appeals had written a vicious opinion on my contempt hearing, and the Government had been able to select the strategic time at which to lock me away. Now, at least, I would have the power to pinpoint the time of my entry into, and emergence from, its clutches. I wasn't afraid of prison; I never had been. I had known many weak, poor creatures who had gone in and out of prison without any great distortion, and my prior experience had shown me that I would do likewise.

I turned myself in quite calmly, and went off to get this particular deal over with on January 8, 1954. However, I found it something quite different from my previous incarceration. That one had been for a misdemeanor, and I had been sent directly to the McNeil Island Prison "farm" where the prisoners slept in barracks, and there was relatively much freedom of movement and activity. This time I was ushered into a cage of stone and iron. The United States Attorney General had done what he could to minimize Judge Murphy's leniency. He had ordered me held in close confinement, as a dangerous prisoner. This meant, among other restrictions, that I should not be assigned to any task which might earn me "good time credits," which could lop a few days off the sentence. I accepted this petty tyranny with the same contempt in which I had held all the retaliatory proceedings of the Government. I was encountering a new and strange aspect of life, and I would add to my understanding of that complex phenomenon without the slightest concern or regret for anything that had placed me in the position to observe it. I must confess, however, that before I was through with it, I had learned plenty to dismay me and to add fuel to my resentment at the universal crime of man's inhumanity to man.

CHAPTER **16**

An Attorney Behind the Bars

SOME years before going to prison I had read the remark made by Dr. Ralph S. Banay—for many years chief psychiatrist at Sing Sing Penitenitary in New York: "If you want to step back into the Middle Ages, you need only enter a typical American prison." Unfortunately, you have to go to prison to understand how well this remark embraces the whole field of penology.

Criminal law is not only the most exciting branch of the legal profession, it serves as the base for at least half of the drama which the public enjoys. Why the fascination? Because the audience can so easily identify with the criminal. Almost everyone is, in fact, a criminal. There are probably few adults who have not committed at least one felony.

There are some 2,500,000 major crimes committed each year in the United States—just those called to the attention of the authorities. The Internal Revenue Department assures us that 76 percent of all income-tax returns are fraudulent. Kinsey Associates claims 93 percent of the population engages in sex practices which are felonies under state laws. Have you ever driven an auto while drunk? Have you ever helped a friend locate an abortionist? Have you ever contrived some twist which is, in truth, a fraud, to an ordinary business transaction? The list goes on and on. If you have been involved in any one of a variety of hundreds of law violations, you are a criminal.

The total number of persons in all the prisons in the country is about 186,000, a tiny percentage of the people who could be there. They are mainly the inept or incompetent who got caught, or those who could not afford defense. Crime, supposedly, is not only reprehensible, but doesn't pay. In movies and on television the criminal always comes to a bad end. In real life he sometimes does—but only exceptionally.

Necessarily, people who commit crimes are just ordinary people. This applies to the professional criminal as well as to those who would be shocked by such a designation. To some extent, the classification is a matter of degree. Sometimes it involves only an honest acknowledgment of status. Certain millionaires, who bribe politicians by subtle devices, would reject these charges with indignation. Yet, I have asked fellow inmates in prison what job they had on the outside and heard them reply proudly, "I'm a thief."

Such angry denial or casual candor in placing oneself in the spectrum of crime varies greatly. It is not permanent. The professional criminal often seeks respectability and safe investments, once he's made his fortune. Typical is the horde of bootleggers of prohibition days who are now respectable, aging businessmen.

Crime involving property goes with our competitive society. Those who acquire and retain property gain status and power. The means and methods of acquiring it are forgotten or glossed over. Most great fortunes in this country were obtained by theft of the public domain, bribery of public officials, and vast frauds upon the public. Violence and murder often accompanied the efforts. It's commonly believed that to become rich and remain honest is all but impossible, and that all public officials are corrupt to a greater or lesser degree.

Contempt for the law runs through all strata of our society, ranging from parking autos in red zones when one is assured he won't be caught, to complicated schemes to violate antitrust laws. Most Americans come to Somerset Maugham's prescription: "Do what you want, but with mind to the policeman around the corner." But most citizens rationalize such behavior, if they recognize it at all. They may know that the bookie and numbers rackets survive by bribing public officials and gang violence. But it has nothing to do, they will say, with betting $2 to show at the corner cigar store.

It is pretended that the stock market is maintained to provide a liquid supply of money for investment. But it is legal gambling. The respectable racketeers who run it go out to the race track to gamble, which is also legal, pretending that the betting is solely to "improve the breed." If the numbers racket was legalized tomorrow, it would be explained, no doubt, that betting really played no part in the business. The reason would be to foster an interest in mathematics to encourage more people to go into engineering.

We live in this exploitative social system. Advancement depends upon exploiting the labors of others. Back in 1776, Adam Smith pointed out that wealth consists in "land and the labor thereon." Things become of value as intelligent and useful labor is expended on them. As the individual's capacity for this is limited, he is seldom satisfied with the product of his effort. He appropriates to himself the work of others. The forms this exploitation takes are infinite. An extreme example is slavery. The commonest is to hire others to create things of value, and pay them part of what is received for them, retaining the remainder. Some become rich by buying cheaply from one and selling dearly to another. Others work with such devices as stocks and bonds to abstract the savings of the uninformed.

These things require capital. Many who have none want more than their own labor can provide. Some resort to criminal means, employing illegal theft instead of legal fraud. They appropriate the fruits of another's labor, not by underpaying, but by the menace of physical injury. They manipulate stolen automobile licenses instead of oil debentures.

They are not concerned with the morality of these activities, but only with their probable penalties. They consider that laws are rules which those who have already won fortunes enact to guard them. They do not make distinctions between themselves and those who enact these laws; and they do not propose to be bound by them. They intend to share in the luxuries of life, and they realize that they cannot do so by legal means.

They systemize this philosophy into a mode of living. Otherwise, they are ordinary people. They have families to which they are devoted in the same proportion as so-called "law-abiding" persons. Many are extremely intelligent. Certain of their schemes are fantastically clever. I have known professional criminals of great charm and kindness. Some have displayed the most admirable courage and fortitude. They cannot be called antisocial. Quite the contrary. The things they seek are those which will give them standing and prestige in the society they occupy. Prison inmates are constantly volunteering for medical experimentation, often at great danger of death or permanent disability. Shortly prior to one of my sojourns in the Federal Penitentiary at McNeil Island, a number of prisoners there had allowed themselves to be inoculated with infectious hepatitis so as to test a new remedy for the disease. Two died and several were invalided in the process. Blood banks in neighboring communities are constantly replenishing their supply through donations made by prisoners in the same institution.

Discussion of inmates' philosophies proves a baffling experience. They compare their trifling thefts with the acquisitions of the most respected and inquire if the latter succeeded through honorable means. They are scornful of suggested alternatives. A young Mexican-American whom I met in prison disposed of my efforts to persuade him to a more acceptable way of life by saying, "I saw my father work himself to death at forty. I am not going to do that. I may spend half my life in jails, but I'm going to have some fun out of the other half."

I ultimately came to the feeling that perhaps these were only the most rebellious of earth's disinherited. Given unity and a purpose, they might have been great revolutionaries.

Sometime during every criminal law course a student will ask if a lawyer should defend one whom he knows to be guilty. The professor has probably been forewarned by previous experience, and has concocted an answer which evades the issue. Ethics would be offended by replying: "A lawyer shouldn't give a damn."

He shouldn't. He has been employed to rescue someone who has been caught in the web of the law. He is not charged with judging the offense. If he were, he should also be charged with judging the system which has trapped his client and the consequences which will attend his conviction.

This would bring him to a consideration of the entire problem of crime and punishment as it operates in our culture. He will discover that it is a barbaric anachronism. It is simple humanity to rescue anyone whom it has enmeshed. Unfortunately, you must go to prison yourself to fully understand this. Everything relating to the criminal law is archaic and irrational. Nobody knows its principles or its purposes. Some say that it is designed to punish criminals. More claim that its object is to prevent crime. Others allege that it is intended to rehabilitate offenders.

A convicted man is assigned a role not embraced in any of these categories. He becomes a sacrificial goat. A baffled and impotent social order vents its anger and frustration on him. He is thrown into a cage, like a wild animal. He is sequestered from view lest his condition disturb the millions who could easily be made to share it with him.

Whatever his capacity, he is assigned to perform menial and inconsequential work. He is treated with disrespect by officials who may be, in every way, inferior to him. He is forced into intimate association with the most vicious and depraved. His outlook on life becomes distorted. He has been degraded and robbed of his human dignity. He is oppressed with a sense of injustice and helplessness. He cannot understand that the solution of his emotional, economic or social problems and crises, requires that he be thrown on a garbage heap to rot.

He loses contact with his family and with his friends outside. Without this support, his morals and principles corrode. In accord with a well-known psychological concept, he tends to become the sort of person he believes others conceive him to be. He becomes tolerant of the sexual perversions which go on around him, and finally descends to them himself. He accepts brutality and even murder.

When he is discharged, he emerges into a still-hostile world. His family has probably disintegrated. He has no base upon which to anchor himself, and he is branded for life. If he applies for a job with any public agency or where a bond is required, he must disclose his past error or misfortune. Failure to do so is an additional felony.

One who goes to prison comes to see crime from a new perspective. Most of all he sees it from an intimate level, and begins to realize how his fellow prisoners, the keepers and the public officials who administer the system, see it. He usually reaches some pretty bitter conclusions.

To officials concerned, for example, prison is just a racket, a means of livelihood. They do not care about the problems or fate of the prisoners. They draw their pay and want as little annoyance and bother as possible. They will keep men locked up in an animal cage many hours, if it will avoid the chore of supervising them in corridors or yards. Everything in a prison is designed to lessen the work load for the guards and officials; to keep the budget within the limits set by some congressional committee; and to stifle complaints which might change the routine. This, of course, is not unique to prisons. It is simply human nature.

My first shock came when I was ushered into the mainline of McNeil Island on September 18, 1954. Towering above me was a mammoth bird cage, five tiers soaring to the ceiling. Some 900 men were confined here, 10 to each 20 by 20 cell. A dull and constant murmur filled the massive room, the voices of society's scapegoats. Here, I thought, here I must live for a year and a half. What if it were life? I was led to a cell, and the door closed behind me. As simply as that I became a "con."

All around me I saw tragedy. On my previous visit to McNeil, I had met one of the saddest cases, a sixteen-year-old Eskimo boy. He was serving a life term for rape. This child victim of a society he did not comprehend had been so frightened by his new environment that guards took his hand to lead him into the dining room, to calm his fears. Here, on my current tour, I met others, some simply victims of the fact that the judge was perhaps drunk the night before. Not that I pretend they were lily white. Only that they were victims of the arbitrary power of Federal judges, men who are not responsive to voters and can indulge their caprices and cruelties as they see fit. Authorities prefer not to recognize that a victim's major initial crime, which started him on his unhappy career, is poverty. The vast majority of prisoners are the children of poverty, ignorance, broken homes, vicious environment—the infected of society's disease.

Typical of the severe and arbitrary power of U.S. courts, were two men who had escaped from a road gang about fifteen years before. Terrified by the hue and cry, they kidnapped a motorist, forced him to drive to the state line, did not harm him and gave him money to return home. They were each given forty-five years, and are now wearing out their lives at McNeil. Again, I met a young man, twenty-seven, who had a wife and two children. He had gotten drunk, picked up a woman in a saloon, and taken her for a ride. To give him the worst of it, he raped her and in doing so broke her arm. It was his first arrest. His attorney made a deal with the U.S. Attorney that the rape charge would be dropped and the defendant would plead guilty to a charge of attempt to commit rape. "You'll probably be granted probation, but you might have to serve six months or even a year in jail," his attorney had cautioned him. The federal judge said "Twenty years!"

But such disparity and caprice is commonplace. Two men I know were serving terms for bank robbery. One, who had served a term in San Quentin before for the same crime, had held up three banks in two weeks. He was serving five years. Another, who had attempted to hold up a bank on his first excursion into crime, was serving twenty years. Similarly, I had met two young men who were Jehovah's Witnesses, on my other trip to McNeil. They had claimed exemptions from military duty as conscientious objectors. The Supreme Court has since ruled that such exemptions are legal, but these twenty-one-year-old lads had served out their sentences before the ruling came down. To add to the confusion, one youth had been sentenced in Montana by a Federal judge, to serve nine months. The other had been sentenced by a San Francisco Federal judge, to five years.

Within a few days after my arrival I found that the legendary "grapevine" of a prison is real enough. Men started sidling up to me, asking me what could be done about drawing up this letter or that legal document. Reluctant or no, I was a prison attorney.

I was determined not to be trapped by the deadly boredom which I knew made prison life a double hell. I had been assigned one of the meaningless tasks which pass for jobs in a prison. I sat in a small room, separating an endless collection of nuts, bolts and screws. But at least the job afforded blissful privacy. I set out to learn Spanish. When I heard the guard coming, I'd drop the book to my lap and be engrossed in the creative task of choosing nuts from bolts.

Also, I saw no reason to ruin my hard-won reputation as a troublemaker. I came across a speech by President Eisenhower in *The New York Times* in which he declared that whenever the Federal Government held power, segregation would not be permitted. I looked out on the grim tiers of steel where Negroes were segregated in cells, as well as in the dining room, living in a prison within a prison. That day I wrote a letter to the warden, calling attention to the *Times* article, and suggesting that dining-room segregation be ended. Further, I said that I would ask other white inmates to help me, so that there would be no disturbing incidents. The letter was ignored.

I turned now to the interrelations committee, an inmate organization which operates, with the support of the administration, as an agency between officials and prisoners. I drew up a petition calling for desegregation in the dining room, and started asking for signatures. I had some when the warden called me in. "If you continue with this, you'll go to Alcatraz Island," he announced brusquely.

The project was temporarily shelved. But about then I was elected to the IRC, and chosen chairman. By then I had drawn up a report on what seemed outstanding defects and injustices. It was no random collection of bitches, but a moderate and fair exposition compiled from talking with many other prisoners. I turned it over to the IRC. "Let's study it, make changes that seem reasonable, and send copies—when it's ready—to the prison administration, congressional committees interested in such matters, and newspapers," I suggested.

But among other elements in prisons, the spy system is efficient. Two guards descended and picked up the offending papers; the warden bluntly notified us that our ideas were "contraband," and that there would be no reform movements at McNeil.

I proposed an appeal. Then the politics got lively. The "company men" among the prisoners—clerks to the officers and other favorites—started a recall movement to eliminate me from the IRC. It failed, but even when I was released months later and asked for the reform papers, they were refused me. It is obvious that prisoners can't do anything to correct conditions, and authorities won't.

If the prisoner can do little in the way of reform in prison, the day he is out is no new dawn. The parole board members— politically appointed stooges—seem devoted to little except preventing adverse criticism of the National Administration which appointed them, and drawing their salaries. Moreover, I am perfectly convinced paroles are sold. I know of too many stories of depositing funds with an attorney under a guarantee of parole, to doubt this. Today the system operates in a most inexplicable fashion. Those obviously worthy are denied, while men with long records are freed—only to be returned as violators. Paroles, it seems, are marketable items. As such, the price is kept high by a limited supply. And what is more logical than to say: "Look at those who have been granted paroles and have been returned. We must be careful"? I believe that properly administered parole laws could reduce the prison population by four-fifths, working toward the release of an inmate before he becomes embittered and convinced that he is not worth saving. Administered by trained experts free from political influence and publicity pressures, the parole law could be a wise and humane measure. Paroles should be a matter of right for a prisoner, and he should be able to appeal to a Federal Court if his appeal is denied. The judge should be able to release him if the board cannot show sufficient cause for refusing his appeal.

A vast array of melodramatic propaganda convinces the public that the "con" is a wild animal intent upon pillage and rape. Writers, movie producers and others involved in selling dramatic situations, have turned for years, quite naturally, to the prison to show characters in conflict in brute circumstance. Obviously to increase dramatic impact, it's always black and white.

A man confined on the mainline at McNeil is housed in a steel and concrete cell before which is a curtain of bars through which only a small-sized cat could penetrate. The cell is closed by a sliding door controlled by a device operated by an officer at the end of the tier. This door is opened for a few moments at a time to permit the inmates to go to work, meals or recreation. Except when on work crews supervised by officers, the prisoners move about within the building which contains the cells. This, in turn, is closed off from the outside by high walls of steel and concrete through which exit may be gained only by doors operated much as those closing the cells. There is an elaborate system of passes, checks and counterchecks involved, even in moving about within this structure.

Outside this is a tall, wire fence, surmounted by barbed wire, and at strategic intervals towers with catwalks are patrolled by guards armed with rifles. All this is contained on an island separated from the mainland by miles of cold water.

If all this paraphernalia of bars, fences and guards were removed, and no preventive to escape provided except a legal penalty, not five percent of the men in prison would attempt to escape. I said this to one of the officers at McNeil, and he answered triumphantly, "That is true—but we don't know which five percent!"

Far too much importance is attached to a possible escape. If there were a handful of professional gangsters who would be dangerous outside and difficult to retake, they could be confined to a place of secure custody without subjecting thousands of ordinary men to the humiliation of being treated like ravenous wild beasts whose presence in the outside world would be dangerous to its inhabitants.

Escape is the great prison taboo. The officers feel that any amount of mistreatment of the prisoners is excusable, as long as none is allowed to get away. It seems to me that if a man succeeded in such an enterprise and was not terrified into some desperate action by the gantlet of roadblocks, sirens, prowl cars and firearms, he would probably hole up and keep safely out of both sight and crime.

During my stay a young Mexican, who had completed about half of a two-year sentence for illegal entry, made good his escape. Nobody believed that the innocuous wetback constituted any special threat to the peace or security of the country by returning to his normal activities a few months early, but there was the same circumstance of sirens, special lockups, bloodhounds, and feverish running around, as if someone nicknamed Machine Gun had accomplished the feat.

Among the most glaring examples of contempt for the rights of the prisoner is the use of "holds" or "detainers" in Federal prisons. When the prison authorities are notified that a warrant has been issued against an inmate by a state or Federal Court, or when they receive from a district attorney a statement that he intends to prosecute the inmate upon some charge—or even when only a police chief or a constable sends in a letter asking to be informed when the prisoner is to be released—a "hold" is placed against him.

This fixes his custody as "close"; prevents him from being assigned to certain more desirable jobs; prevents, except in rare instances, parole; and in effect lengthens the term he serves, without any proof that there is the least merit to the charge pending outside. It is customary for the requesting authority to maintain this "hold" against such a prisoner, even though it has no actual intention of even prosecuting him on the charge, until the day of his actual discharge; then, upon inquiry of the Federal prison, to release the same after having subjected the man to stricter and additional confinement—often for several years.

Letters from the prisoner—and often even from prison officials —are usually sent in vain.

The district attorney of Los Angeles County has a form letter which he returns to all communications. It states, in effect, that no action to release the hold will be taken, and invites a further request "not more than six weeks before the day set for your release." At that time this department of justice takes the trouble to inquire into the merits of its charges.

There is nothing to prevent a state or Federal department from prosecuting a man upon *any* charge while he is an inmate of a prison. Either of them can require the transfer of the prisoner to its jurisdiction for trial. If it does not choose to do so, it is probable that the offense cannot be very serious. Officers of such departments should not be allowed to imprison and punish those against whom they do not care to proceed expeditiously, by having them held in closer custody and for longer periods in the Federal prisons. All such warrants, letters and inquiries, should be ignored, and the inmate treated exactly as if no such "hold" were placed against him. He should be eligible to parole, and not denied it at the caprice of a small-town constable who suspects him of some misdemeanor which he does not care to, or is unable to, prosecute.

In 1955, in the United States District Court in Los Angeles, Judge Ernest Tolin pointed out some of the inequities of this procedure. He had sentenced a man to a term of five years for bank robbery. Thereupon, the district attorney placed a "hold" against the man at McNeil Prison, charging that the prisoner was guilty of armed robbery under the laws of the state of California. Of course he knew that a prosecution on that basis would constitute double jeopardy, but declined to withdraw the detainer. The Federal judge angrily denounced the filing of these requisitions with the prison authorities, calling them a "police-state device" and "an impertinent interference with the judgment of the sentencing court."

Many men are in prison only because they were improperly represented in court. Being for the most part poor and unable to hire private counsel, they are defended by court-appointed lawyers. As these are unpaid, their chief concern is to get rid of a profitless chore. They induce their client to plead guilty to one count or to a lesser charge, make a deal with the prosecuting attorney, and get quit of the case. In this they are aided by an unconscionable device almost universally employed by United States attorneys.

This is a device of splitting a single offense into several separate counts. Thus, a sale of narcotics will be split into four separate charges: (1) possession of the narcotic involved; (2) transportation of same; (3) failure to pay tax on same; (4) sale. There are many cases holding that all these acts constitute but one criminal act and are punishable by one sentence.

The defendant probably knows nothing about such rulings. He is faced with four long sentences if convicted of selling one marijuana cigarette. Indeed, if he stands trial and is convicted, many Federal judges will give him consecutive sentences upon all four counts, being annoyed by the fact that he stood trial. Usually the court-appointed lawyer makes an arrangement with the U.S. Attorney to have his client plead guilty to one of the counts and the others will be dropped.

The defendant is not encouraged by his counsel to risk conviction on all four counts, and he accepts the deal suggested—though he may be innocent. In prison I drew up some writs and wrote some letters on behalf of men who were serving consecutive terms under situations like those stated above, but as too much time had elapsed—and it is almost impossible to attack a record on its face alone—these efforts accomplished little.

Granted that some court-appointed lawyers have done good and even dramatic jobs, the great majority earn exactly what they are paid—nothing. The prisoners have a catch phrase which describes the advice they receive from such advocates: "You tell him you did it, and I'll tell him you're sorry."

The public-defender system is a failure. Defendants are ordinarily given only formal representation by the officers of that office. Instead, a panel of lawyers should be prepared from attorneys who desire to be placed upon it, who would represent indigent defendants, and who would be paid decent remuneration by the Government.

They should not be public officials, but independent lawyers. The defendant should have the right to select from this panel the one he desires to have represent him, and the lawyer should be paid according to the amount of labor and the results obtained. Then those who were the most successful would get the choice of cases and the highest pay; they would have incentive to work conscientiously. Furthermore, they should be paid for taking appeals and carrying them out, and for services rendered the prisoner after sentence. Such lawyers should also be permitted to visit prisons and be available to men who feel that they are illegally imprisoned. There are many such men in federal prisons.

Still another serious defect in the prison system is the waste of the time and energy of prisoners. Great bodies of strong, robust men are engaged in boondoggling enterprises which have no purpose. There is no—or almost no—productive industry in prisons, and no way in which a man can earn enough to place himself in a position of relative safety on release.

Of course, neither private industries nor labor unions will permit prisonmade goods to compete with those produced outside, and such objections are readily understood; but the ruin of the inmate must be balanced against other considerations. Lack of productive or useful labor makes the prisoners shiftless, lazy and indifferent. Over a period of many years such habits make them unfit for work outside.

At McNeil, for instance, a few men worked in the cannery during certain months and earned about seventy-five cents per day; this went to buy them few extra things sold in the commissary or to relieve the state relief agencies of the support of their families. The vast majority of inmates earn nothing. Thus a man might serve five or seven years and then, with his family and friends gone, emerge with the sum of $25 or $30 given by the Government, and have to plunge into a hostile world with this small resource.

There should be industries in all prisons at which all inmates can be employed at wages not too disparate from those paid in similar enterprises outside the walls. These earnings should be protected against assignment or legal distraints, so as to provide the released man a financial foundation upon which he can base his climb back to respectability.

The matters relating to prison are too grim to be termed a joke, but no other phrase adequately describes the "education and rehabilitation" programs. Following the Civil War, an author said that everybody talks "reconstruction," but nobody knows what it means. At McNeil two high-school teachers were employed to give evening classes in English, history and arithmetic to those few interested in learning these subjects. In addition, an inmate presided over a room containing several typewriters at which one was free to learn to type if he could. An inmate ex-truck driver taught geometry and trigonometry to a handful of men, and an inmate ex-elevator operator did the same with Spanish. There were also correspondence courses available in a great many subjects, but I submit, no one ever learned anything by correspondence.

Of course the correct usage of English and a knowledge of American history are very commendable acquisitions, but they are of little value in the struggle of a released prisoner to gain an honest livelihood in a hard and practical world where the use of the *mot juste* falls far behind the value of being able to adjust a carburetor.

If there was a shortage on a job requiring particular skill in one of the prison plants, a promising man with a long term ahead of him was instructed in whatever it might be: plumbing, welding, auto repair, etc.—not for *his* benefit, but to keep the plant in operation and save the paid officials the duties of their performance.

There was nothing like a trade school. There was no opportunity to learn how to repair a car or radio. A man would not be assigned to the auto shop unless he already was skilled in car repair. Perhaps twenty or thirty worked in such shops, and only the release of one would give opportunity to another. A young colored man with whom I was friendly was serving a five-year sentence and was almost in despair. I persuaded him to take the correspondence course in automotive repair. When he had completed it, he went to the officer in charge of such matters and asked to be assigned to the auto-repair shop where he could practice what knowledge he had acquired. He was insulted and sent back to his duties as a janitor.

Schools in such trades as plumbing, automotive repairs, radio, etc., should be established in all prisons. These could be conducted without any expense to the administration, since there are many prisoners skilled in those trades who could be employed as teachers. No extra equipment would be needed, and even the salaries of the high-school teachers could be saved. Classes should be held in the daytime, so that those attending them would have the additional advantage of being relieved from shifting bodies of earth from one place to another and then back again.

A prime and constant problem in prison is sex. Countries more advanced socially than the United States have for many years had programs designed to obviate sexual perversions among prison inmates. Among these are Mexico, Sweden and Iceland. Commissions should be sent to these nations to learn the procedures employed. In these three, private visits from wives are permitted, or the prisoner is permitted to go home for specified periods. Not only should the moral structure of the prisoner be considered, but also that of his wife. If a man so confined will consent to perversions opposed to his mores and feelings, certainly it can be expected that the wife will engage in more normal relations, to the continued disintegration of the family.

Under the circumstances available to me, I was not able to establish the extent of sexual perversion in prisons. The estimates which I could obtain varied according to certain subjective elements. Men who admitted having indulged in such practices made larger computations than those who had not. Their guesses ran between 25 and 90 percent. I venture the opinion that of men between the ages of twenty and forty, confined for a period of three years or more, probably 50 percent engage in some homosexual activity. I had an opportunity to witness the rather extensive manufacture and use of masturbation "machines."

One distressing instance in which I obtained more positive information relates to the institution for youth maintained by the Federal Bureau in El Reno, Oklahoma. Former inmates of this institution, as well as officers connected with it, assured me that there sex perversion reached almost 100 percent. Still more distressing was the revelation that the mode by which the boys committed there arrive at such degradation is by naked force and violence.

The new arrival is forced by the older and more experienced inmates to submit to sodomy and other forms of sexual perversion. "If he puts up a fight," I was told, "the cops grab him. He can't tell what the fight was about, because he'd be a stool pigeon and might get killed; so he gets thrown into the hole. When he gets out they take him on again, and if he fights again, back he goes to the hole. About the third time, he gives in. In a little while it's his turn to take on one of the new kids."

A common result of such experience is that when the prisoner graduates into the adult prison he arrives accompanied by the reputation of a "jailhouse punk," and becomes fair game for older and more experienced prisoners. Compliance with the demands of the latter may be procured by force or fear, or it may be purchased by gifts or even the friendship and protection of the older man.

Strict surveillance should be maintained for the protection of boys sent to such institutions as El Reno, to prevent the first steps on the downward path. I am told that such places are insufficiently and inexpertly manned, and that the conduct of them is largely in the hands of the more violent and strongest of the inmates.

The poor caliber of the men employed as guards in such places as McNeil would suggest that those at the youth schools are scarcely fitted for the important task of rescuing children from vice and crime. In intelligence and personality, the inmates at McNeil appeared to be on a higher level than the guards entrusted with their care.

Those charged with such matters—lawmakers, prosecutors, judges, prison authorities—should get together and determine just what purpose they have in mind in the enforcement of the criminal laws. They will disclaim that revenge is the main consideration. They will mostly assert that an important consideration is to "rehabilitate" the offender and to "return him as a useful member of society." These are ridiculous assertions. If there were a vestige of truth in them, there would be some time limit on the period during which a man who has served a prison term is condemned to outlawry.

There is something extremely malign in the tenacity with which "society" pursues such a "rehabilitated" man. He is prevented from voting or holding public office by practically all state constitutions. In even the most inferior court, he can be impeached as a witness by proof that he has once—no matter how long ago—been convicted of a felony. In many cities he is required to register with the police department and thus expose his past error or misfortune.

While I was at McNeil, there was a man there who, many years before, had served a short term in a county jail for indecent exposure. Many years later he applied for a job as a carpenter on a Government project in Alaska. He was presented with a questionnaire which, among other things, asked if he had ever been convicted of any crime. Anxious to keep his sexual anomaly secret, he answered no. He was given the job—which lasted only six months—performed the work satisfactorily, received his pay and returned home. Months later he was visited by an FBI agent, who questioned him as to the concealment of his jail sentence. The man at once admitted his deception. He was convicted and was sentenced to a term of five years.

The above are among the most glaring of the many faults in our penal system, and they cry out for correction. The entire philosophy behind them should be examined and revised. There should be an end to the conscious program designed to degrade and humiliate the convicted man to the last extent. A prison is an insult to human dignity. As operated in the United States, it is a sympton of a diseased social system. It illustrates the chief crime and folly of which that system is guilty and for which one day it must pay a high penalty—contempt for the individual.

CHAPTER 17

I Go Out and Look
at the World

ALTHOUGH I have attained considerable measure of success as a lawyer, I have always felt that it could have been much greater were it not for certain personal defects to which I must now confess. It must be understood that success in the practice of the law depend upon qualities and circumstances not different than those which insure it in other activities in our culture.

At this point some definitions are necessary. By "success," I mean to become rich and prominent. By "our culture," I mean that social system—also called "our way of life"—whose basis is a selfish, murderous, dog-eat-dog competitive economic system.

In such an order cynicism is a most important quality. This is where I fell down. I consumed a great deal of my physical and emotional energy nursing a chronic slow burn which occasionally flared into self-destructive outbursts at what I conceived to be the follies and injustices of our legal system. Of course they should not have been considered under those designations. They were actually facets of a racket from which much profit may be gained by those who have the proper kidneys to handle it.

In the midst of the trial of *United States vs. Harry Renton Bridges et al,* I passed the thirtieth anniversary of my admission to the bar. The thirty years which had elapsed had involved me in practically every aspect of the law. I thought I pretty well knew all about it. To be sure, long before, I had read some bitter reflections upon it, but I had passed these by with amusement, conceiving them to be mere eccentricities or the diatribes of soreheads. The Bridges case was a catalyst which recalled these few clean elements and united them into a crystal through which the fundamental purposes of our system of laws became apparent.

One night, many years before that, I was driving along a road in France. It was extremely dark. The countryside was completely obscured. It was not possible to discern whether the road ran through open fields, forest or habitations. A storm blew up. Suddenly a great flash of heat lightning illumined the scene as far as the eye could reach. The light endured for less than a second, but thereafter one could not be mistaken as to the nature of the terrain.

So it was with this celebrated case. It was the lightning flash which revealed to me that I had not properly understood the profession to which I had devoted so much time and study. Indeed, it caused me to dismount from that vehicle in which I had been proceeding so smoothly and to search into the dark terrain about me. What I found distressed me, not only in itself, but because I had wasted a lifetime on one small aspect of the law, without having ever known its full extent or having appreciated the significance of the small part with which I was familiar. For the injustices of the law are but one wave in the turbid ebb and flow of human misery, and but one device in the perverted ingenuity by which a small number of men enslave and exploit the remainder.

In Plato's *Republic,* Telemachus, one of its characters, asserts: "Justice is the will of the strong and the laws are the rule under which that class desires to live."

In all human society it is necessary that there be a code to define and punish criminal acts; it is also necessary that rules and forums be established to peacefully resolve disputes. Because these are directly in view, such functions appear to be the most important, if not indeed the only, purpose of the law in our system.

Beneath this necessary aspect, however, it has a concealed design, more important to those who enact and enforce it than those commoner activities with which we are all familiar. That design is to preserve the positions, privileges and prerogatives of a small, immensely wealthy segment of the American people, and to insure the status of society which it conceives to be most beneficial to itself.

For all its babble of "democracy," the United States of America is an oligarchy. It pays lip service to the principles of democracy, but defines it in terms which emasculate it. Thus, in the Republican's Party's election platform of 1956, the definition of social justice involved "equality of opportunity." There is no such thing as equality of opportunity. It is a fictitious, fanciful, egregious fraud. It depends, in its broader implications, upon the assumption that the child of a Mississippi Negro sharecropper, wasted by starvation, pellagra and hookworm, has the same chance for success as one of Nelson Rockefeller's offspring.

As far back as 1913, President Woodrow Wilson warned the American people: "Don't you see that big business . . . must capture the Government? . . . Must capture it? They have already captured it."

In 1930, Franklin D. Roosevelt repeated this warning: "Our liberties are in danger . . . from that concentrated private power which is struggling so hard to master our democratic government." And again, in 1940: "The liberty of a democracy is not safe when . . . the growth of private power becomes stronger than the democratic state itself . . . Among us today a concentration of private power without equal in history is growing."

The process by which this control was effected began before this country had attained national status. It has continued until it is, now, practically complete.

Over a hundred years ago Theodore Parker, the Unitarian minister, cried out passionately but futilely against its growing strength. His grandfather was the captain of the Minutemen at Lexington in 1775, and he cannot reasonably be called a Russian

Red. It was his contention that America was not a democracy; that, having thrown off theocracy, aristocracy and monarchy, it had set up in their place the rule of money—"master of all the rest." He considered that its place in the political scene was open and obvious. He said:

> The Dollar sneers at the poor, at the many, as contempt for the people. It legislates against the poor and for the rich.... Everything must yield to money ... With it there is no absolute right or absolute wrong ... there is expediency or inexpediency ... The millionaire is reckoned by this party as the highest production of society ... he alone has attained the stature of the perfect man.

Control by wealth is not an exclusively American phenomenon; it has been assailed in other nations having our economic structure. In his great satire, *Penguin Island,* Anatole France describes it thus:

> The Penguin democracy did not itself govern. It obeyed a financial oligarchy which formed opinions by means of the newspapers, and held in its hands the representatives, the ministers and the president. It controlled the finances of the republic and directed the foreign affairs of the country as if it were possessed of sovereign power.

The take-over of their Government by financial interests is accepted by most Americans with unconcern. They have been educated into believing that the interests of the country are coincident with those of Big Business. The corollary, that big businessmen should control the Government, follows. Eisenhower's millionaire cabinet lifted few eyebrows. Indeed, the millionaires themselves finally believe their own propaganda, as witness Charles Wilson's statement that what is good for General Motors is good for the United States. Disclosure of the outright purchase of public office arouses indignation in only a few. Some years ago the magazine *United States News and World Report* published an interview with United States Senator Gillette, in which he discussed a recent primary election in Pennsylvania. Each of two candidates filed statements showing that he had spent over $300,000 in the campaign. This was in addition to the amount spent by friends and supporters. The primary election was only to decide which should run as his party's candidate in the final election. In that, the winner would have to run against the successful candidate of the other party. The office itself paid only $240,000 for its entire term.

Representative Clarence J. Brown of Ohio, a member of the Republican Party's National Committee, was quoted in *The New York Times* on the subject of expenditures in the elections of 1956 as follows: "It will be a wild guess, but I would hate to have to pay out of my own pocket all that was spent over $80,000,000 or $100,000,000 in the last campaign."

The big-business interests which provide these funds do not limit their contributions to the G.O.P. William J. McKinney, State Purchasing Agent of Illinois, disclosed during the same election that "outstanding Chicago businessmen" were long-time donors to the Democratic Party machine. He estimated that "at least $100,000 was collected from a thousand firms doing some thirty-five million dollars in state business annually."

Many play both ends of the bet. During the same election, Jesse Jones, Texas financier and Secretary of Commerce under Franklin Roosevelt, admitted: "I am contributing to the Democratic National Committee to help finance their campaign for Stevenson, and to the Republic National Committee for Eisenhower." The implications in such admissions are shrugged off by the American electorate.

Discarded political bosses edit books disclosing their own chicanery, without arousing more interest than an account of how J. Pierpont Morgan fooled Andrew Carnegie when he formed the steel monopoly. The reader chuckles, without reflecting that he was one of those taken.

Even those who accept the evidence of so obvious a situation allow themselves to be persuaded that the courts are not included in the take-over. Beginning in their early childhood, American children are instructed, from books selected by interests involved, that the constitutional division of the United States Government into legislative, executive and judicial branches is designed to curb the powers of the Government and to prevent its arbitrary interference with the liberties of the people. As a matter of fact, these were actually designed to prevent the interference of the people with the activities and accumulations of the wealthy. If the democratic forces get past one barrier, they are practically certain to be stopped by the second or third. Let the tide of democracy sweep too closely to the bulwarks which protect the favored class, and all the instruments of Government rush forth to repel them.

Not only the actions of those who would disturb our economic oligarchy, but even their words, are declared criminal. Repressive statutes pour from Congress and state legislatures. Special committees and constabularies are organized to detect and crush the critics of the established order. Never does the law operate with such ruthlessness, ferocity and efficiency, as when it is called upon for this, its most important function.

Then Government prosecutors throw away every restraint of decency and moderation, and its judges abandon both justice and dignity. The prosecutor becomes a Lord Coke, and the judge a Lord Jeffreys.

This is the way it has been in every period of history. The bravest, the truest and the best of men, whose only crimes were love of humanity and resolve to right its wrongs, have stood in the dock to hear themselves excoriated by Government lawyers and smashed by Government judges, none of whom is worthy to lace the defendant's shoes. That history ultimately exalted the victim and debased his persecutors, was small consolation to the heretic, who learned that his conduct was in no wise justified by its correctness, the nobility of his motives, or the virtues of its purposes.

There was therefore an historic nostalgia in the atmosphere which surrounded our appearance in the United States District Court in the case of *United States vs. Harry Renton Bridges et al.* Its lightning flash illumined the past and foretold the future. The defendants had menaced the existing distribution of wealth as, before them, had Eugene Debs, the abolitionists, the Molly Maguires, and Shays' Rebels. Any assault upon the sacred institutions of the *status quo* were deemed un-American, treason and a sellout to foreigners. This was supported by lofty precedents. Following the American Revolution, the common soldiers who had won it were reduced to desperate straits: the scrips in which they had been paid were worthless; their properties were seized and their persons imprisoned for debt. Finally they rose in revolt. Typical of these uprisings was that in Massachusetts known as "Shays' Rebellion." In a letter dated December 26, 1786, George Washington provided a precedent for the waterfront associations in their controversies with Bridges and the longshore unions. In it he gravely expressed his opinion that the disorders convulsing the new-born country were no doubt due to Great Britain, and that she would "prove every opportunity to foment the spirit of turbulence within the bowels of the United States." When the rebels closed the Worcester Court of Common Pleas, the presiding judge wrote to the governor that he believed that the disturbances were "the effects of British emissaries . . . employed . . . to stimulate the unwary to acts of disorder and violence and to poison the minds of others with unreasoning jealousies of their rulers—suggesting that they are oppressed by them unnecessarily."

Forty-five years after the Russian people emancipated themselves from enslavement by a despotic czar, a dissolute nobility, a superstitious priesthood, and a native financial oligarchy, the American people are still convinced that it was a naughty thing to do. It might be all right to kick out the others, but they should not have molested the millionaires. To an American, there is something charismatic about a millionaire. Even the humblest conceive that he may one day become one himself. The chances against this are about 150,000,000 to one, but those are not considered bad odds. The average American is singularly ignorant of what is going on in his own country, and a fortiori, what is going on in the rest of the world. This is not necessarily to his discredit. Practically from birth, he is engulfed in an endless propaganda designed to convince him that the "American Way of Life"—that is to say, the capitalist economic system—is God given and is the personification of justice, equity, and rationality.

Having had my own eyes somewhat opened by the Bridges case, I decided to put on my rubbers and go out and discover what was occurring in the rest of the world. For a starter I spent a month in the Soviet Union. Prior to that I had read some of the novels of Maxim Gorky, written in the early part of this century, and had a fair picture of the Russian worker and peasant as described by him. They were the products of centuries of poverty, ignorance and oppression. They were drunken, brutal and illiterate. These traits were shared even by their nobility. Back in 1930, in Paris, I had met Russian grand dukes driving taxicabs, who fairly filled the same description. Now these people, and they alone, must be credited with instilling a new spirit into humanity which has propelled it further and faster than it has ever moved before.

What is that spirit? It is a resolve to alter two basic relationships in which men exist: one, that which exists between nature and mankind; and the other, that which prevails among men themselves. The first of these contemplates such study and exploration into the laws of nature as will enable men to use its forces for their own benefit; the second determines to eliminate all exploitation of man by man, whether this involves slavery, serfdom, wage service, or any other means by which one man or group of men can appropriate to themselves the fruits of another's labor. It includes the extirpation of colonialism and imperialism.

The first of these requires all the genius, labor and patience of which man is capable. He descends into the abyss of the atom and journeys among the stars. In this project are enlisted all the true scientists and philosophers.

On the other hand, in his struggles to free mankind from exploitation, he must eradicate greed, avarice, selfishness and cruelty from his own nature. He must rescue the victims of these vices from the grasp of the most ruthless, hardhearted and tenacious of his species. In other words, in the first of these efforts he has the aid of those among us who most resemble the angels; in the second he must combat those who most resemble pigs.

Unfortunately, the pigs have terrible tusks with which to defend their hoards. They have at their command all the repressive forces of the most militarily advanced governments—from police-men's clubs to hydrogen bombs—in a word, from violence to death.

We live in an heroic generation. All over the world people, many of whom we would describe as savages or barbarians, have taken to the mountains, the deserts and the jungles, armed with whatever weapons they can muster, determined to attain these ideals though they perish in the attempt. They accept death that their children may have life; they descend into the darkness that generations they will never see may be lifted into the light.

In this renaissance of the human spirit, the force which most opposes the fulfillment of its dreams is the Government of the United States of America. At home it operates in about the manner I have indicated above; abroad its processes are more direct and more brutal. In 1961, I spent a few weeks in South-east Asia, becoming familiar particularly with the Philippines and Thailand, those "Bastions of Democracy" in the Pacific. Both, nominally independent, are actually colonies; their econ-omies are controlled by Wall Street, and their governments by the State Department. The Philippines is a police state in the worst tradition. It has an Un-Filipino Activities Committee headed by a native McCarthy named Perez. When I was there they were attempting to oust from the university a professor, not for being a Communist, but for being an agnostic. To meet and discuss matters with liberal forces, it is necessary to pursue labyrinthine paths to avoid detection by police spies. It is necessary to contact a guide in some remote spot, drive endlessly and aimlessly to be sure one is not followed, and meet finally in dark and hidden places. A gray terror pervades the Islands: 25 percent of the work force is unemployed; everywhere there is poverty, ignorance, misery and despair. Manila, the capital city, has a population of 2,000,000. Three-fourths of them live in the most awful slums imaginable. I had never before seen square miles of slums. One shack which we examined was six feet wide and nine feet long; eleven people lived in it. Garbage disposal consists of throwing refuse out of the windows and kicking it around until it dis-appears. Every few blocks there is a public toilet containing a series of large earthen pots which are emptied each evening. Similarly distanced are water hydrants from which water is carried in discarded gasoline cans to the squalid homes of the unfortunate people.

The Filipino people, who are among the bravest on earth, have been in constant revolt against Spain, the United States and their own corrupt government. They have finally been smashed by armies maintained, trained and paid by American taxpayers.

Thailand is even worse. It is a military dictatorship. Its sole ruler is Marshal Sarit Thanarat, one of the most brutal and murderous of the American puppets scattered around the world. He has outlawed political parties and labor unions. It is a criminal offense for two or more persons to discuss political affairs. All laws for the protection and amelioration of the conditions of workers have been repealed. Everywhere is poverty, ignorance, superstition, hunger, disease, misery and despair.

I got adventurous with the native food and contracted dysentery in Bangkok. It is a ferocious malady. It twists your guts until you believe you will die of the very agony; the sweat stands out on your forehead; you have a continuing alternation of vomiting and diarrhea. My wife is an amateur doctor and carries with her various antibiotics with whose properties she is familiar. She gave me four Fouroxin pills. I managed to keep the last two down, and in three hours the dysentery was completely cured. I narrate this to illustrate the criminal cynicism of our attitude toward the Thai people: the year before, 10,000 people had died of that same dysentery in Bangkok. Every one of them could have been saved by two Fouroxin pills, and the total cost would not have equaled the price of a single machine gun which we bestow upon our murderous puppet in that unhappy land.

A few days after our return there was a picture in *The New York Times* of two men with their hands bound to posts and their backs turned to a firing squad. It had come from Thailand, and the men were being executed, not on a judgment of a court or even of a court-martial, but on the dictate of Marshal Sarit Thanarat. He had ordered their execution as "Communist conspirators." Both had been duly elected members of the national legislature which he had overthrown in the interests of the American corporations.

Back in 1935, my wife and I went to Cuba for a vacation. We went via the Panama Canal on one of the Grace Line boats which then operated between San Francisco and New York. It laid up for two or three days in Havana Harbor. We spent one day in the capital city and then returned aboard the ship and went on up to New York. We couldn't see ourselves vacationing in the welter of poverty, ignorance, corruption, prostitution, misery and despair, which were the Cuba of 1935. We went back to Havana in December 1960. Fidel Castro and his revolutionaries had overthrown the American puppet Batista, and defeated his army—also maintained, trained, and paid by American taxpayers for the benefit of American big-business corporations. It was the Year of Education, and an islandwide campaign was being waged to stamp out illiteracy. The shacks and slums were disappearing, to be replaced by prefabricated concrete houses. These had sanitary plumbing, running water, gas and electricity. The barren landed estates had been converted into food-producing plantations for the benefit of all. Everywhere there was hope, pride and exultation. The Cuban people had recaptured their country from the exploiters.

In the same way that the American people were educated to believe that the Russian Revolution was bad, a vigorous campaign has been, and is being, waged to convince them that the Cuban Revolution is the same. Castro, an heroic and shining patriot, is depicted as a madman ruining his own country by the exclusion of the benign North American corporations. This has been the classic tradition; an Egyptian leader resisting British colonialism was "the Mad Mullah"; until his capture, the American press always referred to the Filipino patriot Aguinaldo as a "bandit." Going somewhat further back, Julius Caesar in his *Commentaries on the Gallic Wars,* ascribes the resistance of Vercingetorix, the heroic and self-sacrificing chief of the Gauls, as being "driven by personal ambition."

The United States Government, controlled as it is by American big business, now has a program based upon two unalterable principles. One is the preservation, at all costs, of the capitalist economic system. To carry out this purpose, it will use every means to destroy those who advocate its alteration or replacement at home. They are denounced as subversives—whatever that means—and traitors. Dark purposes of violent revolution are ascribed to them. These are "proven" by the testimony of paid informers and professional witnesses to impose brutal prison terms upon the offenders. Others are subjected to social and economic hardship by the activities of the investigative agencies. It is a stinking picture.

The second purpose is based upon the determination that all so-called "backward" regions are proper depositaries for investment of surplus American capital, and that it is the obligation of the American Government to protect these investments from being taken over by the governments of the countries in which they are operating. This is to be accomplished by fair means or foul, and foul are usually cheaper. Open military intervention is avoided when possible. Instead, reactionary native elements are enlisted. These may be feudal despots, as in the oil kingdoms of the Near East; military dictators, as in Thailand, Taiwan, South Vietnam and South Korea. In the Philippines and certain Central and South American countries, the native "business class" is cut in on the take. They are provided with "foreign aid" consisting of military equipment, training and pay, to keep them in power, and a surplus donation to maintain their individual standards of luxury. Naive Americans are accustomed to complain that the amounts so expended by them do not "trickle down" to the indigent native population. They are not intended to do so. They are a bribe to retain the traitorous elements within the camp of American influence. This procedure works excellently. The native compradores descend so far down the road of treason and become so much the objects of hatred and revenge on the part of their own countrymen that they can never turn back. They have become the creatures of the foreign exploiters, and not only their own fortunes but their personal safety are inextricably involved with the interests of their patrons. They will not be abandoned, since it is necessary to instill in these elements confidence in their American masters. Thus Syngman Rhee was plucked, by the U. S. Air Force, from a final accounting with his own people in Korea, to be deposited in a luxurious habitation in Hawaii.

Active military intervention is avoided where possible, but force is available when circumstances require. Thousands of American military "specialists" are interspersed among the native mercenaries as a sort of cohesive network, to save it from falling apart. Operators of the Central Intelligence Agency slip, cloak and daggerwise, through the scene, here engineering a successful revolution in Guatamala, and there a fiasco in Laos.

Whether American big business likes it or not, imperialism and colonialism are over. England and France, far more experienced in these fields, have reluctantly come to that conclusion and are slowly withdrawing from the positions which they had seized and occupied by wholesale murder and unbridled cruelty. The brash American oligarchs expect to take over the loot from which these hardy old pirates have been driven. It is a vain hope. The question is whether it will be frustrated by a series of military disasters such as the defeat inflicted on the French at Dien-Bien-Phu, or by the American people awakened to a realization of the hateful role which their Government is playing on the world's stage.

As for myself, I recall the day I was released from McNeil Island and stood on the boat watching the grim citadel, a monument to man's inhumanity to man, receding in the morning mist as I moved toward freedom.

At least, you son of a bitch, I thought, you're a better place because I went through you!

I hope I can say the same thing as I depart this world.